EXPEDITION TO THE EDGE

EXPEDITION TO THE EDGE

STORIES OF WORLDWIDE ADVENTURE

Lynn **Martel**

Rocky
Mountain Books
VANCOUVER • VICTORIA • CALGARY

Rocky Mountain Books Rocky Mountain Books
#108 – 17665 66A Avenue PO Box 468
Surrey, BC V3S 2A7 Custer, WA
www.rmbooks.com 98240-0468

Library and Archives Canada Cataloguing in Publication

Martel, Lynn
    Expedition to the edge : stories of worldwide adventure / Lynn Martel.

Includes bibliographical references.
ISBN 978-1-897522-09-7

    1. Adventure and adventurers—Biography. 2. Explorers—Biography.
I. Title.
CT9970.M37 2008   920.02   c2008-902779-5

Library of Congress Control Number: 2008930513

Printed and bound in Canada

Rocky Mountain Books gratefully acknowledges the financial support of the Government of Canada through the Book Publishing Industry Development Program (BPIDP); the Canada Council for the Arts; and the province of British Columbia through the British Columbia Arts Council and the Book Publishing Tax Credit for our publishing activities.

Thank you to the Banff Centre for Mountain Culture for its Banff Mountain Grants Program.

To my mom and dad and my sister, Daisy,
for their unconditional support and faith in me.

CONTENTS

INTRODUCTION

For as long as I can remember, I've been attracted to adventure.

As a small child in the 1960s, the biggest adventure for me and my sister, Daisy, happened on those Sundays when my grandfather, Papa Martel, would collect the two of us and our parents from our Montreal apartment to go picnicking in northern Vermont or New York State. Daisy and I were granted the privilege of sitting unrestrained in the far rear of Papa Martel's station wagon, and we lived our own little adventure while he steered the V8 engine down the highway, all of us oblivious to the now unthinkable hazards.

Once over the border, we'd stop at favourite destinations, such as Schuyler Falls, where we'd lounge on plaid blankets spread over dirt and grass plots and snack on dill pickles and Ruffles chips – another special-occasion-only privilege.

I would quietly notice, though, how some of the other families at the picnic area were there for more than just an afternoon, that they had tents and barbecues and campfire pits, and I wondered what it would be like to sleep outside in those woods, amidst splashing creeks and waterfalls and the wind rustling through the maple trees, all soaked in the intoxicating aroma of pine.

Through elementary school, my cravings for adventure were satisfied by the shortcuts Daisy and I took on our daily walks to school with our neighbourhood classmates – down the back alley, through the bushes and around the church via the little concrete path, behind the apartment building, through the parking lot, over the picket fence, a speedy dash through a backyard, behind dumpsters, another clandestine foray around another church – indulging in a healthy exercise so few children are encouraged to explore today.

Everywhere was more interesting than the sidewalk.

My first multi-day encounters with real nature happened at Girl Guide camp, where we slept in big group tents on wooden floorboards and earned canoeing badges and woke up at dawn for an early morning dip in mist-shrouded Laurentian Mountains lakes, an hour's drive and an entire world away from the city.

Through my later teens, however, my thirst for adventure was quenched by Montreal's expert-level discos and punk bars, where I danced to the latest and greatest outfitted in the newest and coolest, the thrill of gaining admittance accentuated by flashing false ID. Then when Daisy's own travel lust lured her to Banff in the early 1980s, although barely aware of the Canadian Rockies' existence, I joined her, and for the first couple of years in that tourist town I wholeheartedly pursued the thrills of its seven-night-a-week bar scene.

Stumbling home in the wee hours, though, I couldn't help but look up at the mountains that surrounded the town like mysterious sentinels and wonder how one began to explore their heights and the valleys cleaved between them that stretched into seemingly infinite forests.

Fortunately, my first job as a salesperson at the Banff Book & Art Den introduced me to *The Canadian Rockies Trail Guide*, the revered bible of Rockies backcountry travel. I put a deposit on a mountain bike, and when my layaway was finally paid off with the meagre remains of minimum-wage paycheques, I pedalled that Kuwahara with goalpost-wide handlebars, bear-trap pedals, no helmet, no spare inner tube or even a patch kit. I explored every fireroad and singletrack leading into the wildness from Banff Avenue, often solo, sometimes overnighting in my tent. Mountain biking through grizzly country on remote Canadian Rockies trails taught me to persevere, no matter how cold, tired, hungry, thirsty, sore, discouraged or scared I was. I explored trails in Hawaii, Whistler, Moab and New Zealand, and the confidence I learned mountain biking eventually transferred to snowboarding, then rock climbing, mountaineering and backcountry skiing.

At the same time, my adventures lured me away from the glossy pages of *Cosmopolitan* to the dirt- and sweat- and snow-packed pages of *Bike* and *Powder* magazines. But as I moved on to work as a retail manager in ski shops and later waited tables in the evenings so I could spend more hours playing outside, and my peers worked as ski patrollers and avalanche technicians and apprenticed to earn professional mountain guide certification, I couldn't help but notice the absence of our outdoor mountain lifestyles in our very own local newspapers.

So I began to record our stories.

For two winters I wrote a snowboard/ski bum lifestyle column for the weekly *Banff Crag & Canyon*. I wrote another column for two more years, called *Postcards from Paradise* for the *Crag*, and later for its sister paper the *Canmore Leader*, which spoke of our particular brand of life in our unique small-town mountain community. I wrote about my experiences in inflatable kayaks, bungee jumping in Queenstown and caving in the Canadian Rockies for a delightful and sorely missed monthly publication called *The Wild Life*. Reaching a saturation point in the restaurant industry, I accepted an income cut and worked as a full-time reporter for the *Canmore Leader* through 2000 and 2001. After covering court and school board meetings and regional politics and traditional sports, and writing about the astounding array of interesting and accomplished individuals who inhabit the Bow Valley, I reached the point where I just couldn't spend another Wednesday morning in court. I decided to freelance.

I really wanted to write about adventure.

My timing was perfect. With two partners, veteran Bow Valley news editor Carol Picard founded the weekly *Rocky Mountain Outlook*, and since 2002 she's welcomed my freelance stories about people who dream big and explore bigger. While all but two of the stories in this collection were previously published in various newspapers and magazines, a great many of them were first printed in the *Outlook*, where Carol trusted me – and still does – to capture the essence of the adventure community in a neighbourhood where so many of that community make their homes, and which attracts so many world-class adventurers to visit.

None of these stories is meant to be a comprehensive tally of any one person's accomplishments in the world of adventure, nor an all-encompassing investigative report of any of their expeditions. They do not portray any definitive roster of top-level participants of any given pursuit, but rather, a colourful cross-section of people who simply follow their individual dreams. Some stories bear only a few changes from the original, while others have been significantly expanded and reworked from the previously published, length-restricted versions.

These stories are snapshots of people who have discovered the pure joy and immeasurable rewards of immersing themselves in the natural environment of rivers, waterfalls, forests, tundra, oceans, mountains and glaciers. They have soared on thermals in the sky, from their own backyards to forbidding landscapes and challenging cultures half a world away. They possess widely different skill sets and experience levels; they follow their passions and their dreams via different modes of travel and exploration, using variously skis, bicycles, kayaks, rafts, climbing boots and paragliders. They harbour different motivations. But the one thing these adventurers have in common is the willingness, the fortitude and the unquenchable desire to embrace their journeys and all they encounter along the way.

FUN SEEKERS

The stories in this section are of fun seekers. They pursue their adventures for the simple joy of the experience. Most have regular jobs, many have families and others are self-confessed weekend warriors. Their outdoor exploits are their recreation, their hobbies and their chosen form of personal expression. In the pursuit of having fun some fun seekers embrace their passions and follow their desires to impressive heights. All of them are content to go wherever their adventures take them.

WEEKEND WARRIOR STANDS HIGH AMONG CLIMBERS (2000)

> Andy **Evans**

As Andy Evans took the final footsteps that led him to stand on the summit of K2 on July 30, 2000, he didn't think about how happy his sponsors would be, because he didn't have any. Neither did he think about updating his blog, calling home on his satellite phone or making any big publishing deals, because he didn't have any of those either.

What he did think about was how he'd just realized a long-time dream and that he'd been fortunate to find the right group of climbers with whom to share the experience. And then he focused his thoughts on getting back down the world's second highest mountain, where one in seven who reach its 8611-metre summit don't make it down alive.

Unlike Everest, which stands 240 metres higher, none of K2's eight established routes offer easy climbing. All follow consistently difficult slopes and steep ridges caked with snow and ice, which demand highly developed technical climbing skills from bodies and minds dulled by the effects of thin air above 8000 metres.

In climbing K2, at age thirty-eight, Evans, who was born in the US and holds dual citizenship, became only the third Canadian to reach its elusive summit – and the second Canadian to have stood on the summits of both K2 and Everest, which Evans climbed in 1997. On that expedition, eleven of the team's fourteen members summitted the mountain over a three-week period, climbing the peak by its North Ridge route "alpine style," ferrying up their own loads of gear and establishing high camps without any guides or Sherpa support.

While he enjoyed appearing on the front page of major newspapers and being met at Calgary International Airport by a TV news crew in recognition of his success on K2, Evans is the first to admit he never sought out the attention.

"I'm a weekend warrior, that's the bottom line. But that doesn't mean I don't have a lot of experience and determination," he says.

To make his historic ascent, Evans joined an expedition that included one British, one Italian, one Ecuadorean and six American climbers, all highly experienced amateurs. Theirs was one of only four amateur expeditions on the mountain during the 2000 season. Evans flew to Islamabad, Pakistan, on May 27, from where he travelled overland to Skardu and then trekked for eight days to base camp. A geologist working in Calgary's oil and gas industry, Evans had twenty-four years of experience climbing in Alaska, South America, the Himalayas and the Pamir mountain range of the former Soviet Union before tackling K2.

On this, his fifth trip to an 8000-metre peak, but his first visit to the Karakoram Range, a region of immense sweeping glaciers, towering granite spires and colossally huge mountains located near the border separating China from Pakistan, Evans figured it would take thirty to forty days for his body to best deal with the effects of altitude. His wife, Janice Ledrew, accompanied him as far as base camp.

To climb K2, Evans and his team, led by American Gary Pfisterer, opted for the most frequently followed Abruzzi Ridge, the same route established in 1954 by the first-ascent team of Italians, Lino Lacedelli and Achille Compagnoni. The mountain didn't see a second ascent until 1977, and when Evans and his team set out, the Abruzzi Ridge hadn't been climbed in four years.

While K2 is the world's second-highest mountain, most climbers regard it as the most difficult, in close competition with another of the fourteen peaks above 8000 metres, Annapurna, which, threatened by avalanches and sérac fall on all sides, offers no safe way up. On K2, climbers rarely employ high-altitude porters, which leaves all the work of carrying gear, setting ropes and stocking high camps to the climbers themselves, with every day spent at high altitude taking a toll on their bodies. While climbers on Everest can usually count on two four- to five-day weather windows during which to launch their summit bid, K2, the highest mountain in its neighbourhood, is subject to unpredictable storms, rendering it nearly impossible for anyone to climb the mountain without being caught in life-threatening weather.

Having read several books by others who had succeeded on K2's steep and treacherous slopes and descended to tell the tale, Evans was aware of the mountain's legends and aura, and also of how many had failed in their attempts.

"It's very spooky," Evans says. "We were aware of all the accidents. On K2 people croak coming down from the summit. One in seven fall off before returning to high camp."

In addition to the objective hazards of rockfall, avalanches and steep ice walls, all at a lung-bursting and brain-numbing altitude, communication between teams speaking different languages and overcrowding in tight places can create difficulties.

"The mountain is so hard. You're quite limited as to where you can put your tent," Evans says.

After a storm ravaged the peak for sixteen days, two members of Evans's team climbed back up to Camp III only to discover that the two tents they had previously set up had been buried. They didn't only lose the tents but also two down suits, food, gas for their cook stoves, ropes and two more tents that were intended for Camp IV. Fortunately, the climbers were able to spend the night in an empty tent belonging to a Korean team before descending to resupply.

"It meant we had to carry a lot more stuff up the mountain for our summit push," Evans says. "After the storm the mountain was a totally different landscape."

It also meant the team had to improvise with their remaining gear. They successfully executed a plan of leapfrogging in small groups between camps in their final summit push, which resulted in six members summitting over three days, nine weeks into their expedition.

Evans's turn came on his fifty-first day on the mountain, and he summitted with four teammates.

"It was kind of this jubilation, an overwhelming feeling of relief that we'd made it and gratitude for this outrageous good fortune," he recalls.

The hour and a half that Evans spent on the summit was also filled with sentiment and emotion when his thoughts turned to the two other Canadians who had been there before him.

Dan Culver and Jim Haberl were the first Canadians to reach the summit in 1993. Culver, however, died shortly after beginning his descent. Haberl was killed in an avalanche in Alaska in 1999.

Apart from the personal pride of having climbed both Everest and K2, Evans says he is most proud of the fact that he is one of a handful of non-

Russians who has earned the title of Snow Leopard – for climbing all five of the former Soviet Union's 7000-metre peaks. After he and Australian partner Paul Walters climbed 7439-metre Pik Pobedy, the highest mountain in the Tian Shan range on the China–Kyrgyzstan border, the local Kazakh climbers were impressed to see a couple of foreigners climb their hardest route. The Kazakhs asked them to join their team for an attempt of Everest's North Ridge route the following spring, and even though Everest had never been a huge desire of Evans's, he accepted.

"I react more to the people situation than to the particular mountain, because you're going to be spending two months together," Evans explains. "I felt it was serendipity, meeting some good people I trusted. I had a good sense that these guys were competent and well organized. But they were also a lot bolder, a lot wilder; they took a lot more risks."

On Everest, four of the Kazakhs spent a night out at high altitude and survived, although one would lose both legs below the knee, the others numerous fingers and toes. Evans and Walters waited out bad weather while three Siberians didn't make it back down on another summit attempt.

"There were a lot of people falling off, freezing and dying. I stuck to my own safety standards," Evans says.

When conditions improved, Evans and Walters set off, and though Walters turned around at Camp II, Evans continued alone until he happened upon a new partner.

"I saw another headlamp in the dark. He was from Slovenia. We introduced ourselves, shook hands in the dark and climbed together," Evans recalls. "It was a real psychological boost, there's a lot of tricky route finding and hard leads there."

The two of them stood alone on the same summit that would see twenty people the following day – a memory that shares space with the discovery of the frozen bodies of two of three of his Siberian teammates.

"When I climbed Everest there was nobody else up there," he says. "We got to enjoy an hour on top of the world with just our thoughts and ourselves. More people climbed Everest that year than had climbed K2 in all of history."

PETER ARBIC UNPLUGGED (2001)

> Peter **Arbic**

Peter Arbic, or P.A., as he is widely known, is one of those members of Canada's tight mountain community whose name instantly evokes a comment or anecdote.

"P.A.? He's a badass partier and he still lives in a shack in Banff."

"P.A.? Did you see him when he dyed his hair blue?"

"P.A.? He greeted his heli-ski group wearing a ball cap that said 'fuck off.'"

Rumours, as far as Arbic's concerned, simply add to the mystique, and he admits he isn't particularly bothered by where the line gets drawn.

"People love to live vicariously through me and it's just as easy for them to do if it's true or not," he says.

With international certification from the Association of Canadian Mountain Guides, Arbic has guided heli-skiers at backcountry lodges for Canadian Mountain Holidays since 1988. On the slopes, the guests see him as a professional mountain guide; après ski as a musician and a comedian.

"He's a Renaissance man," says heli-skier Hank Brandtjen III, who has enjoyed many a good powder run with Arbic.

For most guides, a seasonal work schedule guarantees flexibility, but then Arbic rarely guides in the summer.

"I make a living skiing, but I do live to climb," he says. "I have to make a conscious decision about what I'm going to do next winter, what I'm going to do next summer. But I like having the freedom to choose."

Away from the heli-ski industry, Arbic has worked as part of the safety team for the Eco-challenge events in Morocco and Argentina. In 1999 he travelled to remote northern Pakistan with filmmakers Roger Vernon and Pat Morrow, who were shooting footage for the Hollywood film *Vertical Limit*. Having visited the area before on a climbing expedition to K2, Arbic had the job of schmoozing with the officials and the locals.

"I know how to turn fifteen words of Urdu to my advantage and make everyone work hard," he says with a grin.

Forty-three-year-old Arbic has lived in the same two-room cabin in Banff, Alberta, for eighteen years. Essentially it is a freestanding studio nestled in mature spruce trees. It's cozy, well kept and cheap. To shower, he crosses the yard to the main house in whose backyard his cabin sits.

"I like having a simple lifestyle. If I buy something, I have to get rid of something else," he shrugs.

Arbic's climbing isn't about checklists, or about pleasing photographers or sponsors. He's made impressive and daring climbs of public record and an equal number of stunning ascents that none but his closest friends will ever know about. Climbing is the medium through which he discovers himself, travels to interesting places and explores relationships with people.

In 1993 Arbic, Barry Blanchard and Troy Kirwan attempted the Southwest Pillar on K2, the world's second-highest mountain at 8611 metres. With Kirwan sick at base camp, Arbic and Blanchard climbed to 8000 metres alpine style over three days. On the fourth and planned summit day, they descend all the way to base camp, thinking they'd try again and include Kirwan. The very same day they descended, six other climbers reached the summit, but only three made it down.

"We decided as a team we were not going to the summit," Arbic says. "At the point we turned around, I thought I could follow the rest of the guys and probably make it. But that wasn't why I was there, to climb K2 by myself."

In 1987 Arbic and his close friend Ward Robinson were joined by Blanchard to put up The Wild Thing on the north face of Mount Chephren, a landmark peak on the Icefields Parkway in the Canadian Rockies. Arbic had been attracted to the ice-choked gullies and commanding rock ribs since first seeing the mountain many years earlier.

The team spent three nights on the route in the dead of winter, the only reasonable time to attempt the line, since the crumbly rock would be frozen in place. They climbed only 100 metres on the second day, labouring up a pitch they would later grade an advanced level 5.10 A3.

"P.A. climbed brilliantly on that climb; he led some fantastic pitches," Blanchard recalls.

For Arbic, the experience meant learning about climbing, learning about partners and fulfilling a dream. He and Blanchard collaborated to write "The Wild Thing," one of the classic articles of Canadian climbing literature, published in *Canadian Mountaineering Anthology: Stories from 100 Years at the Edge*. Although a high-school teacher once told him he could make a living as a poet, Arbic says he has not had another urge to write since completing that article.

"A lot of things that stand out in my mind today about that climb are moments of looking around and appreciating what a wild place we were in," he says. "That and trying to have fun when you're scared shitless. I took a few of the moments that really crystallized what that experience was all about, and that's what I wrote."

Born in Guelph, Ontario, Arbic started climbing at the local crags Rattlesnake Point and Bon Echo. Equipped with a chemistry degree, he made his way to Sunshine Village in the Canadian Rockies to learn how to ski. Working as a janitor, he followed the pro ski patrol members enough through his first season that the next winter they hired him for their team. He ended up running the ski patrol a few years later.

"I got some pretty good climbing partners out of it," he admits. "Ward Robinson was a garbage man."

In the summer of 1985, Robinson was bemoaning that his partner for a trip to Europe had jammed at the last minute. With little alpine experience, Arbic offered to join him and Robinson accepted. For three weeks the routes they tackled grew progressively more difficult, culminating in the notorious Eiger Norwand, the 1800-metre-high, steep rock, ice and glaciated north wall of the 3970-metre mountain. If he could remember only one mountain adventure, Arbic said he'd choose that trip with Robinson.

"P.A.'s life is built around climbing. It doesn't matter what kind of climbing, he does it," says Tim Auger, a Banff National Park warden and rescue specialist who's been a steady climbing partner for twenty years. "Hard ice, mixed, high altitude, traditional rock routes, sport climbs, he just loves it all."

Arbic agrees, but adds that he does look at alpine climbing in a different light than rock climbing. "When I've done something [alpine]

I feel like I deserve not to have to do anything for a while," Arbic says. "On the other hand, rock climbing for me is like opening up a toy box. It's really fun and I enjoy it. Alpine climbing is like that nightmare you have to explore."

In August 1992 Auger and Arbic climbed the north face of Mount Alberta, a seldom attempted, let alone ascended, Canadian Rockies Grand Cours route.

"He's a no-miss friend," Auger says. "He's quietly climbed tons, things very few people manage to pull off. I still find out about things he's done and places he's been that knock my socks off."

At the Back of the Lake (Louise) in the Rockies, and at Skaha in Penticton, BC, Arbic continues to be well known and liked for putting up three-star rock routes, many in the 5.12 and 5.13 range.

"I like the exploratory nature of it, of seeing a line, imagining a line and climbing it, seeing it to fruition. I can't imagine anything more satisfying," Arbic explains.

And what does climbing give him?

"Fulfillment, for want of a better word, spiritual fulfillment," he says. "Not total fulfillment in itself, but it's part of the balance. I just really love it."

In 2001 Arbic spent several weeks climbing at Arapiles in Australia's Grampians, as he'd also done the previous year.

"I liked going somewhere where there were so many routes I'd never seen before," he says. "I liked living like a climbing bum, where nobody knew me, living out of a van. It was probably a return to the roots of what I liked about climbing. Making chapatis around the campfire and being really happy because you won the meat raffle that week."

NANCY'S LIST (2003)

> Nancy **Hansen**

Nancy Hansen admits she's a "list person." She especially likes making "to do" lists. And on Monday, September 1, 2003, thirty-four-year-old Hansen finished ticking off items on a "to do" list that earned her a place in Canadian mountaineering history, by becoming the first woman – and only sixth person overall – to climb all fifty-four of the Canadian Rockies peaks that are over 11,000 feet (3353 metres). She completed her mission after climbing Banff National Park's highest peak, 3612-metre Mount Forbes.

Hansen says she decided to climb the "Rockies 54" not long after bagging her first peak, 3543-metre Mount Temple, via the standard southwest ridge scrambling route in 1994.

Apart from the satisfaction of ticking off a list, Hansen says she has often been asked, "Why?"

"I've asked myself that question," Hansen laughs. "It seemed like an achievable goal. It was something that would be continuously challenging over the years because of the variety and difficulty of the peaks."

That technical difficulty ranged from a straightforward scramble up Temple's standard route, to what many climbers regard as the Rockies' most majestic and elusive peak, 3619-metre Mount Alberta on August 28, 2001.

"We climbed Alberta in quite challenging conditions," Hansen recalls. "It hadn't been climbed in two years, and it didn't get climbed again until the next summer."

The outing took "three days and a bit," with two bivouacs, one lower on the mountain and one at 3500 metres on the narrow summit ridge.

"It was very cold," Hansen admits. "We used ice blocks for pillows, looking down on other 11,000-foot peaks."

The challenging conditions on Alberta included mixed snow, ice and rock in steep terrain, enormous cornices along the summit ridge and lots of loose rock – some of it whizzing by in downward flight, a stray chunk of which chopped her rope. Hansen and her climbing partner, Calgary author Bill Corbett – who completed his own goal of climbing the fifty-four 11,000ers in 2002 – were able to continue using the rope to rappel, but it was retired from big-peak duty after that.

In addition to Corbett, four other Calgary men have climbed the 54. The first was Don Forest, who didn't start climbing until he was forty, but, quickly making up for lost time, completed the 54 in

1979. Forest died suddenly from a heart attack in 2003, at the age of eighty-three, while he was out ski touring. Rick Collier was second to climb the 54, finishing in 1994. After Corbett, Forbes Macdonald and Roman Pachovsky completed their quests together when they climbed Mount Alberta in August 2003.

Some of the 11,000ers are recognizable and frequently climbed Rockies landmarks, including the world-famous Lake Louise backdrop, 3464-metre Mount Victoria, 3618-metre Mount Assiniboine and, the Rockies' highest, 3954-metre Mount Robson. Other peaks in the group of fifty-four, such as Mount Harrison, near BC's Whiteswan Provincial Park, are rather obscure. Only seven of Hansen's climbs did not involve an overnight in the backcountry.

Two main factors make climbing the Rockies 54 a challenge: the extreme remoteness of many of the peaks, as many are not even visible from any road, paved or otherwise; and their degree of technical difficulty, often requiring the climber to perform complicated glacier navigation. In addition, some of the climbs are simply long slogs. Climbing 3356-metre Mount Recondite, for example, involves trudging forty kilometres each way, engaging in bushwhacking and three above-knee river crossings, after which the climber is rewarded by loose rock and uninteresting climbing.

By comparison, all fifty-nine of Colorado's mountains above 14,000 feet (4267 metres) have been climbed in as little as sixteen days. Even with the assistance of a helicopter, Hansen says she's certain the technical difficulty of many of the Canadian peaks, coupled with the challenges of lining up suitable partners on those precious few good-weather days (as well as plenty of other variables), render climbing the Canadian Rockies' 11,000ers in a single year virtually impossible. With many of the peaks situated within national park boundaries, helicopter access is rarely even an option.

To pass the time during one long drive to one trailhead, Hansen compiled a list on a notepad. She calculated that to complete her quest she had to drive 25,000 kilometres, 3000 of which were over bumpy logging roads (yes, she wore out a vehicle), hike 1800 kilometres and climb 114,300 vertical metres.

Helping her achieve her goal, Hansen's had "awesome" partners. Who accompanied her depended on who had the days off and who was willing to slog long distances carrying a heavy pack on multiple-day trips that included exasperating sections of bushwhacking and wading through thigh-deep freezing rivers. Hansen says she appreciates the support of her family and friends and especially her husband, Doug Fulford, who shared the rope – and the summit views on the clear days – on about half of the climbs.

Among her favourite trips was a weeklong expedition to climb Mount Clemenceau, 3658 metres, and neighbouring Mount Tusk, 3360 metres.

"Just to get in there was a spectacular drive on a 200-kilometre logging road; then we had to cross seven glaciers," Hansen says. "It had just an incredible feel of remoteness just to get in there."

Her quest yielded some great and some not so great memories, most notably a 200-metre fall while descending the notoriously crumbly summit ridge of 3562-metre South Goodsir in August 2002, a fall that left Hansen battered and bruised with a small broken bone in her neck and ligament damage to her lower back.

Recuperating quickly, she was out climbing just a few weeks later and managed to tick off the items on another of her climbing lists – completing a different route on the vertical south-facing cliffs of Mount Yamnuska (only 2235 metres) during each month of 2002.

Some of the fifty-four summits required several attempts. The most elusive peak for Hansen was Robson's neighbour, 3395-metre Whitehorn Mountain, whose peak she finally reached on her fourth try. On her first attempt she was turned back by –36°C temperatures and a whiteout, the second time – also in winter – by a "manpower shortage" needed to break trail in deep snow. The third time, warm temperatures rendered the snow too soft, making climbing dangerous.

"There are long stories behind every retreat," Hansen admits.

Some of the peaks she climbed more than once, including Temple, which she climbed via the classic, but more technically challenging, East Ridge route on her second trip. Since her first ascent of Temple had been several years before she started her quest for the 54, by counting her second trip up the peak instead of the first she shortened the time span for her feat to seven years and forty-nine days. Perhaps, she suggests in good humour, completing the 54 in the shortest time yet might qualify her feat as a speed ascent on adventurer Will Gadd's website.

With the list completed, does she plan to climb any of the 54 again? "Oh yeah!" she exclaims. "There are different routes I'd like to do on some of them because they're awesome routes."

Not that there's a list, but Robson's Wishbone Arête is among the first she'd like to attempt.

CLIMBING QUEENS LOVE THEIR ICE (2003)

> Abby **Watkins**, Catherine **Mulvihill** and Kim **Csizmazia**

Ask a devoted ice climber what attracts them to the activity and they'll likely say it's the improbability of the act being performed in an improbable medium.

Hooking pointed ice tools into naturally formed slots in a column of ice that's frozen in place like a candle dripping onto itself, kicking sharp metal crampon points into subtle depressions, moving up a pillar of water frozen only by the seasonal temperature of the air, means climbing on a medium suspended in time itself.

Canadians have a great tradition of celebrating winter's miracles of snow and ice – sculpting polar bears from giant ice blocks, skating on frozen ponds and excelling in hockey arenas around the world. In the ice-climbing arena, Canadians have led at the sharp end of the rope since the 1970s, when advances in equipment and techniques led ice climbing to evolve from an element of mountaineering necessary to gain a summit into a highly specialized sport of its own. Canadian climbers, including an exceptionally committed number in the Rockies, continually raise the bar of difficulty and proficiency on the international stage.

Abby Watkins, Catherine Mulvihill and Kim Csizmazia exemplify the passion and wonder that are as essential to ice climbing as sharp tools and frozen waterfalls.

Growing up on Australia's beaches, Abby Watkins learned region-appropriate sports – surfing, swimming, tennis and track and field. Not long after her twelve-year gymnastics career earned her a full athletic scholarship to the University of California at Berkeley, some friends introduced her to rock climbing.

Her first reaction, "It sounds pretty stupid," was fortunately accompanied by, "but I'll try it."

A lifelong professional athlete, Watkins focused on rock climbing with a desire to master it, eventually climbing at the elite level of 5.13 and becoming the US Speed Climbing Champion in 1996. That same year, with fellow Australian Vera Wong, she set women's speed records on The Nose of El Capitan and the regular northwest face route of Half Dome in Yosemite. Two years later, with Wong and Nicola Woolford, she established a new route on 5800-metre Changi Tower in the Nangmah Valley of Pakistan's Karakoram Range.

It should come as no surprise that once she was introduced to climbing frozen waterfalls in Telluride, Colorado, in 1996, Watkins immediately sought to master that too, and by 2002 she placed fifth overall on the Ice Climbing World Cup circuit.

"I just enjoy mastering things," says Watkins, thirty-three. "I like to be able to pull the puzzle apart and figure it out. I like to put myself in adverse situations, having to work things out and rise to the occasion. I'm not interested in doing anything ludicrous or dangerous, or in getting hurt or dying in the mountains."

Certified as an assistant alpine guide with the Association of Canadian Mountain Guides, Watkins teaches ice climbing with the University of Calgary and instructs women's clinics, often spending seven consecutive days outside, ice climbing and backcountry ski touring. In 2002 she performed with Vancouver-based aerial dance troupe Arioso Dance in Taiwan, performing climbing-inspired dance moves while suspended several metres above the ground tied into climbing ropes.

And what's the attraction to ice?

"Ice forms chaotically; it's very aesthetic," Watkins says. "It's extremely satisfying to climb. I love the fact that's it's ephemeral. The fact that the only reason it's there is because it's cold. Maybe part of it is because things don't freeze like that in Australia."

Besides, she says, "What else are you going to do in the winter in Canada? Well, ski, of course, but if you're a climber, well, you ice climb."

> Catherine **Mulvihill**

In 1994 Catherine Mulvihill's background in documentary filmmaking led her to work as Everest base camp manager for IMAX filmmaker David Breashears. There she met one of Canada's most accomplished alpinists, mountain guide Barry Blanchard.

"We fell in love and I moved to Canmore as an expedition war bride and I've had a wonderful life ever since," she laughs.

Mulvihill started rock climbing that summer, but come winter, her friend Margo Talbot, a passionate ice climber, insisted she try climbing Tangle Falls on the Icefields Parkway in Jasper National Park.

"I was in love with it," Mulvihill states. "I thought it was the hardest work I'd ever done."

As a strictly recreational climber, Mulvihill, thirty-three, admits ice climbing is not always easy for her, but the potential for rare days when "it's an exquisite pleasure," continuously draw her.

"The concentration is so profound, it's consumptive," she says. "You have to lose yourself in it. It's a consumptive un-thought."

It can also be unforgiving.

"It makes you accountable for what you can and can't do," she says. "You have to be able to get yourself out of whatever situation you get yourself into. If you don't turn back or don't have a way to get down, that's a quick way to get injured or killed."

Working eighteen-hour days for five months a year as a film industry grip allows Mulvihill to aim for a fifty-day ice season.

"If I have a number goal, it makes me go out on days I wouldn't go out on, 'cause it's too cold, too snowy, it's minus 25 or too windy," Mulvihill explains. "Rather than waiting for a nice day, I put up with the discomfort."

That discomfort often includes thawing frozen fingers that frequently occur after the blood has drained from arms that are repeatedly reaching above the head to make a tool placement – what ice climbers call the "screamy barfies."

"It's an eviscerative knife pain," she describes. "Your circulation is cut off, you get to the top of the pitch and you're just bent over with pain."

How does she deal with it?

"All suffering is ephemeral," Mulvihill shrugs. "You just accept it; it will come and go pretty quickly."

The camaraderie of driving to the climb, the collaboration of climbing and the drive home is Mulvihill's idea of a perfect day in an ever-mutating environment.

"Chandelier, shitty, brittle, it's never the same climb," she says. "The ice changes so much; I change with it. It's the most nonsensical pursuit ever."

> Kim **Csizmazia**

"I never thought I'd be an ice climber. It sounded cold and wet and horrendous," laughs Kim Csizmazia with a smile that sparkles like a sun-kissed column of ice.

This is funny because Csizmazia climbs frozen waterfalls and mixed rock and ice routes beyond the ability of most climbers' – male or female – dreams. She was overall women's winner of the 2000 Ice Climbing World Cup and has won the overall women's ice-climbing category at the X-Games and Ouray, Colorado, ice-climbing festival three times each. In her spare time, Csizmazia, thirty-five, is an accomplished paraglider, rock climber and cross-country skier, who raced on the US national team for two years. A dual US–Canadian citizen, she grew up in Whistler, BC, and now lives in Canmore, Alberta, working as a guide, ice-climbing instructor and technical representative for climbing equipment companies. Already a dedicated rock climber and backcountry skier, when a boyfriend brought her to an ice-climbing slideshow, she was immediately attracted to the ice itself.

"I saw those pictures of climbing on a waterfall and it was totally cool," Csizmazia says. "I thought: it's so beautiful, I have to try and climb that."

And she admits she loves the escape it provides.

"It's an escape because it takes so much focus," Csizmazia explains. "You can't be thinking about other things; you have to be thinking in that moment. The rest of the world kind of melts away. I find ice climbing not to be difficult. Sometimes it makes me frustrated, because I come back to my real life and other things I don't have a natural affinity for – like sitting down and getting some work done."

As a woman who has no difficulty excelling in a predominantly male arena – she is the only woman who's ever climbed the mixed climbing grade of M10 – Csizmazia says she enjoys the exchange of energy she experiences when she's teaching women.

"I think it makes a huge difference. Seeing each other do it is super motivating."

These days Csizmazia says she's interested in doing long alpine climbs that involve more travelling through mountain terrain, but ice will always lure her.

"It's just an incredible medium. You're having this intimate experience with a frozen waterfall," she says. "It isn't there all year and it's changing all the time. How weird is that?"

DULL KNIFE, SHARP THINKING (2004)

> Aron **Ralston**

In November 2002 Aron Ralston was a twenty-seven-year-old recreational mountaineer from Colorado who travelled to Banff, Alberta, to volunteer as a cameraman and assistant at the Banff Mountain Film and Book Festivals.

Just two short years later, he stood on the Banff Centre's Eric Harvie Theatre stage as a 2004 book festival keynote speaker, all because a day hike in Utah's Blue John Canyon, in May 2003, turned into a six-day epic of endurance and survival after a 360-kilogram boulder crushed his right hand against the canyon wall and forced him to save himself by amputating his own arm with a freebie pocket knife.

"It's kind of a surreal aspect of this experience," Ralston admits of being invited to speak at the prestigious festival.

For Ralston, Banff marked yet another stop on a tour that took him across the US, Canada, Great Britain, Ireland and The Netherlands, during which he gave over 250 interviews in six weeks while promoting his book, *Between a Rock and a Hard Place*.

After numerous television appearances and countless newspaper and magazine articles published around the world, strangers recognize him in grocery stores, on trains and in airports, and they ask to have their picture taken with him.

"It's all been positive for me," Ralston says. "It's surprising at times, but I appreciate the feedback I've been getting. In some ways it's really touching to share my story and have people finding strength from it."

Admitting the tour kept him from spending as much time in the mountains as he would prefer, Ralston, who continues to climb and ski in the backcountry with the aid of a prosthetic arm, also says he feels strongly about the ways he has been able to give back to the community because of the book. While in Colorado, for example, he participated in a Colorado fundraiser to benefit environmental preservation, search and rescue organizations and a group working to help youth at risk.

"I feel blessed being able to help and do things for what I see as important causes," he says.

He also says he feels his survival was no accident.

Believing he couldn't possibly make it to safety before bleeding to death after he sawed his arm off, he carried out his plan all the same, only to be met by a rescue helicopter that was searching for him the very minute he reached the first accessible landing spot – an occurrence he views as divine intervention.

"I found what happened to me to be a miracle and a blessing," Ralston says. "My experience reinforced my spirituality and my belief in greater energies and how we react to those. For me it was divine epiphany, it was providence, me making it out of the canyon in time to meet the helicopter."

In a way, he says, his canyon experience was something of a rebirth.

"I spent six days in my grave followed by a bloody and painful birth process, experiencing the same beauty and euphoria of a mother bringing a baby into the world," he explains.

Banff festival audiences are familiar with astonishing survival stories, in particular that of British climber Joe Simpson, subject of the feature film *Touching the Void* and author of an award-winning book by the same title, who crawled for days with a broken leg after being left for dead deep inside a crevasse on a hopelessly remote peak in Peru's Cordillera Huayhuash. Another of the festival's speakers was Vancouver resident Warren Macdonald, an Australian who lost both legs to above the knee after a table-sized boulder pinned him in a creek for two days in remote Tasmania. Ironically, Ralston met Macdonald at the 2002 Banff festival and went ice climbing with him the following winter.

While trapped in Blue John Canyon, Ralston says he thought of both Simpsons and Macdonald's stories, adding he reread Simpson's acclaimed book after his accident, intent on gleaning insight on how to write the best book he possibly could about his own experience. Nominated for the prize in the 2004 Banff Mountain Book Festival's adventure travel category, Ralston – an engineer by profession – emerged from his experience as a talented, captivating and insightful writer.

Appearing in the early chapters of the book as a catastrophe primed to detonate, Ralston writes of himself as a young man with an overdeveloped appreciation for adventure and a dangerously underdeveloped appreciation for the subtleties of nature's dynamic, as he relates his near-drowning in a freezing river, his partial burial in an avalanche and being stalked by a ravenous and very persistent bear.

"I'm not perfect and I've made a lot of mistakes," Ralston admits. "Really what I intended in the book is to show that I've made my mistakes and learned from them. The experience that I carried with me into the canyon was hard learned. I wanted to show a person who can, in a crisis, find the ability to push through."

One thing his experience taught him, he says, was an increased appreciation for the potential dangers inherent in the smaller risks of backcountry travel.

"This was a time of a smaller risk jumping out and biting me," Ralston says. "The kind of risk you encounter a thousand times."

His experience also heightened his appreciation for the personal relationships in his life. During the process of writing his book, Ralston replayed video clips he recorded while in the canyon, watching them alone and then with his parents.

"I know for my mom, it was still too much for her," Ralston says. "Afterward it was the best hug we ever shared."

JUNIOR CLIMBERS REACH HIGH (2004)

> Sean **McColl**, Zak **McGurk**, Celeste **Wall** and Charlie **Hitchman**

In many ways the scene is familiar. Two dozen teenagers gather on a Saturday afternoon, the girls chatting in small groups while the boys joke and challenge each other. The setting, however, isn't a shopping mall but the gravel bank of a tumbling creek at the base of a limestone cliff at Banff National Park's Carrot Creek, an hour's hike from the trailhead.

This group of teens is climbing the vertical and overhanging rock walls with a purpose. Celeste Wall, Zak McGurk, Charlie Hitchman and Sean McColl are among twenty-four members of Canada's Youth National Climbing Team preparing for the 2004 World Youth Championships taking place in Edinburgh, Scotland, in September.

Climbing outdoors, explains their coach and owner of Canmore's The Vsion climbing gym, Dung (pronounced Yung) Nguyen, helps develop essential route-reading skills.

"You have to try out different kinds of rock," Wall agrees. "Climbing inside we can see all the holds. Out here we have to find the holds."

Encouraged by shouts of "Come on, Charlie! You're strong! Hang on…," seventeen-year-old Hitchman determinedly inches his way up Cup o' Joe, a route rated an expertly challenging 5.13b. With downward sloping hand and footholds on smooth, water-polished rock, the extremely overhanging route presents a level of difficulty that demands quick, efficient movement, precise foot placements and advanced balancing techniques. Hanging from one hand to shake out his other, pumped forearm, Hitchman feels his feet suddenly grease off the rock and he drops two metres before his belayer, managing the rope, catches his fall. Dangling in mid-air, Hitchman grins, as comfortable as a circus performer.

Minutes earlier, Vancouver's McColl, sixteen, on-sighted the route – climbing fifteen metres from the ground straight up to the permanently fixed chain anchor, clipping the rope into fixed bolts at intervals along the way without falling or hanging on the rope – without prior attempts or knowledge of the route.

In the fall of 2003, McColl won the 16–17 Boys category at the Youth World Climbing Championships in Bulgaria. For the past four months he and his teammates have trained to improve their strength, endurance and climbing skills. Facing his fourth Worlds, which always take place on indoor climbing walls, McColl says training demands motivation.

"I'd rather be going to the beach and hanging with my friends," McColl admits. "You have to sacrifice, but I think it will pay off. I'll always have the chance to hang out with my friends, but you don't always have the chance to go across oceans and represent Canada."

With nearly 400 competitors from over thirty countries, the world championships sees fifty to sixty competitors in each category. Edinburgh will be Hitchman's second Worlds since he started competing – and climbing – just three years ago.

"I thought I'd prepared myself for the international scene, but when I got there I realized how enormous it was," Hitchman says. "The French are really strong. Last year they only sent their B team; the A team went to adult events. They take it really seriously; there's no parents allowed. It's their national sport. It's inspiring, but you need to look past it. They don't have any superhuman powers. You just need to focus on what you're capable of, not get caught up in what they're doing."

Wall's trip to the Worlds will mark the first time the fourteen-year-old Canmore, Alberta, native has travelled beyond competitions in Vancouver and Saskatoon.

"It's going to be different. I've never had more than ten people in my age group before," Wall said. "It's probably going to be crowded when

I'm trying to warm up. I could have to fight my way to the wall. It's going to be a big learning experience."

Advice from Calgary's Stacey Weldon, who at nineteen is a veteran of the Worlds in Italy, Amsterdam, Austria and France – where she finished seventh – is helpful, Wall admits.

"It's definitely inspiring to watch the older climbers, the experienced ones. You want to get on that route and try it," says Wall, her lithe teenage body showing well-developed arm and back muscles. "If someone gets it, we all feel good for them."

Like several of her teammates, Wall admits she's afraid of heights. "When I first started, I'd go five feet and I was terrified," Wall says. "You get used to it. It definitely boosts your confidence when you do something hard."

While earning a coaching degree at the University of British Columbia a decade ago, national team head coach Andrew Wilson coached junior climbers at Vancouver's The Edge climbing gym (which he now owns). Soon after he began coaching, Wilson began seeking ways to structure climbers' training, which until then had been characterized by a rebellious and undisciplined approach.

"Climbers can train and benefit from training just like triathletes and rowers," Wilson says.

A hockey player and sporadic climber through his teens, Wilson said he became disillusioned as a hockey coach.

"I started to see an atmosphere of kids being introduced to things that were not positive," Wilson says. "Then I went to my first climbing competition and said Wow! The two closest competitors were cheering each other on."

That camaraderie endures, he says, as competitive climbing was welcomed into the World Games in 2005, an important step for the sport toward the Olympics. And Canada is competitive.

"These kids are really focused and really dedicated," Wilson says. "They understand training to get results. This is the strongest team I've even been involved with, for sure. We've got seven or eight capable of cracking the top ten. It's a really exciting time."

That's a tribute to Competition Climbing Canada, Wilson says, and to the generosity of the local indoor gyms where the kids train. With

100 competitors across Canada benefiting from structured instruction from day one, compared to 900 in the US, who have neither a national team to join nor any coaches, Canada's junior climbers profit from the experience of former competitors such as Calgary's Knut Rokne, the only other coach joining Wilson in Scotland. As well, having two dozen parent volunteers on the trip is invaluable, Wilson adds.

From a parent's perspective, competitive climbing isn't much different from other sports, says Fraser McGurk, whose three sons compete in hockey, cross-country skiing and climbing.

"Your kid either finishes school or whatever activity and you somehow try to get food into them and get them out the door to train," McGurk said. "There's not as many competitions as a hockey player has games, but the training is just as intense."

Having Zak make the national team does increase the financial commitment, McGurk admitted. The help of local businesses was invaluable in raising the $20,000 needed to send the team to Scotland.

"It's phenomenal, the support from businesses in town [Canmore]," McGurk said. "It's really good life experience for the kids – the donation is not just given to them. The athletes feel a sense of responsibility, not just to climb well but to represent the country."

And Canmore parents help out during training sessions by billeting visiting team members from other places, such as Vancouver, Calgary, Edmonton and Saskatoon.

"It's really neat. Normally these kids compete against each other to make the team. Now they're working together, building stronger friendships," McGurk said. "They're very supportive of each other. It's an interesting sport, a very calm sport compared to hockey."

Still, competitive climbing is serious business.

At fifteen, McColl won his category at the Worlds in both speed and difficulty events, but he just as quickly lost his title when he tested positive for pseudoephedrine in a routine urine test. He had innocently taken Claritin before the event. A consequence of competitive climbing's first year of drug testing, Wilson admitted it was a learning experience for all. When McColl won again in 2003, his accomplishment was indisputable.

"Now the kids see it's possible," Wilson said. "We know Canadians can be the friendliest team and the best-liked team, but we can have results too."

After winning four World Junior Championships, Sean McColl continued to climb at the highest degrees of difficulty and in 2008 was competing in senior-level events. In their last years as junior competitors, Zak McGurk and Celeste Wall both qualified for the 2008 World Youth Championships in Sydney, Australia. Charlie Hitchman quit competitive climbing, as he realized it would curtail his ability to pursue other outdoor activities, and signed on as a pro ski patroller at Alberta's Sunshine Village resort.

SIX, MAYBE EIGHT, LONG MINUTES (2006)

> Mark **Heard**

It was at least five minutes, maybe eight. Long, tense minutes.

Six months after being trapped in an underwater cave while kayaking a whitewater river near Whistler, BC, Dr. Mark Heard, an orthopedic surgeon from Canmore, Alberta, returned to his practice a very grateful man.

Late one afternoon, after paddling the Soo River near Pemberton, BC, in May 2006, Heard, his son, Jamie, and six other buddies decided to paddle Callaghan Creek near Whistler, rated as Class IV with some "innocuous" Class V drops.

With powerful yet predictable rapids, Class IV kayaking requires advanced paddling and navigating skills. Class V rivers are the domain of expert kayakers capable of negotiating long, violent rapids littered with unavoidable large obstacles, where the consequences of a mishap are usually serious.

A kayaker since he was eleven, Heard has had numerous adventures, including expeditions to remote rivers in Nepal and India. At nineteen, and after countless kayaking days together with his dad, Jamie was old enough to join an adult road trip, and Callaghan Creek was well within both father's and son's abilities.

"This was our first father–son road trip," Heard, forty-six, says. "The last thing we expected that week was an accident. We went out to paddle conservative water."

The kayakers dropped over a three-metre waterfall thirty seconds apart – Heard third, Jamie behind him. Landing in the pool below the falls, Jamie noticed the boaters ahead of him motioning. Something was amiss. Heard had disappeared.

What some locals knew – but Heard didn't – was that behind the tumbling curtain, water was being continuously circulated into a hydraulic hole just below the surface – a kayaker's "room of doom."

Heard remembers none of the accident, nor the better part of two weeks afterward.

"I've had worse swims, and memories of much worse experiences in my kayak," he says. "I'm oblivious to what happened. I think that makes it less traumatic."

His friends surmise that on approach, Heard's kayak bounced off a rock, causing him to briefly stall and land at the base of the falls with less momentum than the other paddlers. Sucking him backward into the cave, the relentless cascade trapped him.

"At first it was total shock," Jamie recalls. "I just felt so helpless. After two minutes we saw his empty boat. Just his actions told us he was in big trouble."

In Class V water, Jamie explained, with numerous rapids downstream, swimming is a last resort.

Finally Heard's limp body appeared, floating face down, arms above his head. The turbulent creek carried him downstream for about "a football field" before a towline could be attached to his life jacket. His face was blue; he wasn't breathing; he had no pulse. He'd been underwater for "five to eight minutes." While Heard was still half in the water, paddling buddy Ian Norn delivered chest compressions while another friend (and an anaesthesiologist), Lothar Schaefer, administered rescue breaths. Then they noticed Heard making a feeble effort to breathe. They continued with mouth-to-mouth, and eventually Heard began, weakly, to breathe on his own.

"When I pulled him from the water, he looked dead," Norn recalls. "Then he started breathing – but he wasn't okay."

Tended to by his friends, including another doctor, Mark Gale, Heard remained unconscious and combative. Absorbing the situation, Jamie helped build a fire. Paddling partner Jean Borduas ran to his vehicle and dialled 911 on his cell phone. A helicopter was summoned – the canyon was too deep to carry Heard out. Guided by the fire, the helicopter arrived two hours later. There was barely enough daylight to lift Heard to an ambulance waiting on a logging road for the fifteen-minute drive to Whistler. Heard was heli-evacuated to Vancouver that night.

"Lots of things helped save my life," Heard reflects.

Comatose for three more days in intensive care, he was intubated and ventilated, suffering from immersion syndrome. He had kidney, bowel, pancreas, muscle and central nervous system damage, as well as a collapsed right lung – all of which he would eventually recover from without intervention.

Heard gradually responded by squeezing people's fingers. Jamie elicited a significant response when he announced, "Well, dad, I'm the alpha male in the family now."

Heard responded by challenging him to an arm wrestle, which Jamie insists he didn't throw.

"I arm wrestled him and I beat him. I still had a tube down my throat," Heard says. "That's when my wife knew I would be okay."

After ten days he was transferred to his home in Canmore, still breathing oxygen through nasal prongs. He'd dropped from eighty-one kilograms to seventy.

As he slowly recovered his physical strength, however, neuro-psych testing revealed that he was unable to drive. Believing he was fine, he was unable to draw a simple cube. "That was stressful, losing that privilege we all take for granted," Heard admits.

In September he took an extensive four-hour test of his brain functions. He passed, and on October 2 he returned to his practice.

"My first day in OR was one of the most happy, meaningful days of my life," Heard says. "It was a very special moment. I'm as passionate about my work as I am about my paddling. Within my first case, as soon as I started operating, it was like I'd been there a week."

Ironically, it was kayaking that led Heard to medicine. He competed on Canada's national team from 1978 to 1983, and one of his coaches, Dr. Bernie Lalonde, was a doctor of sports medicine.

"I realized there was no money in kayaking, so I started looking toward the future," Heard explains. "My sports background led me into sports medicine."

At the time of his accident, Heard was an orthopaedic surgeon at Canmore and Banff, Alberta, and Golden, BC, hospitals, team physician to the Canadian Alpine Ski Team, and consulting physician to several other mountain- and sport-related organizations.

By December, Heard felt he was functioning at "90 to 95 per cent," and was working three shortened days a week. And he'd made a new discovery – power napping. "Before, I'd get home and jump on my mountain bike," he shrugs.

Beyond a heightened appreciation for simply being alive, Heard said he'd also gained a broadened appreciation for his patients.

"Being a patient taught me to be much more caring, to treat the patient more as a person and not just another knee," Heard says. "And I never appreciated how much commitment there is on the part of the family to make those appointments. My wife, Sue, dropped everything to focus on my healing. That's been a great learning for me."

There's no question about returning to his outdoor passions – kayaking and backcountry ski touring, which, he said, bring balance to his personal and professional life. But, he insists, he's engaging in these activities again with a lowered risk factor.

"I'm still going to paddle, I'm still going to ski tour," Heard says. "By going paddling, by having my adventures, my life is better fulfilled. I think it makes me a better husband, makes me a better father and makes me better at work. But before, I probably accepted a touch too much risk. I feel comfortable eliminating the Class V.

"I feel so lucky. I could have easily died. I was more than just a whisper away. But I'm not searching for too many whys. This was an accident. It just was."

1,030 PEAKS AND COUNTING (2005)

> Rick **Collier**

In August 2004, Calgary's Rick Collier reached the summit of his 1000th mountain: 3225-metre Mount Prince Edward. One of the peaks that comprise the Canadian Rockies' Royal Group, it's tucked away in a rarely visited range just ten kilometres west of Alberta's Peter Lougheed Provincial Park.

But he didn't stop there, and the following month he reached a milestone no one else has yet come anywhere close to – climbing all 572 of the peaks listed in the 1979 edition of the *Rocky Mountains of Canada–South* guidebook, written and compiled by Glen Boles, Robert Kruszyna and William Putnam.

Along the way, Collier completed a third milestone when, in 1994, he became the second person to climb all fifty-four of the Canadian Rockies peaks above 11,000 feet (3353 metres), reaching many of the trailheads by vehicle but many others by skis, bicycle or on foot.

Commenting on his accomplishment, Collier suggests the prestige associated with climbing "1,000" mountains is "a bit bogus," since it places mountains such as 2706-metre Grotto Mountain – a stiff but straightforward hike flanking the town of Canmore, Alberta – in the same category as Canada's highest and the world's largest mountain by mass, Yukon Territory's Mount Logan – a remote and daunting objective which he completed with three partners in May 2001. Leaving Logan's more commonly tagged west summit for its elusive and less frequently climbed 5959-metre true summit five kilometres farther, they put in a day that lasted twenty-two hours.

"It was brewing up for a storm, but we said let's do it," Collier recalls. "We got to the summit around 11 p.m.; the temperatures were down to minus 75. We had a couple of cases of frostbite."

Collier, who taught English composition at Calgary's Mount Royal College until 1995, when he joined the ranks of the self-employed, grew up in St. Louis, Missouri. At fifteen, he and a friend discovered climbing at quarries on the Mississippi River. Soon afterward,

Thomas Hornbein, who, with partner Willi Unsoeld, became the first Americans to summit Everest in 1963, took Collier and his friend under his wing.

"It was all uphill from there," Collier jokes.

He climbed in Colorado and Wyoming, and while studying in Wisconsin and Minnesota he developed his technical rock-climbing skills on the steep and overhanging cliffs of New York's famous Shawangunks. After five decades of climbing, Collier says he is continually engaged by the activity.

"There are always new problems to solve," he says. "It's a kind of full-body problem solving."

As well, he adds, climbing incorporates navigational skills, physical exercise and learning to use equipment and skills to solve problems.

"There's not many problems in the city you can't solve with money," Collier says. "You have to go into the wilderness to find those."

Over the decades, he has explored from the Arctic tundra to the European Alps, as well as in New Zealand, South America and the Yukon.

"Every place is the same, every place is different," Collier said. "Climbing peels away all those superficial layers. It's not religious, but spiritual. If I had to choose I'd have to say I'm an animist – I believe every stream, every meadow, every creature has its own spiritual force. It's an odd thing that most churches are in cities – there's not much in the way of the spiritual there."

An accomplished marathoner and long-distance cyclist who has crossed the us several times, Collier says mountaineering offers the opportunity to explore inside himself.

"I think it's a certain amount of testing of yourself," he says. "Not the stupid kind of adolescent stuff, but we don't have many opportunities to see how well we endure, cope under stressful situations. It renews your sense of humanity. There's lots of symbolism in mountain climbing. You can get up to the summit of a mountain, but you can never stay there. It's not yours, but you can go back. The experiences are borrowed."

Climbing all of the southern Rockies, which range from Saskatchewan Crossing, on Banff National Park's Icefields Parkway, to Waterton Lakes National Park, which sits on the Alberta–Montana international border, didn't become an actual project until about 2000.

"I guess it gives you a goal, a way to organize your climbing," Collier says. "And you get to shanghai your friends into climbing these obscure peaks. It's a great way of getting into different places. There's probably not a valley in the southern Rockies I haven't been in."

Collier credits about twenty-five climbing friends with helping him accomplish his milestone.

"They were with me when I needed them, they know their craft and their lore and they had the skills we needed," he says. "It's a kind of teamwork you'll never find in the city."

Over the years, Collier says he's made numerous solo trips too, the longest lasting nine days.

"Solo trips are when you get in touch with those little nodes of higher existence," he says. "I overcome my urban-generated fears of the outdoors and realize the wilderness is a really gentle place."

After encountering at least one or two large, furry, four-legged mountain travellers each summer, Collier says he dislikes popular mythology about bears. Most of those encounters were his own fault, he admits, occurring when he moved through the landscape too quietly and surprised them, as happened in the summer of 2004 when he experienced a chance meeting with a grizzly and her cub.

"She charged three times, coming to about twelve feet from me each time," he says. "She was close enough I could look right into her eyes, and she was terrified. A lot more scared than I was."

Asked to recall his most memorable climbs, Collier replies, "I'm glad you said memorable rather than fun."

He admits he and his partners often asked themselves, "Why do we do this?"

"I always answer, 'It may not be fun, but it sure is memorable,'" Collier laughs.

Among his most memorable climbs was 3119-metre Mount Swiderski, the last of the named peaks of the southern Rockies to sit unclimbed, until 2005, when Collier, with fellow members of their "Old Goats Group" Martin Taylor and Rick Homes, navigated a route through broken rock towers to the summit. Devoid of any cairn or evidence of a previous ascent, this summit marked for Collier one of "about eight first ascents."

"Most of those, people have never heard of; they're in areas people never go into," he admits.

Directly east of the Kootenay National Park warden station, 2921-metre Split Peak, his last of the 572, was also quite memorable, with an approach that involved several unbridged creek crossings.

"It was very difficult. We're calling it 'Little Alberta of the South,'" Collier says, referring to the notoriously crumbly smaller neighbour of the Rockies' famously challenging Mount Alberta. It was his third attempt.

"I had a very good crew with me," he says. "We spent seventeen hours on it. There was snow cover, loose rock up to 5.7 – some interesting stuff."

With his tally sitting at about 1030 mountains, Collier doesn't have any intention of slowing down.

"As long as you keep your aerobic fitness, you don't ever have to quit."

I interviewed Collier for this article in the fall of 2005. By the winter of 2008, his tally stood at 1,150 mountains.

"CINDERELLA CLIMBER" REACHES SUMMIT OF DREAMS (2007)

> Karl **Griffiths** and Grant **Meekins**

Nearing the end of his first year as a full-time resident of the town of Canmore, nestled in the bosom of Alberta's Rocky Mountains, Carl Griffiths beams with pride at a poster displayed on the wall of his home office. In the photo, he's standing on a mountaintop against the backdrop of a stunning panorama.

Behind his left shoulder looms Mount Everest. Beside him stands Grant Meekins, the Canmore-based mountain guide Griffiths credits for getting him to the 6857-metre summit of one of the Himalayas' most dramatic peaks, Ama Dablam.

More than three months after that summit photo was taken in October 2006, Griffiths was still smiling, grateful to Meekins for helping him fulfill a dream.

Griffiths started climbing recreationally while studying at Britain's University of London in the 1970s. In 1997 he discovered climbing in the Canadian Rockies with Canmore guide Alison Andrews, launching an annual tradition of increasingly challenging ascents. In 2005 Griffiths and Andrews summitted 5199-metre Mount Kenya, Africa's second highest peak. Unlike Africa's highest, 5895-metre Kilimanjaro – the highest mountain in the world that can be walked up – Mount Kenya involved 450 metres of technical rock climbing.

"It was enjoyable rock climbing, but it was a real struggle dealing with the altitude," Griffiths admits.

Despite the difficulties, however, Griffiths harboured one more alpine goal.

"I thought I'd like to take it one more step – perhaps the Himalayas," he said. "I was in love with the idea of being able to climb a serious Himalayan peak. I really wanted to be over the 20,000-foot threshold."

Griffiths began researching potential climbs and settled on Ama Dablam, an exquisite peak regarded by many as the most beautiful in the region, which also offers some enjoyable climbing challenges.

Next, he visited Yamnuska Mountain Adventures' Canmore office for advice about guided trips to Ama Dablam, where the staff suggested he speak with Meekins, who had previously guided the mountain. An alpine guide certified with the Association of Canadian Mountain Guides, Meekins had guided Griffiths once before, on Guides' Route, a 655-metre rock climb overlooking Canmore on EEOR (the locally used term for the east end of Mount Rundle).

"That was a big route for me. I'm just an enthusiastic amateur," Griffiths says. "It gave me an excellent introduction to Grant; I thoroughly enjoyed climbing with him. I appreciated his calm demeanour."

They began planning their Himalayan adventure.

For five months, fifty-one-year-old Griffiths trained. Once a week he tackled a route from Alan Kane's guidebook *Scrambles in the Canadian Rockies*. He lifted weights. He raced up Banff's Sulphur Mountain trail, trying to match Meekins's time of forty-three minutes. His best was forty-six.

In September 2006 they climbed the east ridge of 3480-metre Mount Kitchener, near the Athabasca Glacier, an outing that involved camping overnight and negotiating an exposed ridge. Meekins set up a fixed line to mimic the climbing Griffiths would experience on Ama Dablam.

"Grant felt that represented an excellent testing ground for me," Griffiths says. "It gave us both the confidence that we were on the right track."

Ama Dablam's southwest ridge would involve fifty-five-degree ice climbing and mixed terrain, including a slightly overhanging section at just under 6100 metres – all while carrying a heavy pack.

"Ama Dablam is physically demanding," Meekins says. "I set up an obstacle course for Carl to work on his fixed-line technique forward and backward. Then all we had to think about was acclimatizing and slogging on."

Meanwhile, Meekins arranged for food, lodging, base camp cooks and Sherpa support in distant Nepal.

"Communication is difficult; it can be a month and a half between e-mails," Meekins explained. "Sherpas can't communicate until they go down to a village that has e-mail. Then there's the language barrier, so you get an e-mail back that doesn't clear up anything you've asked for, and you know it's going to be another month before you hear back."

In late October, after flying to Kathmandu, then to Lukla, trekking for six days and staying in local teahouses, Griffiths finally saw their objective for the first time.

"I was looking at a serious Himalayan peak," Griffiths admits. "When I saw it, it was intimidating."

The pair spent ten days on the mountain, climbing to progressively higher camps and descending to base camp at 4790 metres for rest days.

Then, the night before starting their summit push, Meekins became violently ill, first with vomiting, then with diarrhea.

"It was pretty intense. I was very sick," Meekins says. "I'd experienced something like it before on previous trips to Nepal. But I felt it wouldn't last long, usually I'd bounce back in twenty-four hours."

They started walking together in the morning, but Meekins's diarrhea stopped him. He'd nearly catch up to Griffiths but was forced to stop – ten times. At advanced base camp, Meekins suggested Griffiths continue to Camp I at 5703 metres, believing a Sherpa would soon be there. Around 3 p.m. Meekins learned the Sherpa wasn't coming, so he pushed himself to join Griffiths.

"He just could not leave me alone – he felt it was his professional responsibility," Griffiths says. "That level of self-sacrifice is uncommon. It spoke volumes."

At Camp I, Meekins set about the task of replacing precious body fluids for both of them.

"Water is always a big challenge," Meekins explains. "It all comes from snow melt, and it takes a long time."

Fortunately, by morning Meekins felt better. They climbed to Camp II, which Griffiths likens to "setting a tent on the torch of the Statue of Liberty."

Steep climbing the following morning was a rude awakening, he adds.

"We were straight into steep, in-your-face mixed climbing," Griffiths says. "It was exhausting, scrambling over snow-covered rocks, rock climbing up sixty-foot vertical pitches."

From Camp III, at 6405 metres, they would climb to the summit, then return for the night.

"It was very hard. I was tired by the time we got to Camp III," Griffiths says. "I was worried about my energy level, knowing what we had to do. I started having a lot of feelings of self-doubt. The last 300 metres nearly killed me, I almost wanted to quit. But I couldn't do that to Grant, not after what he'd done for me. I thought of my wife and daughter. There was no way, after all their support for the past six months, that I wanted to put people through that humiliation."

ANDY EVANS IS ALL SMILES ON THE SUMMIT OF K2, KARAKORAM, PAKISTAN.

PETER ARBIC TAKES IN THE VIEW ON HOWSE PEAK IN THE CANADIAN ROCKIES.

ARON RALSTON.

ABBY WATKINS CLIMBS ROCKY MOUNTAIN
HORROR SHOW, AT THE CINEPLEX,
CANADIAN ROCKIES.

KIM CSIZMAZIA SWINGS ONTO
AIN'T NOBODY HERE BUT US CHICKENS,
CANADIAN ROCKIES.

CATHERINE MULVIHILL LEADS UP
THE PILLAR ON ICE NINE ON
THE ICEFIELDS PARKWAY,
CANADIAN ROCKIES.

ZAK McGURK TRAINING
HARD AT GRASSI LAKES,
CANADIAN ROCKIES.

MARK HEARD.

RICK COLLIER IN THE VOWELLS, BUGABOOS, BC

KARL GRIFFITHS CLIMBS ABOVE CAMP 2
ON AMA DABLAM, NEPALI HIMALAYAS.

Sliding hand-held ascenders up the fixed rope, Griffiths pushed on – eight steps, rest, eight steps, rest. Then a Sherpa began moving in tandem just ahead of him.

"The moral impact of having him there made me think I just might do this," Griffiths says. "I got through that period of self-doubt."

At 12:30 p.m., five hours after leaving Camp III, they summitted.

There's a great difference between climbing recreationally in the Rockies around Canmore, Griffiths says, and climbing a big mountain at altitude.

"I have such a high respect for Canadian guides," Griffiths says. "They've earned such high credentials that I'm capable of investing great trust in them. Custom trips are not cheap, but the experience justifies it. We had a truly remarkable trip. This was, to me, a lifelong ambition fulfilled. I owe Alison and Grant an enormous debt. It's a very special relationship between the guide and the client to make people's dreams come true.

"I call myself the Cinderella climber. I'm not one of the elite you see in this town; I never will be. I won't do anything like this again. That's what makes this a particularly special achievement. It was the greatest moment of my life."

EXPLORERS

This section features adventurers who are, first and foremost, driven by a desire to break new ground. They seek to make first ascents of unclimbed peaks, first descents by kayaks and inflatable rafts on unexplored rivers. They seek to establish new routes on vertical rock walls or aim to accomplish their adventures in a manner or style that has not yet been achieved. Explorers thrive on the unknown, and they live to create their own paths.

RAFTERS DODGE RAPIDS, CROCODILES AND GUERRILLAS (2000)

> Colin **Angus**, Scott **Borthwick** and Ben **Kozel**

After spending five months navigating the Amazon, the world's most voluminous river, in an inflatable rubber raft, three intrepid adventurers returned to their home base of Canmore, Alberta, to dry out their gear and allow the magnitude of their accomplishment to soak in.

"It's good to be back. You forget how beautiful it is in the Rockies," says Colin Angus.

Angus, twenty-eight, Scott Borthwick, twenty-three, and Ben Kozel, twenty-six, gratefully rested their weary and soggy bodies at the home of Angus's sister after becoming the first people to travel the 6300-kilometre length of the giant South American river from source to sea in an inflatable raft.

"I've always been fascinated by the Amazon," Angus says. "I thought, 'What a great way to explore it, from source to sea.'" No beginner in the pursuit of adventure, at nineteen, Angus embarked on a five-year sailing odyssey across the Pacific Ocean, completing much of his journey solo.

To kick off their Amazon adventure, the trio flew to Lima, Peru, and headed out from the sprawling city of 15 million on September 8, 1999. In addition to paddling the river, the team also made a self-propelled crossing of South America from the Pacific Ocean to the Atlantic. They hiked for three weeks along old roads and through deserts into the Andes mountain range to reach the South American continental divide, and the source of the great river, a cliff at 5170 metres on Nevado Mismi, a glaciated volcanic peak in the Arequipa region, about 650 kilometres southeast of Lima.

From there, a stream descends the mountain's northern slopes, then runs its course through other tributaries and rivers which eventually form the Amazon.

"Going down in whitewater with views of 6000-metre peaks on both sides was incredible," Kozel says.

For six weeks the team navigated whitewater, dodging boulders and waterfalls and sometimes getting stuck in narrow chutes.

"Sometimes the river would disappear into a crack between two cliffs," Angus says. "We had to run those sections blind."

At one such section, Borthwick fell into the surging water and had to climb up the rock wall to a small ledge from where he hoped to be rescued. Angus and Kozel, however, were swept downstream in the raft, stranding Borthwick and leaving him to swim back to the raft through treacherous Class V rapids.

"It was nerve wracking," Borthwick admits.

Four months after the whitewater section of their trip, all three adventurers still had vivid memories of the trip.

"When you've got that much adrenalin pumping through your system every day for a month and a half, it's a constant mixture of fear and exhilaration," Kozel states. "Every day you ask yourself, is this the day I make a fatal mistake?"

The whitewater section ended very abruptly when they entered the jungle and were suddenly surrounded by tropical rainforest, chirping birds and swinging monkeys. The nastiest hazard they encountered on this section of otherwise calm water was an attack of gunfire delivered courtesy of some forest-dwelling Shining Path guerrillas. Luckily, the paddlers eluded the bullets as they rounded a bend in the river.

By the end of bouncing and floating all the way to the Atlantic Ocean, their raft had flipped six times, and its occupants had performed a combined total of thirty-three unintentional swims. At night they listened to small crocodiles splashing in the chocolate-brown water, and during the daytime they enjoyed the company of friendly pink and grey dolphins.

For the flat, broad section of the river, they built a frame of balsa logs, on which they mounted oars. The frame also supported a table of sorts, constructed of bamboo and vines, where they placed their cooking stove.

"It was quite homey," Angus jokes.

Meals consisted mostly of boiled rice and beans, which were sometimes augmented by wild bananas or freshly caught trout. While the first two-thirds of the voyage were spent in relative comfort, however, Angus says the rainfall became relentless toward the end of the trip, causing their belongings to become mildewed because they couldn't dry them out.

"We were rotting inside our raingear," Angus says.

After becoming the first team to travel the entire length of the Amazon in a rubber raft, retracing the 1986 route of Polish adventurer Piotr Chmielinski's historic first descent of the Amazon from source to sea by kayak, the rafters admitted their return to the modern world left them with somewhat mixed feelings.

"There's a feeling of accomplishment, but it's kind of sad in a way," Borthwick says. "We've got to go home, but we're relieved, too, after all the hard work. It does feel good to be in civilization, though, and to be able to go and buy a pint of milk."

EAT, SLEEP, SKI (2004)

> Kari **Medig**, Merrie-Beth **Board**, Guy **Edwards**,
Dan **Clark and** Karsten **Heuer**

The wind is everywhere at once, a brutal, tangible force with gusts capable of pushing you uphill. It tests your steadiness on your skis as you carry a thirty-kilogram pack. With your head tucked deeply into your hood, you fix your goggle-encased eyes on the ground ahead: a constantly swirling sheet of snow spontaneously changing direction like schools of scurrying fish. Before the skier five metres behind you reaches your tracks, they are erased by the wind like a vigorously shaken Etch-a-Sketch. Ice-plastered rock cliffs suddenly appear close enough to touch, towering a thousand metres above you in a swirl of cloud, then disappear as if someone switched a remote control back to a screen of churning wind and snow.

Whiteout, blizzard conditions are a common encounter for anyone skiing across a glacier. While powder-hungry resort skiers attach climbing skins to their ski bases in search of an afternoon's worth of freshies within minutes of the parking lot, others set out on multi-day trips through wilderness made all the more remote, and at the same time more accessible, by a deep snowpack and freezing temperatures.

And while those skiing from hut to hut on the four-day Classic Wapta Traverse straddling Banff and Yoho National Parks look forward to eating and sleeping in warm and well-equipped cabins, skiers embarking on more remote journeys, such as the 130-kilometre, two-week Bugaboos to Rogers Pass Traverse, look forward to the shelter of a −30°C down sleeping bag and nylon tent under the night sky, whether filled with twinkling stars or blizzard-driven snow.

In April 2003 twenty-eight-year-old Merrie-Beth Board of Golden, BC, hitched a ride in a Zodiac from Haines, Alaska, that dropped her and three companions across Haines Inlet at Davidson Point. They walked along the beach in their ski boots and followed a drainage onto a glacier. Unstrapping their skis from their packs, they clicked their boots into their bindings, where they remained for most of the next fifty-four days as the group skied 700 kilometres across the Saint Elias mountain range. Along the way they spent eighteen days climbing to the summit of Canada's highest peak, 5959-metre Mount Logan, up the east ridge and down the west.

"It's very mysterious to see a half-erased mountain; you only see a rock buttress or piece of a ridge," Board says of skiing in a whiteout. "The surrealness of spending a night out there just takes over."

After two months of skiing preceded by several months of planning by phone and e-mail, poring over maps and arranging food drops with bush pilots, the group was fifty-four kilometres shy of their journey's end when Jacqui Hudson lost her balance on an icy slope and tumbled into a crevasse.

"She landed on her head; she was in quite a bit of pain," Board recalls. "It was like watching someone do a backflip into a crevasse. It was a terrifying moment."

Despite neck and rib fractures, Hudson extricated herself, and, with her teammates carrying her share of the food and gear, the group skied the final five days to Cooper River near Cordova, Alaska.

"We had a serious wake-up call," Board admits. "You're not at the end until you're at the end."

Travelling on skis hundreds of kilometres away from the nearest snowmobile track is not without its risks. Every group member must be proficient at route finding, map and terrain reading, crevasse rescue and first aid. Even with a satellite phone, help is hours or sometimes days away.

"If there's any kind of objective danger, you have to be very clear about the decisions you make," Board says. "The littlest mistake could cost you your own or your partner's life."

Added to the objective hazards presented by crevasses and avalanche terrain are the challenges of physical discomfort, emotional weariness and friction between individual personalities brought on by extended journeys in remote wilderness.

The solution, Board says, is to look at the trip one day at a time.

"There were definitely more days of 'this is amazing.' I don't know if it's fun or if it's the challenge or honing your patience with yourself, or honing your patience with your partners. It was more fun to take things step by step than to look too far forward."

For Cranbrook, BC's Kari Medig, twenty-nine, the only male on the Saint Elias Traverse, long wilderness ski trips necessitate a welcome simplification of priorities.

"I love that aspect of having a daily purpose – the main purpose is to cover ground," Medig says. "I just love waking up and knowing that. You have to get back to the basics. You have to streamline and analyze every detail, try to make your days easier. Linking one place to another, by foot, twelve hours a day. It's quite simple – eating, sleeping and skiing."

With food caches ten days apart, the skiers towed sleds constructed from modified Crazy Carpets.

"It was sort of like dragging a little pet across the glacier; the sleds sort of took on a life of their own," Medig recalls.

Rest days are rarely planned, he explains, because a fierce storm could suddenly keep the group tent bound, eating the food required to sustain them until they reach their next food cache. Accurate location readings are crucial, he adds, because if the marker wand is blown over, the food can be difficult to find, even with a GPS. As well, careful menu planning helps.

"It's so easy when you're sitting in the comfort of your home, but after you've been out there for a while you start hating what you've got."

Medig should know. The year before, he skied a two-month section of the first complete Coast Mountain Traverse. Guy Edwards, thirty, and John Millar, twenty-four, were the only two group members who skied the entire traverse, leaving Vancouver in February to ski across vast glaciers, climb up and down 1800-metre passes and bushwhack through dense valley bottoms to arrive five and a half months and 2015 kilometres later in Skagway, Alaska.

Spending nearly half a year skiing offers a unique freedom, Edwards says.

"The longer I'm out there, the calmer my mind gets," he explains. "You get stuck in such a meditative and reflective mindset for so long, you become much more open and aware of the world around you. If you're a weekend warrior you never get to get out of your daily regular workday mindset."

Benefiting from those who broke the first trail decades ago, today's adventurers are linking shorter ski traverses into longer trips. One of those pioneers was Calgary native, mountain writer and guide Chic Scott. In 1967 Scott, Neil Liske, Don Gardner and former Resorts of the Canadian Rockies ski-hill mogul Charlie Locke successfully completed the first Great Divide Traverse, skiing from Jasper to Lake Louise, Alberta, across remote glaciated terrain of the Canadian Rockies in twenty-one days, raising the bar of ski touring possibilities.

"The Great Divide Traverse is still a really big trip," says Dan Clark, twenty-eight, a Calgary native who was a key organizer and participant in the Coast Traverse. "It's got some of the biggest and best terrain anywhere; it's really stunning and really impressive."

As a university student, Clark was inspired by Scott's *Summits and Icefields* – the guidebook that's ignited many a ski touring dream trip – to attempt the first complete ski traverse from McBride to Kimberley,

BC. In 1998 Clark and Chris Gooliaff set out on a sixty-one-day, 700-kilometre trip, skiing through the Cariboo, Selkirk and Purcell mountain ranges. North of Mica Creek, BC, the two encountered steep side valleys with avalanche slopes that threatened to sweep them into the canyon below and hastily bury them in debris. In one section, slowed by impenetrable forest, they travelled only six kilometres in two days as rain increased to a torrential downpour. While some days brought knee-deep barefoot crossings through numbingly cold creeks, others provided panoramic views of untouched snowy peaks under brilliant azure skies.

While modern technology has created lighter, yet extremely resilient, boots, bindings, skis, packs, stoves and tents, and, increasingly, GPS units and satellite phones have become essentials in any ski tourer's pack in case of emergency, sometimes primitive means are invaluable.

In March 1999 Canmore, Alberta, resident Karsten Heuer, thirty-four, and companions Leanne Allison and Jay Honeyman skied 450 kilometres in twenty-eight days, from Jasper, Alberta, to Kinuseo Falls, BC, as part of Heuer's eighteen-month Yellowstone to Yukon journey to research the migration paths of wolves and grizzlies. More than once, Heuer and his partners found themselves following wolverine tracks through small, narrow canyons.

"We soon learned if we didn't follow their tracks our time was ill spent," Heuer says. "When the wolverine tracks went in, we were usually able to get through and when they didn't we usually ended up at a frozen waterfall."

The wolverines' example wasn't the only one Heuer and his team benefited from on their ski trip. During a three-night outing to place a food cache prior to their departure, Heuer was joined by Don Gardner, who insisted they travel using wax instead of skins and without stove or tent, instead making small fires and sleeping in tree wells.

The same light and simple approach served Gardner well in 1992, when he walked out the back door of his downtown Calgary home and began following the shore ice of the Elbow River. Gardner ultimately skied 900 kilometres in twenty-eight days carrying only a nylon jacket, down coat, extra pair of socks, sleeping bag and food.

For Dan Clark, long ski trips are all about the satisfaction and rewards of reaching the top of a pass after two weeks of travelling, the intensity of relationships that develop through hard work and stress, and the wonder of experiencing places few people ever get to see.

Any advice?

"You just need a really good sleeping bag," Clark said.

In April 2004 Guy Edwards and John Millar disappeared while attempting a new route on the unclimbed north face of Devils Thumb, on the BC–Alaska border in the Stikine Icecap region of the Coast Mountains.

NEVER SAY "NO" TO A DETERMINED WOMAN (2005)

> Arlene **Blum**

When Arlene Blum was deciding which university to attend to work toward her Ph.D. in chemistry, she was thrilled to be accepted at Harvard. Not only a highly respected academic institution, it also boasted the Harvard Mountaineering Club (HMC), and during her undergrad years at Portland, Oregon's Reed College, Blum had developed a great passion for mountaineering.

Her enthusiasm was quickly extinguished, however, when the HMC president informed her she was not eligible to join, because the club didn't accept women members.

Blum was stunned. It was 1966 and while women were beginning to gain a tiny foothold in the academic, professional and social world, they had enormous mountains to overcome in the climbing world.

For Blum, however, being told she couldn't do something because she was a woman served as a powerful motivator rather than a spirit-flattening deterrent. Raised in a Midwest home filled with cigarette smoke and the din emanating from a blaring television, Blum was forbidden to do much of anything, including swim at the beach or play piano.

"I was constantly told I couldn't do anything," Blum says. "I loved being outside, so I'd go and shovel snow. I always found a great sense of freedom and escape in the cold and the wind."

In mountaineering, Blum discovered the wonders of the high alpine while also exploring the limits of her own resolve. And she discovered significant obstacles among a fraternity that believed women were not strong enough to carry heavy packs or endure the rigours of high altitude.

Having climbed 5500-metre mountains in Mexico and the Peruvian Andes with friends, Blum knew otherwise. But after she was rejected from an expedition to North America's highest, Alaska's Denali (Mt. McKinley), by a man who told her women weren't strong enough to carry heavy loads or emotionally stable enough to handle the challenges of altitude, Blum began contacting experienced women climbers from as far away as Australia and New Zealand.

On July 6, 1970, the six "Damsels on Denali" became the first women's team to reach McKinley's 6198-metre summit. Then, with their leader suffering from the effects of altitude and exhaustion, Blum suddenly found herself taking charge in an emergency with a storm fast approaching.

"I didn't have time to think about it," Blum says. "I had to solve the problem and get her down. In the end, it was a very empowering experience. It gave me a real impetus. It jump-started me on the path to leadership. Women could do hard physical things, function and deal with life-threatening experiences and solve them."

She then dreamed up a greater challenge: in 1978 she led the first all-women's expedition to a giant Himalayan peak – 8091-metre Annapurna.

"No woman from any country had even climbed to 8000 metres," Blum says. "Because of my experience on Denali, I knew women could."

Annapurna is considered by many to be the most difficult of the world's fourteen 8000-metre peaks, but Blum's expedition placed two climbers and two Sherpas on the summit.

"I felt we did quite a good job," Blum said. "I'd done a lot of expeditions before, and we picked a strong, experienced team. Ours was the fifth (and first American) ascent."

Unfortunately, after the climbers succeeded in summitting, two more members of the thirteen-woman team died on their attempt to be the second team of the expedition to reach the summit. "It was such a tragedy, it overwhelmed climbing it for us," Blum says. "Right after the climb, I wished I could have told them they couldn't go."

After the 1978 expedition, Blum wrote *Annapurna: A Woman's Place*. Not only was their expedition a first, so was her book, capturing the challenges, triumph and tragedy of a Himalayan expedition – for the first time from a woman's point of view.

Not long afterward, Blum began working on her second book, *Breaking Trail: A Climbing Life*.

As featured guest at the Banff Mountain Book Festival in November 2005, Blum shared the story of *Breaking Trail*, in which she attempts to understand why, after losing half her friends to climbing accidents by the time she was twenty-five, she continued to climb and lead expeditions to high, dangerous mountains.

What she learned, Blum says, was that a childhood of denial led her to seek out improbable challenges.

"There's a lot of challenge in trying to do really hard things," Blum says. "People can do so much more than they think they are capable of."

After watching a movie about surfers seeking an endless summer, Blum embarked on a series of expeditions from 1971 to 1973 in search of endless winter climbing. In 1981–82, she made the first traverse of the Great Himalayan Range of Bhutan, Nepal and India.

"Once I get a picture in my mind of a challenging thing, I have to do it," she admits.

The approach has also served her well as a scientist, as her research led to the banning of a cancer-causing chemical previously used as a flame retardant on children's sleepwear.

"I discovered that a lot of the processes of science and climbing were similar for me," Blum says. "Dreaming up improbable but possible things and making them happen."

A successful inspirational speaker who lives in Berkeley, California, from where she runs a small adventure travel business, Blum quit leading expeditions to dangerous mountains in 1987 when she became a mother, but she continues to trek through the Andes and Himalayas.

Most recently she climbed Mount Kenya and Oregon's Mount Hood, and in the summer of 2005 she and her daughter trekked and scrambled up small peaks in Slovenia.

While the mountains continue to lure her, Blum says she hopes to return to public policy work, particularly to research harmful chemicals prevalent in North America.

"People are so afraid of terrorism, but the chemicals in our bodies are so much more harmful," Blum says.

"It's a hard mountain to climb, but I'm an optimist."

MOUNTAINEERING IS A VEHICLE FOR LEARNING (2004)

> Carlos **Buhler**

His résumé reads like a five-star anthology of small, lightweight first ascents of the world's most formidable climbing challenges.

After a thirty-four-year (and still climbing) career, he's participated in more than forty expeditions to remote places including Peru, Argentina, Uganda, Pakistan, Tajikistan, Kazakhstan, Russia and Tibet, and he is credited with putting up some of the world's most difficult and committing high-altitude routes, from which retreat was rarely possible once the climb was begun. Most notable among these is his 1983 ascent of Mount Everest by its last unclimbed face, the Kangshung (east) face starting from the Tibetan side of the mountain, as part of an American team that established the mountain's most technically difficult – and still unrepeated – route.

Growing up a lot closer to some of the world's tallest buildings, in Harrison, New York, than to the world's highest mountains, Carlos Buhler received his first climbing exposure in 1970 at the age of fifteen on a National Outdoor Leadership Course at Wyoming's Wind River. From the very beginning he recognized the experience was extraordinary.

"I knew that something very special was going on," Buhler says. "The interactions between myself and nature, and myself and people, were more intense than anything I'd ever experienced."

Later living and attending high school in Barcelona, Spain, Buhler joined the local mountaineering club, Peña Guara – of which he remains a member. The experiences and relationships he formed in Spain shaped the rest of his life. After university his Spanish language skills allowed him to guide hikers and simple climbing ascents in Peru, Ecuador and Bolivia for an adventure travel company.

"It was my way of seeing the world, an opportunity allowing me to travel as a young man without the financial worries of paying for airline tickets," Buhler says.

Then, in 1978, the American Alpine Club invited Buhler to be part of a joint US/Soviet climb hosted by the former Soviet Union's mountaineering federation in Tajikistan, in Central Asia's Pamir Range.

"That exposure to our Cold War opponent was life changing," Buhler says. "We learned about a culture that was theoretically our enemy, but our experience was one of warmth."

On what was his first trip to Central Asia, Buhler and a couple of teammates ended up in hospital suffering from altitude sickness.

"We experienced extraordinary hospitality in a land so foreign from our own," he says. "It led me to realize what kind of politics must be involved to name people our enemies. I grew a different way of looking at things."

The following year, the Soviets invaded Afghanistan, not far from where he'd been climbing.

"These are the kinds of geopolitics happening now," Buhler says. "I could be climbing with an Iraqi mountaineering team, and very happily, but our governments are at odds."

In subsequent years, Buhler shared intense experiences on many other mountains with the same Russian climbers he first met in 1978, experiences that constantly expanded his view of human relationships and his understanding of how mountaineering serves as a conduit for personal and spiritual growth.

"It allowed me to realize the breadth of the mountaineering community and the influence it could have on the world," Buhler says. "I was exposed to those methods and people and systems that were so different from our own, drawn from the same love of nature and sense of camaraderie as in the us. The opportunity to climb with Russians broadened my horizons immensely."

The opportunity didn't hurt his technical skills either.

In 1985 Buhler and one American partner made the first ascent of 6817-metre Ama Dablam's daunting northeast face in winter. Three years later Buhler became the first American to summit Kangchenjunga, at 8591 metres the world's third highest mountain. In 1990 he reached the summit of 8172-metre Dhaulagiri I with a Lithuanian and a Nepali, in the process becoming the first North American to summit four of the world's 8000-metre peaks. In August 1996 – his third attempt on the mountain – Buhler reached the world's second-highest peak, the fearsome 8611-metre K2, with two Russians. Buhler is one of only two North Americans to have summitted the mountain via the Chinese north face route.

Eleven months after he summitted K2, he and a Russian partner became the first American and the first Russian to climb Pakistan's 8131-metre Nanga Parbat, and in 1998 Buhler and the same partner spent sixteen days ascending the sheer-vertical 1586-metre north face of Changabang in the Indian Himalayas, topping out on the 6864-metre summit with three more Russian teammates.

His most memorable climbs, Buhler says, are those that were instrumental in changing him as a person and helped define his very being.

"Mountaineering is just a vehicle for the learning that goes on," Buhler says. "That's definitely been the result of my experiences in climbing. It's an activity that I certainly enjoy and pursue with reckless abandon, but I realized very early what I was taking from my experiences in the mountains was much more than just the activity."

Throughout his career, Buhler, who currently maintains his primary residence in Canmore, Alberta, with his partner Crista-Lee, has appreciated climbing in the Canadian Rockies as well.

"The Canadian Rockies are easily accessed by automobile; at the same time they provide a very intense environment consistent with what people are forced to learn in the Himalayas," Buhler says. "There are issues with snow, avalanches, glaciers, insecure anchor challenges and intense cold. The mental problem-solving is very similar to mental challenges you'd have to work out anywhere."

As in the Himalayas, however, small mistakes can lead to enormous disasters.

"The Rockies have a steep learning curve, which many of my friends didn't survive," Buhler says. "The Canadian Rockies has a stinger in its tail that's taken out numerous climbers in their quest to learn."

And have his climbing objectives changed over the decades?

"They're easier, I'm getting old," he jokes. "My focus is still to explore that inner journey with people on the stage that is created by the mountaineering challenge. Mountaineering is problem-solving. That's the essence of climbing. You use a number of different tools to solve problems."

VETERAN MOUNTAINEER IS AN ARTIST AND A GENTLEMAN (2006)

> Glen **Boles**

In nearly half a century of climbing mountains, Glen Boles has accomplished much.

He's climbed about 525 mountains, reaching the summits of all but six of the fifty-four Canadian Rockies peaks higher than 11,000 feet (3353 metres), and all but one of the seventeen peaks above 11,000 feet in BC's Columbia Mountains. A talented artist and photographer, he's amassed a library of over 34,000 slides and 25,000 black and white negatives, and many of his photos appear in guidebooks and climbing books. He's made thirty-seven first ascents, pioneered new routes and received awards for his contributions to the Canadian climbing community.

But the first thing anyone who knows him is likely to remember is that he's one of the nicest people they've ever met.

"Glen epitomizes the grace a person can gradually acquire through a lifetime of passion for mountains and mountaineering," says Rockies author and historian Bob Sandford. "There is no better person to honour in terms of the qualities he inspires in others, and in particular in younger climbers who have the privilege to meet him."

Born in New Brunswick in 1934, Boles arrived in Calgary in the early 1950s. Soon after taking a job with the City of Calgary – for which he worked as a planner and draftsman for thirty-five years – Boles joined co-worker Heinz Kahl for a climb on Mount Yamnuska's steep south-facing cliffs.

"I was just scared to death the first time we went out, but I was back at it two weeks later," Boles recalls.

In the 1960s Boles pioneered new routes on Mount Edith and Storm Mountain with Brian Greenwood. In the early 1970s he teamed up with Mike Simpson, Gordon Scruggs and Don Forest (the first person to climb all of the Rockies 11,000ers), forming the nucleus of the Grizzly Group – so named because of a 1974 encounter with one of the furry beasts. In subsequent years, the group expanded to include Leon Kubbernus, Jim Fosti, Lyn Michaud and Walt Davis.

"Glen's just a really easygoing, compassionate guy," Simpson says. "If you wanted anybody on the other end of your rope who was reliable, Glen would be the first one you'd pick."

Year after year, the Grizzly Group flew into different remote and rarely visited areas of the Rockies and Columbias, established a base camp, and explored and climbed. Boles's meticulous records of those trips and climbs have since become a valuable resource for climbers venturing into those regions.

"I like exploring and getting into new areas," Boles says. "It's like the bear went into the mountains to see what he could see, what's over the other side."

After retiring from his job in 1991, Boles began drawing black and white pencil sketches based on his mountain photos and experiences, which have since become popular collector's items among the mountain community. The basement of his Cochrane, Alberta, home is a captivating climbing museum displaying photos of great mountains and good friends. Boles has also contributed to two books, *The Climbers Guide to the Canadian Rockies* and *Place Names of the Canadian Alps*.

In 2004, he embarked on a new project – printing about 3000 of his favourite photos, culled from his inventory of black and white negatives, in his basement darkroom. The images were taken over a period of more than forty years and capture hundreds of Rocky Mountain peaks, as well as the partners he climbed them with. Gillean Daffern, co-founder and editor of Calgary's Rocky Mountain Books, painstakingly trimmed that number down to 300 before finally settling on 140 images to fill the pages of *Glen Boles: My Mountain Album*, a hardcover collection of Boles's photography and artwork.

More than a photo album, the volume is a 168-page coffee-table-sized ode to the Canadian Rockies and to the profound bond between steadfast climbing partners. Boles's crisp photos capture the intricate textures of icy crevasses, the striated profiles of rockbands, snow runnels as sharp as comb's teeth and séracs standing like ice castles – the details are all palpable in his artwork. Like his climbs, each page is a new adventure, an intriguing balance of photographs and sketches, from expansive panoramas to a single mill hole, intricately featured glaciers to a sun-kissed glacier lily, or a mother and grizzly cub's tracks preserved in mud.

"It's harder to take good black and white pictures than colour. It's harder to get the contrast," Boles admits.

Black and white images, he adds, better capture the mountains' moods and personalities. Boles's photos, however, also capture an era, showing climbing gear and clothing from the 1950s well into the 1990s. They also remind viewers of the significant shrinking of the Rockies' glaciers.

My Mountain Album is not simply a visual album, either. Nearly every cutline comprises a lighthearted anecdote capturing the sense of camaraderie between Boles and his climbing partners, and reverence for his mountain surroundings.

"Those stories are the things I remember better than anything," he says.

Many of his images also include numerous obscure, distant and rarely visited mountains that even the most prolific Rockies climbers wouldn't recognize – Kitchi Mountain, Mount Blane,

Mount Peleg. In other cases, Boles captures familiar skylines from uncommon angles.

Asked if he has a personal favourite among his images, Boles says it would have to be the shot where fellow Grizzly Group members Gordon Scruggs and Don Forest appear in sharp silhouette while climbing the ridge on Mountain Livingstone, located in the Rockies' Clemenceau area.

Despite suffering a surprise heart attack in early 2005, Boles was hiking by the start of the summer season only months later, by summer's end taking in the fall colours at Highwood Pass and Sunshine Meadows.

He last reached a 10,000-foot summit at the 2004 Alpine Club of Canada General Mountaineering Camp in the Lyells.

"The last few years I was doing the easy ones," Boles admits. "I was saving them for last – just scrambles, like Eiffel and Fairview and Castle."

Although not a technical climb by its standard route, the latter is a twenty-eight-kilometre round trip.

An honorary member of the Alpine Club of Canada, long-time member of the Calgary Mountain Club, Calgary Mountain Rescue, Canadian Ski Patrol and more recently the Lake Louise Ski Friends, Boles says one of the benefits of a lifetime of climbing are the friendships.

"Through the mountains you meet some wonderful people," Boles says. "They're a little different; it's a close community. I've made some really good friends."

PUT UP AND PULL DOWN! (2002)

> Chris **Perry**, John **Martin** and Peter **Arbic**

It didn't take long after he'd moved to the Canadian Rockies from his native England in the early 1970s for Chris Perry to run out of routes to climb and for him to start seeking out new ones.

"When I came here in 1972, I climbed everything there was to climb in about six months," Perry says. "So, I've always climbed new routes."

While most of Perry's routes are traditional climbs up thousand-foot cliffs using removable gear for protection, two of his most recent routes are single-pitch sport climbs at Cougar Creek, in the Bow Valley. After more than a dozen outings and over thirty hours of labour, Perry is gratified to see his routes completed.

"Doing this, you realize just how much work some of these sport routes are," Perry comments after the final bolts are drilled, hangers attached and fingertip-wide ledges brushed clear of dirt.

Christened Full House and Poker Face – both are situated on a wall named Casino Crag – the two new routes join the ranks of more than 1,800 sport climbing routes that lead up walls in dozens of cragging areas between Kananaskis Country and Field, BC. And they were all put up, bolt by bolt, by individual climbers. Averaging twenty to thirty metres in length, sport climbing routes are equipped every few metres with eight-centimetre-long, one-centimetre-diameter stainless steel bolts drilled into the rock, and with permanently fixed anchors at the top. A metal hanger is attached to each bolt, which together can support thousands of pounds. The lead climber hooks a carabiner into the hanger, then threads the rope through a second carabiner, which is attached to the first by a nylon sling, while a belayer controls the rope from the ground. That way, if the lead climber slips off the wall, his belayer can stop him from falling more than a metre or two below the highest carabiner the rope is threaded through.

"Sport climbing is essentially an urban activity," explains Calgary climber John Martin. "It was devised to eliminate objective hazard and to minimize chances of injury so you can concentrate on the actual climbing without worrying about staying alive."

In the early 1980s, bolt holes were drilled by hand, an exercise that often took twenty minutes for each bolt, said Martin, the Rockies' most prolific route builder with over 400 sport climbs to his credit. He put up Cougar Canyon's first sport route, Bob's Yer Uncle, in 1988, before a trail even existed, and he's been building routes ever since.

"Sometimes I think too many people think the route fairy did it," Martin jokes. "It's fascinating for me; as soon as you get one done, you want to do another."

Sometimes routes are built from the top down, with the climber lowering himself on rope threaded through a fixed anchor at the top of a previously established route adjacent to the intended line. Others must be set from the ground up, with the lead climber working his way up the face until he finds appropriate features in the rock face and a balanced, comfortable stance from where he can stop and drill a bolt into the rock, clip the rope in and climb up farther. To work on his routes, Perry hiked up easy ground to the top of the Casino Wall cliff, where he carefully tied one rope around one strong tree and tied a second rope to another tree. Then he rappelled down, using jumars (ascending devices) to move up and down the rope to work on his routes.

With the average climber – though certainly not all climbers – being a 5'9" male, ideal bolt placement requires careful consideration, including solid rock and accessible hand- and footholds. There's a degree of craftsmanship involved in creating first-rate, physically and aesthetically enjoyable routes.

"It's a matter of your imagination allowing you to see holds," says Peter Arbic, a long-time Rockies resident, internationally certified mountain guide and widely respected climber with dozens of quality routes to his credit, many on the quartzite cliffs known as the Back of Lake Louise. "Then you create protection so it doesn't add anything or take away from the climb to be there. It's nice not to have to stop the flow of the actual climbing."

Many of the few veteran climbers who put up routes a decade ago continue to follow their imaginations, while several younger climbers are setting new routes at the high end of the difficulty scale – such as those in the Rockies at Acéphale and Bataan, a vertical cliff high on the south-facing slopes of Grotto Mountain overlooking the town of Canmore, Alberta.

Initially, Martin admits, he put up new routes so he'd have stuff to climb. But eventually he discovered that after so many years of climbing he wanted to give back to the sport.

"I have a satisfaction that I've provided fun for people, nice clean, safe fun. Not a single person has ever told me they didn't appreciate my effort."

Unlike climbing, which is very partner oriented, route building, he says, tends to be a solitary pursuit.

"You have to develop your own very strict safety protocol," Martin says. "This is actually more dangerous than going climbing. It really is a solo effort. When you spend hundreds and hundreds of hours dangling on a rope, you have to know what you're doing."

On good quality rock, a full-length sport route shouldn't take more than a half day's work, Martin says, but at many limestone crags, such as Cougar Creek, a single route may require two to three full days of work to complete.

"You have to clean off the stuff that's loose or might possibly become loose (from the top down)," Perry says. "Once you're below them they'll fall down on top of you."

That includes prying off loose rocks with a crowbar, smaller rocks with a large flathead screwdriver. What's left underneath is the route that gets climbed.

"Sometimes you're left with less than what you started with, other times more than what you started with," Martin says. "It takes a certain amount of experience to assess a piece of rock before you start."

Afterward, a wire brush or whisk broom cleans off lichens and moss.

"If I spent as much time cleaning my house as I did cleaning that route ..." Perry laughs.

Route builders often end up with unique scars on their legs from having hot drills hanging from their harnesses, Arbic says. Their $200 ropes also suffer from the heat of the drills, and the ropes' life spans are severely shortened. While bolts and hangers are relatively inexpensive, costs do add up, with the average sport route costing $45, not to mention up to $1,500 for a cordless hammer drill.

Once a route is complete, the route builder stamps his or her creation with unique monikers such as Wicked Gravity, Cerveza Sundae, Fiberglass Undies and You Ain't Nothin' but a Hangdog.

"While a new traditional route is more about exploration and adventure, with sport routes it's all about the end product, what you're going to leave behind," Perry says. "You have this nice feeling that you've created something worthwhile. Then sometimes people actually stop and say, 'Thanks for doing that, I'm looking forward to climbing it.'"

ROCKIES CLIMBER SAMPLES
SCOTTISH CLASSICS (2007)

> Sean **Isaac**

With over 1100 established ice and mixed climbing routes, the Canadian Rockies are the dream destination of climbers the world over.

But for Canmore, Alberta, climber Sean Isaac, who by thirty-four had spent half of his life ice and mixed climbing, establishing dozens of new routes and authoring a guidebook – *Mixed Climbs in the Canadian Rockies* – in the process, the destination of his dreams was none other than Scotland, birthplace of technical ice climbing.

In February 2007 Isaac got his wish and spent six days as a participant at the British Mountaineering Council's fifth Scottish Winter Meet. Held every second winter, with a similar event organized alternating summers, the gathering draws representatives invited from climbing clubs around the world, including France, Slovenia, Norway, Greece, China and South Africa.

Although it had been seven years since Isaac first learned of the meet, he was finally able to attend, representing the Alpine Club of Canada, which covered the cost of his plane ticket, making him only the second Canadian ever to participate.

"Ever since I started climbing, I wanted to go to Scotland," Isaac says. "We live in a great spot for ice and mixed climbing, but Scotland it where it all started. It's always good to go back to your roots. It was an incredible week of cross-cultural exchange in addition to sampling the best mixed climbing I have ever done."

With all expenses covered by the British Mountaineering Council once there, the visiting climbers teamed up with a local host each day to experience a Scottish adventure.

Climbing activities were halted on two days due to stormy – even by Scottish standards – weather and extreme avalanche hazard, but for his first outing Isaac climbed a Scottish classic, Indicator Wall on the famed Ben Nevis, a route one finishes by climbing through a cornice and throwing a sling around a summit marker.

At 1344 metres, Ben Nevis – taken from Gaelic words for "poisonous or terrible" – is Britain's highest mountain, and it attracts some of the nastiest weather anywhere as climbers test themselves on its 700-metre north cliffs.

"It's a great training ground, and a big reason why some of the best alpinists have come from Scotland," Isaac says. "Hard technical climbing in full-on nasty conditions. You have to be prepared; you have to have your systems down."

Some of Ben Nevis's classic routes were first climbed at the turn of the twentieth century, including the Northeast Buttress, which saw its first ascent in 1895 and its first winter ascent only a year later.

Another day during his visit, Isaac climbed with "Mr. Scotland," Simon Richardson, a father of two and a guidebook author with a full-time job who climbs every weekend, usually putting up a new route each time.

"He wanted to show me the true Scottish wilderness climbing experience," Isaac says. "So he arranged to get me a bike, and we rode bikes for about an hour and a half, then hiked over the moors until we were way on the backside of the Cairngorms at a little quarry. It was a five-hour approach – a twelve-hour day for three pitches of climbing. But, it was a new route."

The first pitch consisted of climbing vertical frozen grass, Isaac describes, "with all four tools and feet stuck solidly in the turf." Once they were actually on rock, the final pitch featured an overhang and seventy-degree snow.

"In the Rockies, if you come across seventy-degree snow, it's dry powder on loose slabs," Isaac says. "In Scotland, the snow gets so solid, it actually squeaks."

Scottish climbers practise a very different style of winter, or ice, climbing, Isaac says, due to the local climate and the nature of the rock.

Rockies ice climbing happens on steep, pure, frozen waterfalls, he explains, with mixed climbing consisting of climbing dry rock to get to the huge icicles. Since the Rockies consist largely of limestone, which does not easily offer cracks in which to place protection, climbers drill permanent bolts into the rock.

By comparison, Scottish rock is granitic and laced with cracks and features that lend themselves well to traditional climbing protection – removable cams and nuts.

"Plus it gets hammered by storms. It's more like snow-covered and rimed-up rock," Isaac says. "You go up and scrape off all the ice and climb the rock."

As well, local Scottish style strictly adheres to a "no bolt" rule, not to mention a ground up, on-sight climbing ethic.

"Which is a great thing; they're really trying to keep the adventure aspect to climbing," Isaac says. "They've got a limited resource, especially compared to what we have in the Rockies, and that way they're preserving what they have for future generations. They've turned little mountains into big adventures."

For his last day, "a dream come true," Isaac teamed up with British climbing star Ian Parnell, with whom he once climbed on the Rockies' famed Weeping Wall. Their day resulted in a five-pitch new route on Ben Nevis, which they rated the equivalent of expert level Rockies M7.

"It was steep, technical, challenging. It took all day and we topped out in the dark," Isaac says.

They christened the route Curly's Arête, in honour of Karen McNeill, the passionate Canmore ice climber known for her plentiful dark curls who died in 2006 on Alaska's Mount Foraker.

"It was definitely an eye-opener for me," Isaac says. "Climbing in Scotland takes skills, not just climbing skills, but navigation too. On Ben Nevis, you need a map and compass and goggles – always. I would love to go back, maybe guide some of the classic ice gullies."

With plenty of evening entertainment too, Isaac was invited to present a slide show on his home country, which left the Scots impressed.

"They were really psyched; we're the envy of the world for ice climbing," Isaac says. "Especially this winter, since Europe has virtually no ice."

As always, he adds, climbing in a new area meant he had lots to learn.

"They talk about double Gore-Tex days," Isaac laughs. "I showed up in my soft shell, and my underwear was soaked before we even started the route. You pretty much need a full change of clothes. I came home every day drenched."

After drying off, Isaac was schooled in the other classic Scottish tradition – single malt.

"It was great to try a different Scotch every night. I definitely got an education in Scotch."

STYLE IS THE SPICE OF CLIMBING (2005)

> Marko **Prezelj**

Style, says Slovenian alpinist Marko Prezelj (pronounced Prey-zell), is the only thing in climbing that really matters to him.

As applied to climbing, he explains, style is exactly as described in a dictionary – the manner of conduct or action; the mode of expression or execution in any kind of art. On giant, high-altitude mountains comprised of labyrinths of rock buttresses, vertical ice pillars and glaciers corrugated with crevasses, Prezelj's brand of alpine style means moving quickly with one or two partners, carrying the bare minimum of climbing equipment, food, clothing and bivy gear, and making solid decisions in survival-challenging situations.

"Just doing things – that's empty or plain," Prezelj explains in his thick Slovenian accent, punctuated by a hearty laugh. "Without style – it's like eating something that has no taste, eating just to fill your stomach. The style gives the taste to what you're doing."

Arriving in Canada a week before appearing as featured speaker at the Banff Mountain Film Festival in November 2005, Prezelj spoke at the home of his good friend and frequent climbing partner Barry Blanchard, considered by many to practise the best style of any of Canada's alpinists.

While style is important, Prezelj says what draws him to pursue increasingly challenging mountaineering objectives is the curiosity to explore new and different experiences. When Prezelj was a child, his parents introduced him to mountaineering. On one outing when he was about twelve, foggy conditions led them to turn around, but

Prezelj noticed others were continuing. While he thought the decision to turn back was a wise one, he realized more experienced climbers could go farther. Too young at the time to join any mountaineering clubs, and without any friends his age who shared his interests, Prezelj explored the mountains on his own for about three years until he was able to join organized climbing schools. Discovering that pushing his mental and physical limits delivered continually fresh experiences, Prezelj teamed up with partners who shared his interest in seeking out increasingly difficult climbing objectives – learning more with each challenge.

"The learning process is constant," Prezelj says. "I learn about me, about my personality, the personality of others. You make decisions, which look sometimes simple, banal, but even the banal decisions are important at the end."

Although trained as a chemical engineer, Prezelj makes his living as a mountain guide and photographer in Slovenia, where he lives with his wife, Katja, and two sons, aged five and eleven. As a professional guide, Prezelj said his clients pay him to be the decision maker.

"As a guide, it's my job for him to have fun, to be safe, and for him to come again," Prezelj says. "I like guiding. When you are climbing, you make decisions for you and your partner, and your partner is doing the same. When I'm guiding, I'm making all the decisions, and sometimes against the client's wishes."

Since they are growing up with a father who pursues far and long travels, Prezelj says he expects his sons will learn from him to be responsible for their own decisions and respect the decisions of others.

"The family works as a kind of expedition," Prezelj says. "You can't blame other people for their decisions."

Learning from, and accepting, responsibility for the decisions you make is one of mountaineering's greatest lessons, he says.

"If you make decisions you have to take responsibility for your actions, the good and the bad, not just the sweet taste."

While on a Himalayan expedition to 8476-metre Kangchenjunga South in 1991, Prezelj first tasted climbing's bitter side when two teammates died near the summit. Prezelj recalls communicating with them by radio from base camp: "Their voices were already on the other side of life."

While Prezelj and Andrej Stremfelj were awarded the prestigious Piolet d'Or for their five-day alpine style ascent of a new route on the peak, Prezelj said his personal success was clouded by his friends' deaths.

"I learned the mountains are dangerous," Prezelj says. "Before, the mountains were a more romantic place I went to have fun. Since then, I know that it's serious. The decision-making process is not fun. Certain decisions – you can lose your life."

Already having accomplished numerous first ascents and new routes on 6000- and 7000-metre peaks in Alaska, Pakistan, South America and Tibet, in April 2004 Prezelj and American Steve House started up one of the Canadian Rockies' most daunting alpine challenges – the 1500-metre north face of the North Twin, a partially glaciated and relentlessly steep limestone wall, often plastered in rime and slick with verglas. This route had seen only two previous ascents: the first by George Lowe and Chris Jones in August 1974, and the second by Barry Blanchard and Dave Cheesmond in August 1985.

Carrying sufficient food and fuel for five days, a carefully pared climbing rack and sharing a single synthetic sleeping bag, the pair were perched on a thirty centimetre by fifty centimetre ledge for their second night on the face and preparing dinner – soup and dehydrated mashed potatoes – when House decided to change his socks. As he replaced the outer shell of his left boot, the loop at the back broke and the two stared in horror as it plummeted down the face into darkness.

After much cursing and some discussion, they decided to keep climbing, arguing it would be easier, quicker and safer to reach the top of the route, from where twenty-three kilometres of non-technical glacier travel would deliver them to the Columbia Icefields Centre on the paved Icefields Parkway. After climbing for a third full day, House following Prezelj's lead with one fully functioning boot and the other inner boot wrapped in athletic tape, they bivouacked just below the summit for a third and final night before their long march the following day – in a complete whiteout.

Continuing to live and climb in style, shortly before celebrating his fortieth birthday in September 2005, Prezelj accomplished his most difficult rock climb yet, rated 5.13b.

"For a sport climber, that's not so great, but for a mountaineer, it was a good challenge," Prezelj says.

CZECH START, CANADIAN "PINISH" (2007)

> Lilla **Molnar** and Jen **Olson**

As soon as their plane touched down in Islamabad, Pakistan, in the middle of September 2007, Lilla Molnar and Jen Olson steeled themselves for an adventure.

Ever since they'd won the John Lauchlan Award a year earlier, they'd been planning their dream trip: to establish a new climbing route in the far west of Pakistan's Karakoram Mountains on a 6000-metre granite spire called Bublimating, or Ladyfinger. The women had chosen their objective, a subsidiary peak of 7388-metre Ultar Sar, which towers over Karimabad, for its striking physical features and also for its remoteness.

"It's aesthetic," Olson says. "We were attracted to the nature of how the peak looks, and also we thought it would be a good granite rock climb."

Although the peak had previously been climbed, they had plans to establish a new route, which would involve about 1000 metres of technical rock climbing that would be similar in nature to that in BC's Bugaboo Mountains, where both women have put up new routes. But this time, they'd be in the thinner air of 6000 metres.

"I'd been wanting to go to Pakistan for a really long time, knowing there's good granite there," Olson says. "Also, this is a relatively undisturbed area. It's quite remote and it hasn't seen as much climbing as other Himalayan regions."

The women chose their objective partly on the recommendations of other climbers who had been to the area. But some of the encouragement to apply for the grant came from their friend, climber

Karen McNeill, who disappeared while climbing a challenging route on Alaska's Mount Foraker in May 2006.

McNeill, who had organized and participated in numerous climbing expeditions to the Himalayas, Alaska, South America and China, had asked Olson if she ever simply dreamed of something and then made it happen.

"You don't think you can make it happen, and then all of a sudden you do," Olson says.

Only the second all-women's team to be awarded the prestigious – and substantial – $5,000 John Lauchlan Award, their proposed climb embodied all of the award's criteria as a bold and innovative expedition that was exploratory in nature, environmentally sensitive and non-commercial. Presented annually at the Banff Mountain Film Festival since 1996, and voted upon by a judging committee comprised of half a dozen seasoned Canadian Rockies alpinists, the award was created in memory of Lauchlan, Canada's top climber of the late 1970s and early 1980s, who died in 1982, and who was admired and respected for his bold and adventurous spirit.

When Molnar and Olson disembarked from the plane in Islamabad with their passports, both also carried professional certification with the Association of Canadian Mountains Guides. They also possessed years of climbing experience earned in venues such as Alaska, Peru, the French Alps and the big walls of Utah's Zion National Park, including a one-day speed ascent of Denali's Upper West Rib route for Molnar and a first ascent of the east face of Sunrise Spire in Alaska's Kitchatnas for Olson. Once off the plane, however, they carefully wrapped scarves around their blond heads and joined the designated "Women and Children" line.

While they had followed the political happenings of the troubled country for months prior to leaving Canada, Molnar said they felt relatively secure when they were met at the airport by Ghulam, owner of Blue Sky Tours, an outfit that came highly recommended by friends who had previously travelled and climbed in the region. The following day, the women hopped a small plane north to Gilgit and then boarded a "decent" Toyota minibus with their good humoured guide/cook,

Imran, for a five-hour stomach-churning ride to Karimabad along the notoriously terrifying Karakoram Highway.

"Before we left, we were definitely concerned about politics and the overall state of the country," Molnar says. "But knowing we'd have a local looking out for us was a huge help, and a huge benefit for our safety. We specifically asked for Imran; everyone said he'd been very helpful on their trips. He took care of hotel and travel logistics, and he arranged the porters for us."

Trekking through the Ultar Meadows in the Hunza Valley of the Batura Muztagh Range, they stopped to set up a base camp from which to launch their Ladyfinger climb. But while the rock looked good, as they hiked higher to have a good look at the glacier beneath Ladyfinger (which they would have to negotiate to reach the base of the spire), the approach did not. They decided to abandon their objective.

"We had a pretty good look at the approach, and we decided not to follow through with our route," Molnar says. "It posed too much potential rockfall hazard for our liking, and also because we would have to shuttle our own gear, which meant too many trips with too much exposure. We had heard of another potential approach from the opposite side of the mountain, but Imran informed us that an earlier expedition had been unsuccessful there due to similar hazards."

Equipped with Imran's local knowledge, they backtracked to Gilgit and followed the raging Indus River by minibus to Skardu, their sights set on the Husche Valley and its namesake village, starting point to five separate glaciers, including their new destination, the Nangmah Valley. Their knees scrunched around their ears, they bounced and rattled up the Husche Valley and stopped in the village of Khane, where, to their complete surprise, Imran hosted the women in his home, which was constructed of mud and plaster with a squat toilet, small garden and grass roof.

"He had six kids and another eighty members of his extended family in Khane village," Molnar recalls. "It was a really neat experience. We stayed in an open room with a carpet and pillows on the floor. His family greeted us and treated us to wonderful meals and tours of the village with amazing views of Masherbrum."

Stopping in the last village before the Nangmah Valley, at the K6 Hotel guesthouse, they found an informal sign-in book, in which Czech climbers had drawn information about a route they had started on a mountain named Brakk Zang. Unable to finish it, they encouraged others to try. Coupled with information gleaned through a twenty-minute Internet session undertaken when they passed through Karimabad, the climbers now had a new objective.

With twenty porters carrying their five fifteen-kilogram duffle bags loaded with several manufacturers' catalogues worth of gear to ensure they were prepared for any type of climbing they might encounter, they made their way up the Nangmah Valley, lush with deciduous trees showing fall colours of reds and oranges and yellows.

"We had everything we needed for aid, for rock, for ice," Molnar laughs. "We were really going for a rock climb, but we still had two pairs of crampons each."

Fortunately, they also packed a few everyday North American over-the-counter drugs, which the porters made enthusiastic use of, since most of the porters in the area are accustomed to working for large expeditions that travel with their own doctors who habitually pack a fair quantity of drugs. Some large expeditions intent on climbing Pakistan's K2, the world's second highest mountain at 8611 metres, which typically involves a two-month effort, employ as many as 700 porters.

Perceived as North Americans to be in possession of medications, Olson and Molnar ended up handing out a few cure-alls.

"We dispensed a few ibuprofens and some Pepto Bismol," Molnar says. "One guy had a few pimples on his face, so we gave him some Polysporin. They all claimed to feel better in the morning."

Unable to find any detailed topographical maps, they set up a base camp at 4100 metres and scouted the area.

"With a hand-drawn map, we tried to piece together where we were," Molnar says. "It's difficult in Pakistan to get good, detailed topo maps. They might exist, but we couldn't find any. There were steep granite walls everywhere. It was really hard to get a grasp of how big things were, until you were standing on something you thought was really high, and looking around at other things that were twice as high. The

Czechs had described their route to be on a rock face with a huge hole in it. We set up our base camp and looked up, and oh – that looks like the hole the Czechs mentioned."

On their first day of climbing, the women reached the Czechs' high point and carried on to add three more pitches. Then they fixed three ropes before descending to camp. After waiting out some poor weather, two days later they returned to their high point and climbed five additional pitches. Reaching the ridge at 4800 metres in a snowstorm, they descending via a route they'd scouted on their rest day.

"We topped out in about two inches of snow in rock shoes," Molnar says. "It was pretty much a whiteout at the ridgetop. It was definitely more involved than we had anticipated, because of the snow. We had to pitch it out in terrain that, had it been dry, we would have soloed. Our day ended up being seventeen hours."

By the time they arrived back in camp in 10 p.m. darkness, Imran had hiked down the valley to hire porters for the trek out. The camp helper, Hussein, was sound asleep.

"He jumped out of his sleeping bag, and although he didn't speak much English, based on his body language he was relieved," Molnar says. "He seemed pretty happy. We were pretty happy, too. We felt good that we'd finished it. And we were really happy with our alternate objective. With these kinds of trips you can have an objective, but you have to be willing to walk away from it and not be pressured because you got a grant."

Overall, the quality of the rock was as excellent as they had hoped, despite a few memorable extra features.

"Generally, it was really good rock, especially the second half," Molnar says. "The whole route required a lot of cleaning of all the cracks, though; there were a lot of small bushes. We laughed a lot at how much dirt we had on ourselves. We were thinking in hindsight that goggles would have been a good idea. They were in base camp – we never thought of doing a rock route with goggles on!"

"Actually, we didn't climb so much as we extricated plants and harvested dirt," Olson adds jokingly. "If extreme gardening were an Olympic sport, we'd be medal contenders."

Thinking of Imran, they christened their route Czech Start Canadian Pinish.

"Imran would look at us after dinner and say, 'Pinished?'" Molnar recalls. "We loved it, and we wanted to incorporate it into our route."

While it was without doubt an unusual scenario for two women to be climbing mountains on their own in remote Pakistan, Molnar and Olson say the locals were friendly and receptive.

"Several times we did get asked how many were in our party, and we'd say just Jen and I," Molnar says. "You could tell they were trying to figure out what that was all about. We wore head scarves the whole time, around the villages and with the locals. In Islamabad we were told we'd be fine without headscarves, but we just felt more comfortable with them on. We didn't even wear short sleeve shirts – we were in full sleeves and pants the whole time. Then once we were in the camp with the staff, it was fine."

"We definitely stood out and felt like we were stared at a lot," Olson adds. "We had a different status from the local women. Often people didn't seem to really understand what we were doing there. I expect most of them thought we were hikers. We both wore wedding rings and were accompanied by Imran most of the time, so we didn't get hassled by men in a negative way."

Molnar, whose husband, Marc Piché, is also a climber and an internationally certified mountain guide, says when people noticed the wedding ring on her finger, they would ask if it was a love marriage or an arranged marriage. When Molnar asked Imran if his daughter would get a job and work outside of the home, his answer was definite – no. Asking if she had a husband yet, Imran replied no – but made it clear that he was looking.

"The Balti people were kind and poor. They're devout Muslims and they have a strong sense of family and community," Olson says. "They live in traditional ways; they're farmers, hunters/gatherers – it's survival living. I loved meeting the people and learning about the culture and about what people like Greg Mortenson (founder of the NGO Central Asia Institute) are doing for the Balti. I feel lucky that we got a new route in before bad weather ended our trip, and I'm very excited that I visited the Karakoram. I would love to go back."

Molnar agrees.

"Overall, I thought people in Pakistan were very generous and very helpful," Molnar says. "In Khane, we really experienced the warm generosity of the Balti people."

ICONIC ALBERTA IS A COOL CLIMB IN WINTER (2005)

> Raphael **Slawinski**, Scott **Semple** and Eamonn **Walsh**

Of all the jagged, crumbly, daunting peaks in the Canadian Rockies, none has a more fearsome reputation than Mount Alberta.

The sixth highest of the Rockies, and the last of the range's major mountains to allow climbers on its long, narrow, persistently corniced and highly exposed summit ridge, Alberta didn't see its first ascent until 1925 – an accomplishment that wasn't repeated until 1948.

But in February 2005 three of Canada's fittest, fastest and most technically skilled alpinists stamped their own mark on Canadian mountaineering history by making the peak's first winter ascent.

Raphael Slawinski, thirty-eight, an instructor of physics at Calgary's Mount Royal College and one of Canada's more proficient mixed rock and ice climbers, along with equally skilled Canmore residents Scott Semple, thirty-one, and Eamonn Walsh, thirty, climbed up 800 metres of steep, snow-coated rock ledges, see-sawed their way along the kilometre-long summit ridge until they reached the 3619-metre pinnacle, then retraced their steps back down.

"It was nice to have done it," Semple admits.

Unlike other Rockies peaks, Alberta offers no easy scrambling route up its back side. The kind of mountain that follows any person within its sights like a large, powerful, supernatural presence, Alberta rises like a steep-sided layer cake terraced with narrow ledges on its south-facing front side.

The approach hike follows the banks of Woolley Creek over jumbled scree piles before rising to a masochist's crescendo at the summit of Woolley Shoulder, the slopes of which are steeper, looser and take much longer to slog up than the more frequently travelled – and cursed – Abbot Pass trail below Mount Victoria.

Alberta's most straightforward ascent route, the Japanese Route, established by the first-ascent party, includes about ten pitches of consistent 5.6 climbing on rock that is notoriously crumbly, difficult to protect and prone to falling with semi-automatic frequency, before climbers finally reach the tightrope-wide, repeatedly broken summit ridge. Consecutive summer mountaineering seasons pass without anyone topping out on the towering giant.

It wasn't until the early 1970s that anyone was able to establish a second route up Alberta's treacherous flanks. In 1972 American alpine master George Lowe and partner Jock Glidden successfully forged a route to the summit via the peak's steep north face, the highlight of which included a 600-metre vertical ice wall. A third route, following the committing northeast ridge, was established in 1985.

When they arrived at the mountain's base in the dead of winter with designs on the highly committing north face, which they would not be able to descend by backtracking, Semple, Walsh and Slawinski also looked at the northeast ridge. Finding the mountain plastered with an abundance of snow on all three of its nearly vertical faces, they opted for the standard Japanese Route.

"We had hoped we might be able to do the north face, because it would offer the most intense experience," Slawinski says. "But the cold temperatures and snow-plastered rock on the mountain made us go for the Japanese Route."

"Even the steep rock was holding snow," Semple adds. "There was enough snow to cover the scree and the cliff bands below."

To their delight, however, the abundance of snow worked in their favour, allowing for faster travel on the lower scree slopes.

While it was Semple's and Walsh's first time on Alberta, this marked Slawinski's "fourth and counting" successful climb of the remote and isolated peak, including another impressive first – a single-day ascent via the Japanese Route in eighteen hours from car to car in the summer of 2004, with Calgarians Dana Ruddy and Tim Haggerty. Most parties take three fully exhausting days to hike in, climb the mountain and hike out – with many spending an impromptu night high on rocky ledges.

"I have always thought Alberta would be a cool objective in winter," Slawinski says. "The summit ridge is a wild enough place in summer. I could only imagine what it would be in winter. Plus, I admit that the idea of a first winter ascent of an iconic Rockies peak was appealing."

The trio skied from the Icefields Parkway to the Alpine Club of Canada's Lloyd McKay hut in an impressively speedy six hours, then the following day they cruised up steep cliff bands to tag the summit late in the afternoon of February 19, only nine hours and ten minutes after leaving the rudimentary, yet cozy six-person shelter.

With clear skies to the west, clouds bumped right up to the ridge on the east side, Semple says, making for impressive views of neighbouring peaks, including the sinister, vertical and sunless north face of 3730-metre North Twin.

"The ridge was spectacular," Semple says. "It was quite sharp, so you had to walk carefully. But I think it's a much better route in the winter."

Descending the gangplank ridge, the climbers found a spot sheltered from the strong winds and light snow, crammed into a small nylon refuge they'd carried to be on the safe side, and spent the night out.

"We didn't know what to expect," Semple says. "Since we had full bivy gear, we just stayed up there."

"There were some pretty good views," says Walsh – easily the largest of the three men. "Squeezing three men into a two-man Bibler was memorable. It was cozy. We were warm."

While Semple, Walsh and Slawinski each carried a backpack and years of experience in moving quickly, efficiently and comfortably on steep, strenuous and technically difficult mixed rock and ice routes, the 1925 team of six Japanese climbers, led by Yuko Maki, along with Swiss guides Hans Fuhrer and Hans Kohler, and amateur Swiss adventurer Jean Weber, travelled from Jasper with forty horses and five wranglers. To overcome the obstacle presented by a four-metre overhanging rock wall high on the mountain, they formed a three-man human ladder.

A mountain of many legends, Alberta's most romantic is that which recounts how the Japanese team left an ice axe crafted of solid silver – reportedly given to them by Japan's emperor – on the summit to mark their success.

They made the journey from Japan with the specific goal of scoring the first ascent of the last unclimbed Canadian Rockies giant. After successfully topping out, on their descent the climbers plunged an ice axe into broken rock below the summit as evidence of the accomplishment.

When two American climbers, Fred Ayres and John Oberlin, made the mountain's second ascent in 1948, they found the axe, and attempting to wrench it from the rocks, they snapped the very ordinary wood and steel axe in half. Back home, they presented the shaft to the American Alpine Club in New York. Half a century later, Jasper Park warden Greg Horne negotiated its return to Jasper. The head of the axe was retrieved from the mountain in 1965, when nineteen climbers from the Nagano High School Old Boys Alpine Club in Japan made the mountain's fifth ascent and took the lower half home with them.

In 1997 the two halves were eventually reunited in a formal ceremony before Japan's crown prince and prime minister and 800 members of the Japanese Alpine Club. In 2000, the two jagged ends fitting together perfectly, the ice axe was placed on permanent exhibit in Jasper's Yellowhead Museum.

With such legends augmenting their experience, the team that made their own history by succeeding on the first winter ascent of the most feared and revered mountain in the Canadian Rockies admits the peak is nothing short of spectacular.

"It's a pretty cool, remote mountain," Walsh says. "Just spending a night at the hut is amazing."

On September 15, 2007, Eamonn Walsh and Raphael Slawinski made the first ascent of Mount Alberta's west face, which they rated at a put-hair-on-your-chest grade of V 5.10+.

THE BLACK HOLE OF THE ROCKIES (2004)

> George **Lowe**, Chris **Jones**
> and Barry **Blanchard**

Climbers invariably describe it as massive, black, icy, scary and dangerous.

Seeking shelter from midsummer snowstorms, aspiring ascensionists have surveyed the coveted face – 1500 vertical metres of partially glaciated and relentlessly steep Canadian Rockies limestone, usually plastered in rime and slick with verglas – only to conclude, "It scared the bejeebus out of us."

Thirty years after George Lowe and Chris Jones climbed the north face of the North Twin, the mountain had lost none of its reputation. Tucked in an area at the north end of the Columbia Icefields known as the Black Hole, the face has seen only two successful ascents since their 1974 accomplishment. In his compendium of Canadian mountaineering *Pushing the Limits*, Chic Scott likened it to the north face of Switzerland's Eiger. Respected Canadian alpinist Barry Blanchard, who with Dave Cheesmond made the second ascent of the North Twin's fearsome north face via its north pillar in 1985, is less subtle, writing in the 2002 *American Alpine Journal*, "At times it makes the Eiger look like a kiddies sandbox."

"It's a really, really serious face in the summertime," Blanchard says, two decades after his and Cheesmond's impressive ascent. "The rockfall can be life-taking, literally. A lot of people would just turn around when they saw the rocks smacking into the glacier at the base. It's the steepest, longest face of the Rockies. The headwall is so much steeper than the Eiger. There's a number of great faces in the Rockies, but none have the sheer, black, serious nature of the Twin."

It's only natural, Blanchard says, that the Lowe/Jones climb has endured as a Canadian Rockies legend.

"For two guys walking up to a face with two packs and a rope and climbing it, I don't think anything in the Alps at that time measured up to the difficulty and the commitment of the North Twin," Blanchard declared.

In November 2004, to celebrate the thirtieth anniversary of their landmark climb, Lowe and Jones shared their story at the Banff Mountain Book Festival.

Both leading climbers of their generation, Lowe and Jones established some of the most difficult routes in the Rockies, on the north faces of Columbia, Alberta, Deltaform, Kitchener and Geikie. Their ascent of the North Twin, however, is repeatedly hailed as the singular hallmark alpine climb of the 1970s.

"George and I had been skulking about the Rockies for some years with the idea to climb the most challenging routes," Jones says. "After we'd done those, regrettably, the North Twin was next on the list. If there had been an intermediate climb, somewhat harder than Alberta, then we would have done that. But there wasn't."

By their fifth day on the face, the duo realized they no longer had sufficient gear to retreat even if they'd wanted to. Stymied by apparent dead ends, they spent another night out in the open at the mercy of an escalating snowstorm. On the sixth morning, Lowe discovered a snow patch leading up a gully to an overhang, which he mounted by pressing his knees into the mature snow, which miraculously held his weight. After climbing another fifteen pitches through hail, with avalanches running all around them, they reached the summit, where heavy snow collapsed their tent twice during the night.

The north face of the North Twin was well known among climbers as a "great problem," Jones says, adding that he and Lowe were quite pleased after accomplishing the first ascent.

"We knew it was the hardest climbing in Canada," Jones says. "It was probably as difficult as the two most difficult climbs put together that either of us had done previously."

Neither the Lowe/Jones nor the Blanchard/Cheesmond route has ever been repeated. But in April 2003 American Steve House teamed up with Slovenian Marko Prezelj to make the face's third ascent, following a different line before joining the Lowe/Jones route for the upper pitches.

A strenuous full day's hike from the Icefields Parkway, just reaching the base of the North Twin involves fording the icy Sunwapta River and trudging up the ankle-gouging, endlessly treadmilling scree slopes of notorious Woolley Shoulder. The area, Blanchard suggested, is likely frequented by more bears than people.

Soaring above the moon-like glacier surface, the vertical to overhanging north face offers no continuous crack systems and very few ledges. Once above the first quarter, rescue by even the most modern means would be, quite certainly, impossible.

"The climbing was pretty much what I had envisioned – half-serious loose rock and half-great rock and great climbing," Blanchard admits. "But knowing the Rockies like I do, I was even taken aback by the amount of rockfall."

His scariest moment came when a large chunk of rock holding their anchor broke off. He and Cheesmond spent four nights on the face, another on the summit of Mount Stutfield. In all, their climb took seven days.

The ascent was hailed by Scott as "one of the finest achievements ever made by Canadians in their own mountains." Blanchard says his strongest memories of the climb are those of Cheesmond, who disappeared in 1987 on Mount Logan's Hummingbird Ridge.

"It was one of the last big routes we did together," Blanchard says. "We were laughing, having fun leading, getting gripped and swearing. Him with his wry South African humour."

And while Blanchard reveres the Lowe/Jones climb as one of the greatest of their era, the respect is mutual.

"I'm sure what Barry and Dave Cheesmond did was quite an extraordinary effort as well," Jones says.

EXPEDITION TO THE EDGE OF UNKNOWN (2005)

> Katy **Holm**, Katherine **Fraser** and Aidan **Oloman**

Within days of landing in Chengdu, a city of about ten million people located in Sichuan, the most populated province in China, the world's most populated country, Katy Holm, Katherine Fraser and Aidan Oloman expected to be pretty much alone.

They had travelled halfway around the world from their homes in British Columbia to explore a region of China that even the Chinese know little about, intent on making first ascents in the remote and largely unclimbed Four Girls Mountains of Sichuan's Qionglai Range. Within that range, they had their sights set on granite peaks flanking the valleys surrounding the impressive 6250-metre Siguniang Shan.

Opened to travellers only in 1999 and home to the Himalayan vulture, the golden monkey and people of mixed Gyarong Tibetan and Qiang ancestry who continue to live traditional lifestyles, the region has seen few Westerners, let alone climbers. And for those locals, the very idea, let alone the reality, of three women climbing on their own was a novelty indeed.

"The area is a mixture of cultures; it's right on the edge of Tibet," Holm, thirty, says. "People graze yaks in the meadows. I actually felt quite safe there. As women, though, it was quite interesting. While there have been some climbers in the area, there've been relatively few, and certainly not women. I don't know if they knew what to make of us at all, we were definitely a novelty. People stared at us in town. Plus we were always laughing, doing things people thought were totally crazy. I think people were pretty amused by us."

But when some of the local men felt obliged or perhaps were economically motivated to offer their assistance to the women, it was the climbers who were amused.

"They would offer to guide us," Holm laughs. "Big men with pot bellies and cigarettes hanging from their mouths. They weren't even from the mountains. They weren't shepherds or farmers, but city men. It was quite funny."

Before venturing into the mountains, the climbers first navigated Chengdu's crowded markets and shops to purchase a month's worth of food supplies, snapping up familiar items such as quick cooking oats and Tang, and not so familiar items including condensed chocolate milk in tubes.

Their shopping chores completed, they woke early one morning to catch the public transit bus for the 230-kilometre ride to Rilong. Obliged to split into two taxis in order to make room for themselves and all their gear, Holm rode alone with most of their bags. Arriving at the bus depot first, she found herself standing amidst piles of luggage, wondering how she might keep an eye on them and move them inside at the same time, when suddenly a tiny Chinese woman started hauling the bags away.

"She was so light and teeny, she couldn't have weighed more than 100 pounds, but she was amazingly strong," Holm says. "At first I wasn't sure what the heck she was doing with my bags, but it turned out she was just an industrious worker. She was really efficient, and by the time Katherine and Aidan got there, we were ready to go."

With six duffels and three food packs strapped to the roof and stacked high beside the driver, they boarded the bus for a six-hour ride on a twisting, bumpy, potholed and muddy road to Rilong, the village at the foot of the Four Girls Mountains in the National Reserve Siguniang Mountains. The trip was made all the more uncomfortable by the other passengers' smoking and phlegm-purging habits.

"It was the locals' bus, packed with mountain people commuting," Holm says. "There were people sitting on luggage at the back of the bus, smoking and spitting on the bus. We were lucky, we had seats up front."

As they drove through Chengdu, the scene was typically Chinese, she says, with all modes of transportation jostling for position on the streets, trying to force their way through the chaotic traffic. They often saw two passengers sharing a moped, one catching a few winks on their way to work.

"The city was filled with dense smog, just so much hustle and bustle and noise," Holm recalls. "There was construction everywhere, just building, building, building, people taking apart buildings by hand. It was a jungle of civilization, with people growing little patches of food right beside the sidewalks or beside a factory belching fumes. There were highway workers and their sleeping platforms six feet from the road. We drove by a ditch with boards across it where the workers slept. It seemed like the whole country was in a state of transformation."

Finally, the bus escaped the urban cacophony, and began climbing into the mountains.

"That was the most beautiful thing," Holm says. "The road zigzagged like a ribbon up the mountainside, through lush forest, and it got steeper and steeper, and really narrow. The only other traffic was other buses and transport trucks, and scooters and all-terrain-style vehicles towing these trailers piled high with toilet paper or hay or produce. There was barely enough room for two vehicles to pass each other; they would each have to pull in their side mirrors."

After cresting Balangshan Pass at about 4500 metres' elevation, and passing through the Wolong Giant Panda Reserve, the road dropped down to the town of Rilong.

"It was a beautiful town on the flanks of a mountain, with a stream gushing through the middle of town," Holm says. "It was so great to be in the mountains. There was good food, people were smiling, they had rosy cheeks and some of them were in traditional Tibetan dress. But it's hard to say how much of that was for the Chinese tourists – there were a lot. It was funny, too, that for tourism they'd made Chinese-looking buildings, but that wasn't what the Chinese tourists wanted, so they were redecorating it all again so it would look Tibetan."

Despite the area's status as a hot spot for Chinese tourists, finding reliable information about their alpine objectives outside of Rilong presented a challenge, since no topographical maps of the region were available to the public. Before departing Canada, the climbers had gained limited information from a report posted on the website of a Slovenian team who reported having climbed rock routes up to the grade of 5.11 in the Shuangqiao Valley on previously unclimbed mountains.

"We figured that was right up our alley," Holm says. "I think we were all at a stage where we wanted to push our limits climbing. We picked the area because we wanted to climb alpine rock routes, cracks and granite. It was a wild, new world to explore. But we wondered how it would be, climbing technical rock at elevation. Everything was a little bit of an unknown. There was some information about what had been climbed, but it was hard to get the latest information and it was tough to know if we had all the information."

Once in Rilong, they negotiated with a local horse packer, Mr. Mah, whose walls were decorated with Chinese, Japanese and Russian flags from previous climbing expedition clients. The negotiating required Fraser – whom Mah appeared to favour – to smoke and drink the numerous cigarettes and small glasses of weak beer offered her. During the course of the bartering, Mah enlisted the assistance of a passing English-speaking tourist from Hong Kong to translate.

"I was probably the most assertive person in the group, and the most willing to bumble my way through conversations, so I guess that's why he picked me," Fraser, twenty-nine, says. "It was fun interacting with Mr. Mah. He had a good sense of humour, and negotiations were very much a sit down, smoke cigarettes, drink tea kind of affair. My most memorable moment was being taken to eat hot pot with him and his wife and two Chinese tourists – a big steaming pot in the middle of the table, beaks and all, and lots of beer and toasts. And there's me, trying to figure out what exactly I was getting in my bowl."

While the climbers did catch a glimpse of a 1:50,000 Chinese military map, Mah drew the curtain before it could be of any use to them. In the end, they resorted to cross-referencing line-drawn tourist maps with Japanese and Chinese photography books, and matching Chinese characters with English names to identify peaks and determine approximate elevations.

Negotiations finalized, they set out from Rilong on a rainy morning to travel the twenty kilometres to their base camp with twenty ponies carrying bags bulging with ropes; glacier-, rock- and ice-climbing gear; and twenty days' worth of food; and with Mr. Mah simultaneously smoking, walking and shouting commands to his horses.

Their destination was the twin river valleys of Shuangqiao (Long Terrace) and Chiang Pin (Double Bridges), which are joined at the north end by two 4900-metre passes. Each valley was about forty kilometres long, and both were flanked by huge granite walls on 5000- to 6000-metre peaks, most of them unclimbed.

Some 500 metres below the valley, however, Mah stopped and refused to continue any farther, insisting his horses would drown if they attempted to cross the river. Advising the women to climb slowly so they would not become sick from the altitude, and telling them to take their gear to high camp with them so it would not fall prey to thieves, he left them to spend three subsequent damp days ferrying eleven loads in backpacks across teetery logs spanning a turbulent river to reach their base camp at 4200 metres. Finally, high above the golden larch trees and valley-bottom villages, they settled into camp beside a cascading mountain creek tucked in a cirque rimmed by 5000-metre granite peaks – three of which had yet to be climbed.

As a small, lightweight and self-sufficient expedition, the women's trip had garnered enough interest to become the first all-women's expedition ever to receive the prestigious John Lauchlan Award, sponsored by the Canadian Himalayan Foundation.

To win the award, a proposed expedition must be bold, innovative, exploratory, environmentally sensitive and non-commercial, with at least half its team members Canadian. The women were thrilled and honoured to receive not only the financial assistance but also the peer recognition the award conferred.

Because they were all strong and experienced climbers, they had been earning peer recognition for some time: Holm as a Vancouver-based wilderness educator with Class 4+ first descents by kayak under her skirt and first ascents on remote big walls in Greenland; Oloman as a 5.12c rock climber, V7 boulderer and one of only three Canadian women to have earned her full rock guide's certification with the Association of Canadian Mountain Guides (ACMG); and Fraser as an ACMG assistant rock guide and rigger with Vancouver's film industry whose résumé includes 5.12c routes on Squamish's giant granite walls and a speedy (fourteen hours, car-to-car) ascent of the twenty-nine-pitch northwest face of Yosemite's Half Dome.

In addition to the Lauchlan Award, the climbers had also garnered support from the Alpine Club of Canada's Jen Higgins Fund and sponsorship from Mountain Equipment Co-op and Integral Designs, who supplied their invaluable, sturdy tent for the expedition.

At base camp, the team waited out days of rain and snowstorms that blanketed the valley and surrounding peaks and sent avalanches thundering down distant mountain faces as they peered anxiously out the flap. During intermittent afternoon sunny breaks, they would hurry outside to wash clothing and work out on a chin-up bar they hung in a large rhododendron above camp, with a blue sheep perched on a rock slope for an audience.

"Our base camp was very secluded," Fraser says. "During the days that we were moving gear up from the main valley to our hanging valley we saw some hunters, but apart from that we saw no one. Aidan and Katy slept in a big three-person tent and I had the little single-wall Integral Designs. We also had a cook tent set up. It was quite a pretty location with a stream nearby and the weather was quite warm, even though it was wet, and we only had two days of snow. But we did spend quite a few days tent-bound. I ended up ploughing my way through eight books, wrote a journal on my Blackberry and slept."

Eventually their patience paid off, as the weather improved and they accomplished first ascents on 5250-metre Chiwen, 5466-metre Chibu and on an unnamed 5006-metre peak which they christened The Little Prince – all via technical rock routes.

Descending from their 800-metre climb on Chibu, its western skyline a series of sharp, wave-like fins with walls dropping sharply from its ridges into a deep turquoise lake, the climbers rappelled rope length after rope length in mist-filled darkness, finally reaching flat ground after fourteen hours of climbing.

"Rapping into the mist played games with our perspective of reality," Fraser says. "Every rap felt as if we were dropping into some great abyss. For the person who went first, your eyes were open so wide they got dry from looking so hard. And the headlamp acted like a bright light in the fog, reflecting whiteness and creating a dense halo of illuminated water particles."

For Holm, who suffered from incessant altitude sickness even after taking Diamox, the technical climbing turned out to be the easy part.

"Hiking to the climbs was the hardest part," she recalls. "I had to go so slowly, I couldn't go fast enough to even sweat. I was full-on

COLIN ANGUS, LEFT, AND BEN KOZEL EXPLORE
THE AMAZON RIVER DELTA.

KARI MEDIG PULLS HIS SLED TOWARD MOUNT LOGAN
ON THE HUBBARD GLACIER, YUKON TERRITORY.

ARLENE BLUM TREKS IN THE HIMALAYAS.

JOHN MARTIN, LEFT, AND
CHRIS PERRY AT THE BASE
OF CASINO WALL, COUGAR
CREEK, CANADIAN ROCKIES.

CARLOS BUHLER.

GLEN BOLES ON MOUNT
KARNAK, PURCELL
MOUNTAINS, BC

ABOVE: CLIMBING THE NORTH FACE OF THE NORTH TWIN IN THE CANADIAN ROCKIES IS A LONG, COMPLICATED AND DANGEROUS UNDERTAKING.

ABOVE: EAMONN WALSH NEGOTIATES MOUNT ALBERTA'S PRECIPITOUS SUMMIT RIDGE, CANADIAN ROCKIES.

OPPOSITE: SEAN ISAAC WORKS HIS WAY UP SLOVENIAN DEATH WATER, CAIRNGORM MOUNTAINS, SCOTLAND.

BELOW: JEN OLSON, LEFT, AND LILLA MOLNAR ON THE SUMMIT OF BRAKK ZANG, KARAKORAM, PAKISTAN.

MARKO PREZELJ SUSSES OUT THE ROUTE UP THE NORTH
FACE OF THE NORTH TWIN, CANADIAN ROCKIES.

FROM LEFT,
KATHERINE
FRASER,
KATY HOLM,
AIDAN
OLOMAN
IN THE
FOUR GIRLS
MOUNTAINS,
CHINA.

JEFF BOYD, TOD GOURLEY AND MARK HEARD PADDLE THE
LOHIT RIVER, ARUNACHAL PRADESH, INDIAN HIMALAYAS.

LOGAN GRAYLING IN
VIETNAM'S CENTRAL
HIGHLANDS.

BEN FIRTH EXPLORES
THE CLIFFS OF WADI
RUM, JORDAN.

KAREN McNEILL, LEFT, AND SUE NOTT,
MOUNT McKINLEY, ALASKA.

PAT MORROW SAVOURS HIS MOMENT
ON THE SUMMIT OF MOUNT EVEREST.

vomiting. It was so frustrating, to be in a group and being the person who was slowing the group down, when you know there are time deadlines, and you're not able to do anything about it, and knowing you're really so much better than that."

After three first ascents, however, the women were happy to escape incoming snowstorms and return to the bustling mountain town of Rilong, where they appreciated the hospitality of the local Tibetan people, as well as the remoteness of the nature reserve.

"The green valleys and towering granite peaks of the Four Girls Mountains and the adjacent Wolong Nature Reserve stood in such stark contrast to the very polluted and industrial landscape east toward Chengdu," Holm recalls.

And while feasting at a local noodle shop, the women learned a team of American climbers had become stranded on bivy ledges on a nearby peak waiting for the snow to stop falling.

"We felt really happy to have climbed three first ascents and to be finished," Holm says. "And we were really grateful to be in Rilong – safe, dry and warm."

While I had met both Katy Holm and Katherine Fraser before their trip to the Three Girls Mountains, and spoke to them afterwards, I never did meet Aidan Oloman, even though I attended a slide show all three women presented at The Vsion climbing gym in Canmore, Alberta, one of several such shows they shared in western Canadian mountain towns. Tragically, just one week after their Canmore presentation, on January 14, 2006, Aidan was killed by a rogue avalanche while collecting weather data in what was confidently considered a safe place at a cat-skiing lodge near Fernie, BC. She was twenty-nine.

ROCK CLIMBING, INDIANA JONES STYLE (2007)

> Ben **Firth**

While enjoying a leisurely rock climbing vacation in Spain during the depths of the Alberta Rockies' frigid January temperatures, Canmore resident Ben Firth received an e-mail.

Coming from Canadian photographer Aaron Black, currently based in Wales, the message inquired if he'd be interested in joining a climbing trip to Jordan's historic Wadi Rum region.

Although the two had never met, Black knew through the tightly connected climbers' grapevine that Firth was a skilled climber who had spent time in the Middle East, that he understood something of the culture and that he spoke some Arabic. Eager to climb in an entirely new environment about which he knew very little, Firth jumped at the chance.

"I knew nothing about Jordan," Firth says. "I like going to places with not too much knowledge, so I don't damage the impression too much. Looking at pictures, going on the Internet – you create impressions. I knew there was climbing in Jordan; I was thinking of Petra. I remember when I was a kid watching Indiana Jones and loving it, and thinking 'Do people climb that rock?' I've always dreamed of going there."

In early March 2007 Firth met up for the first time with Black and Colorado-based climbers Heidi Wirtz and Chris Kalous at the airport in Amman, Jordan's capital city. The team also included Canadian cameraman and filmmaker Jean Gamilovskij.

Proudly touted by Jordan's government and His Majesty King Abdullah II Ibn Al Hussein as one of the world's premier tourist destinations, the Wadi Rum consists of uniquely shaped massive mountains that rise vertically out of the pink desert sandstone.

From valley floors that rest 900 to 1000 metres above sea level, the towering cliffs rise as high as 550 vertical metres, their faces eroded by millennia of wind and occasional rain into shapes resembling the images of men, animals and monsters. Near the border of Saudi Arabia, the region became the setting of *Lawrence of Arabia*.

"Our base camp took an hour to walk to from town," Firth says. "We didn't have water in our camp; it was a classic sand-dune environment. Every five days we'd walk back to the village for water, then hire a jeep to get back."

And although the setting was exquisitely beautiful, climbing on the desert cliffs proved quite treacherous and, ironically, left

Firth grateful for his extensive climbing experience on frozen waterfalls.

"The climbing was actually quite dangerous," Firth says. "It's really soft sandstone. We worried about holds breaking off all the time. You can't get in any protection. We got to one place where some pillars had formed. We used a nut tool and dug a hole through the back of the pillar, and threaded the hole with a sling. That was the best pro you could find. It was pretty crazy."

Despite the hazards, the team worked for about three weeks of their month-long stay to put up a new, eight-pitch, 320-metre route on the southeast face of a mountain called Nassrani North. With some bolts drilled into the rock for protection, they rated their creation at an expert level 5.13a.

"It started out at about 5.8 on the first pitch, and it gradually got harder and harder and harder," Firth says. "Just finishing the route was a lot more work than climbing. But that was the best part, working on that type of project with everybody."

When it was done, they christened the route Dar-al-Salaam, the rest of the group vigorously vetoing Firth's suggestion they call it Bahka Lahka Dahka Street from the Trey Parker puppet movie *Team America: World Police*.

Climbing in the desert was a unique experience, Firth says, particularly on the one day it rained.

"It was strange for sure," he says. "It turns into a big mud pit, then it gets sucked right back into the air."

The area is home to the traditionally nomadic Bedouin people, who live in the desert and travel by camel. While some still live in tents, others inhabit stone houses built by their government. Those who own vehicles drive thirty- to forty-year-old Land Cruisers, he says.

To supplement the locally purchased foods they brought into their camp, the climbers also bought a sheep, which their jeep driver nonchalantly slaughtered and butchered for them.

"They don't care, they just hack it apart," Firth says. "It was climbing in a completely different environment and situation than what we're used to."

To mark his twenty-ninth birthday while he was there, Firth smuggled some Johnnie Walker Red Label into the alcohol-free country. Sitting around the evening campfire in down jackets, Firth says he appreciated its warmth.

"It was actually quite cold there. At night I had my down jacket on; in the daytime, it went up to 25 degrees," Firth says. "I've worked in 50 degrees in the desert – it wasn't nearly as hot as that!"

Prior to his climbing trip in Spain, Firth spent the months of October and November doing seismic work in southeastern Libya, sweating in Central Saharan 50°C temperatures near the Chad–Sudan border. In previous years, he worked two two-month stints in Oman, soaking in the ancient desert culture of the Middle East.

During his time in Libya, Firth and some colleagues made their own Indiana Jones discovery, unearthing what they were convinced were dinosaur bones.

"It was like – what's that?" Firth says. "We kept on digging and found some teeth. I found this full alligator jaw. We spent a bunch of time doing that."

After contacting the Royal Tyrrell Museum in Drumheller, Alberta, they learned their find was not quite as old as dinosaurs, just a little younger – but still tens of millions of years old.

"They were really soft; they'd break really easily," Firth says of the bones and teeth. "They were really friable, it looked like rock, but you know they're not. Full-on teeth."

In the Libyan landscape that Firth describes as similar to the Drumheller Badlands, they also discovered a massive petrified forest, with some trees over thirty metres long. They also discovered the area was surrounded by land mines, likely placed there to discourage pillaging.

The sheer harshness of the environment and social conditions in northern Africa, however, presented enough challenges, Firth says, as he witnessed refugees coming over the border from Chad, standing by the hundreds in giant transport trucks amidst heaps of personal goods.

"There are hundreds of people walking across the desert, and many people – they don't make it. They die in the desert," Firth says. "They're malnourished; they have no water. It's pretty real."

Many of the refugees find work in the oil and gas industry, he adds. Back in Canmore, Firth says he is happy to stay home for a while. "Over there, you're reminded how good it is here," he admits.

Before boarding his flight home, however, Firth did manage to fulfill a long-time dream – climbing one of the giant pyramids in Egypt. "I paid off one of the guards," he admits. "I've always wanted to climb those. It was only about 90 metres vertical – there's a huge amount of rock in them, but they're not that high. Coming back down was easy scrambling, but I had to move quickly."

PADDLING A FAST BOAT THROUGH INDIA (2004)

> Jeff **Boyd**, Tod **Gourley** and Mark **Heard**

Take three very keen paddlers; add three kayaks, a retired Indian Army major general and a virtually unknown river coursing through a narrow mountain valley in northeastern India; and you've got a once in a lifetime trip. That scenario partly describes the experience of a team of Albertans comprised of orthopaedic surgeon Mark Heard, emergency physician Jeff Boyd and firefighter Tod Gourley.

To sweeten the deal, theirs was the first foreign expedition (which included several British paddlers travelling as a separate team at the same time) paddling the first kayaks on the Lohit River for the first complete descent of the river that demarcates the eastern edge of the Himalayas in India's Arunachal Pradesh region bordering Myanmar and China. Until their expedition – the logistics of which were facilitated by river guide Kim Hartlin, whose Thunderbow Expeditions has run trips on remote Indian rivers since the early 1990s – only small sections of the river had been rafted by members of the Indian Army.

All three teammates being experienced whitewater kayakers, with expeditions to Nepal, Ecuador, Honduras and New Zealand under their spray skirts, the paddlers said it was the combination of intense rapids and cultural differences that made the trip spectacular, as each mountain drainage in the area is home to its own unique tribe.

While paddling down the Lohit, the kayakers occasionally sighted members of one especially colourful local tribe, the Mishmi, peering out from the rainforest along the riverbanks.

"This is an unknown valley in an unknown area of the world," Heard says. "The tribal people were very pastoral and friendly; for them it's totally rare to see white people."

Historically known for their penchant for cannibalism, Boyd adds, the Mishmi people are subsistence farmers of Burmese descent whose crops include opium, and whose older generations still wear traditional tribal clothing. Although some of the more isolated tribes are just now seeing their first Westerners, these days the Mishmi are becoming increasingly aware of the Western world. Boyd says he couldn't help but notice a look of wonder on the Mishmi's faces, but also a look of yearning to connect with the modern world that was passing them by.

"It's inevitable that they get drawn into the modern world," Boyd says. "Last year they were wearing tribal dress, this year the younger ones are wearing blue jeans."

Identified by the World Wildlife Fund as a preservation priority, the region supports a significant stand of tropical *Dipterocarp* – a native hardwood commonly logged in the region – and is the only place in the world inhabited by four big cat species: jungle leopard, clouded leopard, snow leopard and tiger. It also is home to the red panda, pangolin, Himalayan brown bear and Himalayan black bear. All of these species are vulnerable to poaching and the black market trade of coveted body parts, such as tiger claws and bear gall bladders.

Although the area is sparsely populated, the Indian state of Arunachal Pradesh, having learned from the devastating effects of floods created by excessive logging in China and Tibet, made a commitment in 1999 to protect the area. To that end, efforts are underway to create a biosphere reserve in the eastern sector of the state. The proposed 5000-square-kilometre Anjaw Biosphere Reserve would allow the local tribespeople to continue living in the area, while preserving their culture and the natural environment.

As they paddled through the region, the kayakers admit, they repeatedly presented a significant curiosity to the local villagers.

"When we were at a village we'd get lots of visitors," Gourley says. "They'd never seen a kayak before and very few Westerners. It was quite a road show."

Once back in their boats, the kayakers navigated long stretches of Class V whitewater – only for strong, experienced paddlers equipped with lightning-fast reflexes – as they followed the Lohit down an enormous valley bordered by 4300-metre mountains covered with pine forests in the upper reaches and jungle vegetation on the lower slopes.

Heard, a former Canadian national team paddler, whose love for kayaking was sparked when he was an eleven-year-old outdoor education student, says the medium-volume river was unlike any other he'd ever experienced.

"It was probably the most sustained whitewater river I've ever paddled," Heard says. "It was just rapid after rapid after rapid. I think we paddled about 300 rapids. We thought it would ease off, but it just never did."

For six consecutive days they bounced through more rapids and more rapids in sparkling-clear green water.

"It was just rapid after rapid and big huge waves and huge holes," Gourley grins. "It was great paddling."

Unlike many regions of India, Heard says the water and food in the area were very clean and the population free of diseases and infections.

"We didn't worry about getting sick up there," Heard says.

After they descended through the mountains, the river abruptly emerged onto the flat plains of Assam, where vast tea plantations date back to the early nineteenth century.

The kayakers initially learned of the river through Indian-based Aquaterra Adventures, which waded through the daunting rivers of paperwork required for the group to visit the militarily sensitive area, as well as arranging transport to and from the put in and take out for the Canadian group's kayaks, and those of a Welsh–American group that travelled on the river at the same time.

Although the two groups saw each other from time to time, Gourley, Heard and Boyd travelled independently for six days, camping at night and joined on some days by two young, less experienced Indian kayakers, who found the relentless whitewater quite overwhelming.

For the Canadians, however, it was the bureaucracy that was daunting.

"It's a very difficult area to access; you need a restricted-area permit," Gourley says. "You have to shake the right hands, make the right people feel important. The bureaucracy is quite different from here."

Fortunately, Aquaterra provided the team with the expertise of a retired Indian Army major general who worked to get the kayakers through sensitive checkpoints in the region, where in the early 1960s India and China fought a war.

"Without him we wouldn't have gotten even close to the China border," Heard says.

The group had hoped to start their trip about forty kilometres higher on the river, but the Chinese Army presence forced them to start lower down, at the historic site of a major battle.

"You could see where they'd dug fox holes; you could see military infrastructure," Heard says, adding they were advised not to walk in certain nearby fields because of possible land mines.

But once on the water, the kayakers felt right at home dodging waves and holes and rapid after rapid after rapid.

KAYAKERS SPLASH DOWN ON VIETNAMESE RIVERS (2007)

> Logan **Grayling**

Hiking through a field in the central highlands of Vietnam, Logan Grayling and his four kayaking buddies marched right through giant swaths of stick-like plants covered with teeth-like thorns. And they learned the hard way what those teeth were capable of.

"They stick to your skin with their teeth and if you don't pull them out right away they will hurt for days," Grayling recalls.

This little bit of knowledge was but one of many the adventurers learned the hard way during a two-month exploratory kayaking trip, from Vietnam's Mekong Delta north to the Chinese border in early 2007.

"We found out a lot of stuff the hard way," Grayling admits.

For instance, the group wasn't aware that they'd need special permits to travel in northern Vietnam, where the rivers and the waterfalls they hoped to run form the border with China, and where soldiers patrol with authority.

"The Chinese threatened to throw us in jail," Grayling says. "They just weren't pleased we were there. We didn't know we needed permits, and they weren't pleased we didn't know that."

Born and raised in Canmore, Alberta, Grayling, nineteen, grew up skiing, snowboarding, surfing in California and excelling in gymnastics. He took up kayaking in 2003 and hasn't been dry since, pursuing adventures in Africa, Norway, Switzerland, Ecuador, California, Oregon and western Canada.

He made the Canadian national team at sixteen, and despite finishing dead last at the World Championships that year, he found the experience to be enormously valuable.

"I didn't care about the contest; competing isn't my main focus," Grayling says. "I'm into creeking and making videos. And at Worlds, I met a lot of key people."

Among them were other young filmmaking kayakers who comprise Young Guns Productions. In November 2007 Grayling teamed up with fellow kayakers Anthony Yap, Ben Marr, Brooks Baldwin and Pat Camblin – from Australia, the US and Ottawa – to run some Vietnamese rivers that had never seen kayaks before, timing their trip to arrive during the smaller of two annual rainy seasons, partly at the urging of Yap's father, a native Malaysian living in Kuala Lumpur.

"No one's been there, no one's done it," Grayling says of the rivers. "We thought we'd get it."

Financing his airline ticket and travel expenses by working at northern Alberta oilfields as a roughneck, Grayling flew to Kuala Lumpur with his buddies. Once there, they based themselves at Yap's father's house. They rode a bus to Singapore and flew to

Ho Chi Minh City (formerly Saigon), from where they launched their five-week, 2500-kilometre road trip north into green and lush mountainous country.

"It was a little chillier than the rest of the country, because of the altitude," Grayling says. "But there were lots of waterfalls, some three or four tiers, 120 to 150 feet in total. They were Class V, some waterfalls were seventy feet high."

Just road tripping through the country presented an adventure in itself, he says.

Thinking they'd hire a HiAce (Toyota-made minivan-sized motorhome) and attach a Thule rack on top to hold their kayaks, they contacted the local Thule representative (a Young Guns sponsor).

"We thought we would put the rack on and throw the boats on," Grayling says. "But they said no, you can't do that. We said why not, we do that at home. And they said, 'It's against the law to have anything on the roof.' So we asked for another model van, and they said, 'We don't have any.' The last thing left was a bus, a forty-seater for the five of us, and the driver was part of the deal. So we told them we really needed a driver who was young, who would be cool with what was going down, and who spoke good English. But our driver turned out to be forty, with like six kids, and he didn't speak a word of English."

To make the situation workable, they hired a translator, who rode with them for their entire road trip and afterward boarded a bus for home.

Despite their initial misgivings, the kayakers found both their driver and their translator to be enormously helpful as they travelled through remote villages in search of enticing waterfalls.

"It got pretty funny after a while," Grayling says. "They ended up really helping us, and got the locals to help us find waterfalls."

For the most part, though, the villagers thought the kayakers were nothing short of insane.

"They'd say, 'No, not possible,'" Grayling recalls. "And we'd say, 'We'll be fine,' and they'd say, 'Not possible!' and we'd say, 'No, we'll be fine.' Then, after watching us do it, they'd just say, 'You crazy!'"

No one in the region had ever seen a kayak before, let alone five young men dropping over sixteen-metre, vertical, frothing waterfalls. People lined the shores to watch them, including magazine photographers and two TV crews who covered their story.

Although the group never found copies of the print story, they did record the segment as it appeared on local TV news to bring home as a souvenir.

"After that, a lot of people recognized us," Grayling says. "They'd make waterfall sounds and say, 'You famous!'"

The local kids knew a cool thing when they saw it. Watching the kayakers gear up beside the highway, some kids offered to carry their paddles down to the water for them.

"Then we put two kids in boats and all the others wanted a ride, too," Grayling says.

Throughout their trip, kayaking didn't present the only source of challenges for the crew, as the local menus offered plenty of adventure.

"My stomach's pretty bombproof," Grayling admits. "I can eat pretty much anything and I'll be fine. Half the time we didn't know what we were eating. We ate some dog, we ate some rat, pig intestines and chicken esophagus and a bunch of other stuff I had no idea what it was. Dog is actually quite tasty. Up north, dog is on every menu. Lots of rat, too."

While Grayling wasn't too concerned about getting sick from roadside food stands, he does express concern about other hazards, including land mines, adding that many local people still bear scars from the Vietnam War of the 1960s and 1970s.

"In some areas the people were not pleased we were there because we were white," Grayling says. "There are still lots of land mines in the central highlands area. It was definitely a little scary for us hiking through the jungle – plus the spiders and snakes and other things that hurt and bite and kill you."

Despite that, he and his buddies can't wait to return.

"We want to go back in October for the big rainy season," Grayling says. "We want to get the stuff we didn't do. And it's so cheap."

A VIEW TO ETERNITY (2004)

> Karen **McNeill** and Sue **Nott**

The Cassin Ridge is big.

It rises 3720 metres from the Kahiltna Glacier to the 6100-metre tip of the Kahiltna Horn, just below Mount McKinley's 6194-metre summit – North America's highest point.

Climbing the Cassin Ridge Route (first accomplished in 1961) involves negotiating seventy-five-degree ice pitches, a 305-metre knife-edge ice traverse, 5.8 rock-climbing moves, snow slopes, mixed rock and ice gullies and a 610-metre traverse along a steep ridge where falling is not an option. And in May 2004, Canmore, Alberta's Karen McNeill and Vail, Colorado's Sue Nott became the first women's team to climb the Cassin.

With the average party spending three to five days on the route, McNeill and Nott carried food for four, knowing they could stretch it out to last six. In all, they spent eight stormy days on the route, plus a ninth on the approach – the last three without any food.

Their third trip together since meeting as ice-climbing competitors at the X Games, their mission marked McNeill's fourth Alaskan expedition and Nott's second.

On her first Alaskan expedition in 1994, McNeill and a partner retreated from Denali's West Buttress at 5185 metres, after a storm inflicted second-degree frostbite on McNeill's fingers – an experience she admits was "huge on the learning curve."

McNeill returned in 2002 with fellow New Zealanders Anna Keeling and Patricia Deavoll, and they became the first women's team to climb the Colton Leech Route on 3730-metre Mount Huntington. Benefiting from uncharacteristically fine weather, they made several other ascents, including a new route. The following year, McNeill and Deavoll's sister, Christina Byrch, put up a new route on 2909-metre Mount Dickey.

"Alaska's incredibly beautiful," McNeill says. "I could sit there every day and look at the scenery and not get sick of it. And it's easier to organize and cheaper than other big trips."

After climbing in India, Nepal, Tibet, Peru, Bolivia and Greenland, including her personal high point of 7600 metres on 8201-metre Cho Oyu in the Himalayas of central Nepal, McNeill says any route on McKinley is a big deal.

"It's a huge mountain. It's intense," McNeill says. "It can have really severe weather; the winds can be horrific."

On one visit, gusts were clocked at 165 kilometres per hour. When a friend suggested they climb the Cassin a few years ago, McNeill declined.

"I thought it was something that was too hard for me," she admits.

Due to the Arctic's atmospheric pressure, climbing in the Alaska Range is equivalent to climbing at 600 to 900 metres higher than at the same elevation at the equator. In May the sun barely sets. The unique Alaska Grade System, which in addition to considering technical difficulty and the usual hazards of glacier travel and avalanche potential, also takes into account extreme temperatures, length of time on a route, camping options, the sustained nature of the route, difficulty of descent and difficulty of retreat.

By comparison, the summit of the Canadian Rockies' highest mountain, 3954-metre Mount Robson, is slightly lower than the Cassin's base – the elevation at which the effects of altitude first take their toll.

While camped at 4270 metres to acclimatize, Nott – who had never been sick on other high-altitude climbs – was stricken with high-altitude pulmonary edema. After camping with about sixty others in a large snowfield, including park rangers who administered oxygen, the women descended to 3350 metres.

After resting for a couple of days, Nott was fine, so they climbed higher, and even helped rescue a Korean climber who had been found with one bare hand at 5640 metres in bad weather. Thankfully, he recovered.

Finally, McNeill and Nott broke their camp at 4270 metres around 2 p.m. and started up the West Rib. Two hours and only 215 metres higher, they hauled out their tent and pitched it in a whiteout. By 11 p.m. they were moving again, down climbing toward the base of the

Cassin, when bad weather stopped them again at 3355 metres on the Kahiltna Glacier, and they crawled back into their tent. Starting out at 9 a.m. in thick fog, they finally reached the Cassin's base twelve hours later.

"We just got in the mode," McNeill says. "The weather was terrible the whole time. But there was never a day when we didn't climb."

After bits of progress, strong winds would surge later in the day. Fortunately, they managed to find good bivy spots every time.

"The wind came up; it was just desperate," McNeill says. "On every pitch your hands would freeze. The sleeping bags were wet for days on end; we were just pulling them apart. For three days we were like, 'We're going to get to the summit and down today.' But we just couldn't."

Climbing the last three days without food, they fortunately had plenty of fuel to melt snow. On dealing with hunger, McNeill shrugs. "I think it's a whole mindset. You can't pine for it, you just deal with it."

Finally, they spotted the wands that announced the summit. In howling winds and yet another whiteout, they pitched their tent on a flat spot. They descended to 4270 metres the next day, and reached base camp at 2045 metres the day after. Along the way, park rangers gave them food. At base camp people asked, "Are you the girls who slept on the summit?"

McNeill credits her years of experience in the mountains for surviving – particularly remembering to stay hydrated.

"It's learning how to use the resources you have in yourself, using what you've learned to survive in different circumstances," she explains. "It's very rare you get perfect conditions in the mountains."

A substitute teacher at Morley Community School on the Stoney Nakoda First Nation reserve in the foothills of the Canadian Rockies west of Calgary, McNeill also teaches women's climbing clinics, where the participants constantly inspire her.

"It never ceases to amaze me to see them so empowered and feeling so good about themselves," she says.

And what attracts her to climbing?

"I love being in the mountains, where you're free of faxes and phones and e-mails," she says.

But why climb week-long, difficult and dangerous routes instead of going for a pleasant hike or a comfortable night in a backcountry lodge?

"I guess it's the intensity," she replies. "Keeping it together when you accept that it's not going to get easier. It takes full focus. And the experiences you have together are so intense."

With a smile, McNeill recounts how, as she and Nott walked off the summit, they found a single square of chocolate lying in the snow. They shared it.

"I'm pretty excited; it is a big deal," McNeill admits. "People talk about the Cassin. It's a big route. I'm really proud that we did it, that we just dealt with what was given us."

On May 14, 2006, Karen McNeill and Sue Nott hoisted their packs, crammed with sleeping bags and enough food and fuel to last them eight to fourteen days, and started up the Infinite Spur, a difficult 2865-metre mixed rock and ice route on 5303-metre Mount Foraker, in Alaska's Denali National Park.

Three weeks later – a week after their food and fuel would have run out – Denali Park rangers launched a search for the missing climbers. They found Nott's backpack, which contained a functioning radio, about 150 metres from the start of the route. Several other items were retrieved nearby, including a sleeping bag and jacket, all of which had fallen a significant distance. Using a high-altitude LAMA helicopter, the rangers also found tracks at 5000 metres, above the route's major technical difficulties and where no other climbers had been that season.

Several days into the search, the rangers were forced to suspend their activities as storms engulfed the Alaska Range. On June 11, the search was scaled back to a recovery mission. Some speculate the women were blown off the mountain by winds that had gusted to 150 kilometres per hour while they were on the upper part of the peak. Others suggest they might have taken shelter in a crevasse and grown too weak to come out.

No sign of them has since been found.

Shortly before she left for Alaska, I asked McNeill how the Infinite Spur compared to the Cassin Ridge route. She told me it would be longer, and that it would involve some pitches of harder climbing. Then the conversation turned to stress, through which she was characteristically sharing advice on how I might cope with a mishap in the mountains I'd recently experienced.

"It can come back and affect you when you least expect it," she said, adding that nearly two years later, she still had times when she felt the stress of the Cassin climb.

"And you're going back to do it again?" I replied.

With a shrug, her answer was optimistically determined.

"Yup."

THE COST OF THE CLIMB (2003)

> ❯ Pat **Morrow**, Lloyd "Kiwi" **Gallagher**, John **Amatt**, Tim **Auger**, James **Blench** and Colleen **Campbell**

Fifty years ago today, New Zealander Ed Hillary and Sherpa Tenzing Norgay became the first people to reach the 8848-metre summit of Mount Everest and descend safely to celebrate. Their achievement generated great national pride in New Zealand, Britain and Nepal, and also marked a long-coveted milestone in mountaineering history.

On October 5, 1982, Calgary's Laurie Skreslet, climbing with Sherpas Sungdare and Lhakpa Dorje, became the first Canadian to stand on that 1-by-4.5-metre mountaintop. Two days later, his teammate Pat Morrow reached the summit with Lhakpa Tshering and Pema Dorje. Their achievement also generated great national pride, earning them lunch with Prime Minister Pierre Trudeau, speaking engagements and TV and print interviews.

Canada's 1982 Everest expedition, however, was riddled with controversy and discord, much like crevasses on a glacier. It was also marred by four deaths. In the process of fixing ropes and ferrying supplies to establish a series of camps up the mountain, three Sherpas – Pasang Sona, Ang Chuldim and Dawa Dorje – were killed in a massive avalanche. Two days later, CBC cameraman Blair Griffiths died in an icefall collapse.

Those tragedies, in conjunction with differences in opinion on leadership and climbing styles, as well as more basic personality conflicts, would eventually lead to nearly half the team leaving the mountain halfway through the expedition.

"It wasn't an easy trip," expedition manager John Amatt admits. "Everest is a dangerous mountain and a very unpredictable mountain. There are places on Everest that as a climber you wouldn't go if they weren't on Everest – the Khumbu Icefall, for example. But you tend to put your fears aside because it's Everest."

The team that trekked the 250-kilometre approach route from Kathmandu – a distance now routinely shortened considerably via ready helicopter access, despite the trek's exceptional value as a means of properly acclimatizing – was a diverse group that had been assembled over nearly five years of planning. Consisting of two distinct subgroups of older, British-born Canadian climbers and younger, Canadian-born climbers, the team was following its third leader since the climb's inception, Bill March, a University of Calgary physical education professor who had been appointed a mere five months before the team left for Nepal. Lloyd "Kiwi" Gallagher, a mountain rescue specialist, served as deputy leader. With previous experience in organizing and funding expeditions, Amatt had secured funding from Air Canada, one of over 150 sponsors. Expectations were as high as the mountain itself, and all manner of media were working to let every Canadian know about the extravaganza.

With sixteen climbers, five support personnel and thirty Sherpas, the team was seen by many as appropriately large, given that Canadians had no experience climbing into the fruitless air above 8000 metres, and its members, although experienced climbers, were not experienced Himalayan climbers.

"We decided to go with a strong team, knowing some would likely become ill when they got to the mountain, since they didn't have a lot of high-altitude experience," Amatt recalls.

For some, however, more climbers meant more strong personalities, more gear and supplies to ferry up the mountain, and more people committed to spending greater periods of time in extremely hazardous places, such as the Khumbu Icefall, a 600-vertical-metre constantly shifting maze of tottering ice pillars.

"Ours was a group that came together in a very diverse way, and it was a very diverse group," recalls Tim Auger, a mountain rescue specialist with the Banff National Park warden service. "Not much thought or stock was put into putting together a team that would work well together. Only one or two of the team members had more than none in terms of Himalayan experience, and those who did have some didn't have personalities that were open to sharing."

Expedition members had been selected from more than 100 applicants on the basis of their individual strengths and skills rather than for their ability and inclination to work well within the confines – and demands – of a large, structured team. At that point in mountaineering history, some climbers had begun to move away from large, siege-style expeditions to lighter, faster teams, an approach some of the expedition members, including Auger, favoured.

"A big team like that means many more tons of protein that needed to be hauled up the mountain," Auger says. "You're going to burn out your climbers hauling loads for all your climbers."

In addition to a large team, the expedition also had large ambitions – to leave a uniquely Canadian stamp on the mountain and in mountaineering history by establishing a new route up the mountain's difficult south pillar.

At that time, with only a handful of permits granted annually, Everest had seen about 127 successful ascents by six different routes. By comparison, in 2002, more than eighty climbers summitted by the standard South Col Route in the spring season alone.

While he admits his participation in the 1982 expedition, and his good fortune in being one of the two climbers to reach the summit, definitely benefited his photography career, Pat Morrow says today a great many climbers who follow fixed ropes up the same South Col Route the Canadians ultimately climbed seek to climb Everest primarily as a career move.

"I can't deny I used it as a stepping stone for other adventures in the future," Morrow says. "It came at a really good point in my career as an adventure photographer. And the lessons I learned were how to launch an expedition to anywhere on the planet. But these days an alarmingly large number are going there purely as a stepping stone in their careers, and sadly, once they're on the rubber chicken circuit back home, their involvement with the mountain world will dry up." After Everest, Morrow became the first person to reach the highest point on all seven continents in 1986, and with his wife and creative partner, Baiba, has travelled to remote regions of the world photographing and filming those natural and cultural wonders ever since.

Today, he says, very few Everest climbers seek to establish bold new routes, as Canmore's Barry Blanchard attempted in 1988, reaching 8400 metres on the unclimbed northeast face with a single climbing partner and without Sherpas or supplemental oxygen.

"Climbers then went to Everest because they wanted to make a mark in climbing journals," Morrow says. "Now people use it as a career lever, rather than going there to up the ante for Himalayan climbing standards. It's rare to see harder climbs done in good style on Everest nowadays. But the mountain still has difficult routes for people who want to make their mark in the climbing history books."

As the 1982 expedition unfolded, however, the Canadians were forced to modify their ambitions after the accidents spurred six climbers, including Auger, to leave Nepal for home, while the remaining climbers restructured their team and plotted their course up the standard South Col Route.

"We had the cream of Canadian climbers on the team," Morrow says. "Then we were hit by a major avalanche and an icefall collapse and that turned the tide of the momentum of the whole team. In the end it was just survival. Our objective was completely changed by the accidents that happened. The people who stayed learned how to change gears and change objectives.

"Looking back now, it's a bit like surviving a war. You're not sure you should celebrate. But being on the summit was wonderful. We had the whole route to ourselves. Nowadays you've got to have pretty sharp elbows to move up there."

Overall, Morrow says, the complicated expedition required an enormous amount of teamwork.

"Taking on such a large mountain – we had to get through an icefall that you wouldn't even attempt on any other mountain," Morrow says. "We had to learn how to build a route through it just to get to the base of the mountain, then start climbing the actual mountain. Even if you're the only one who gets to the top, there's a huge effort of others who helped you get there."

For deputy leader Gallagher, who stayed through the expedition and climbed as high as 7900 metres, just shy of Camp IV, the weeks spent on the mountain were rewarding but stressful.

"On a trip like that, you're putting yourself on the mountain for six weeks, not like here [Canmore] where we go out for a day and come home," Gallagher says. "Many expeditions go out all the time and nothing happens, but then, when you're in the wrong place at the wrong time and something does, it teaches you so quickly you can lose your life on a mountain like that. You realize there's a lot more things in life you can do, and Everest was just one of those things."

Retiring in 1997 after twenty years as head of public safety for Kananaskis Country, which included being head of safety for the 1988 Calgary Winter Olympic Games' Kananaskis skiing events, Gallagher continues to work as a mountain guide and safety instructor.

For Amatt, who had dreamed of climbing Everest for sixteen years but never ended up climbing above Camp I, the tragic turn of events on the mountain presented him with an entirely different mountain to climb. Unable to establish an effective radio link from base camp, and intent on protecting the expedition's valuable sponsorships, Amatt flew by helicopter to Kathmandu, where he spent the duration of the expedition working eighteen-hour days liaising with media in response to an avalanche of inaccurate news stories that had begun reaching the Canadian public.

"Back in '82 we didn't have the communication links we have today," Amatt recalls. "There were 150 miles and 24,000 feet of mountains between base camp and Kathmandu. And I felt a strong responsibly that the sponsorship be protected and that the facts were the straight facts."

Amatt returned to Canmore unemployed and founded One Step Beyond, developing motivation strategies for people in fields other than mountaineering using the metaphor of mountains and Everest in particular. Two decades later, he says his Everest experience taught him many valuable lessons.

"You have to accept reality as it exists and have to adapt by challenging the status quo – what you've accomplished in the past – and strive to move one step beyond your previous experience," Amatt says. "Everest has become a very powerful metaphor, even though as it is being climbed more and more and it's becoming devalued in the process, it's still the highest place on earth and a symbol of reaching as far as you can reach.

"What I learned from our expedition is that in life there are things you can predict and things you can't predict, things you can control and things you cannot control, and you shouldn't spend your time worrying about things you can't control. The things that happened were possible but not predictable. Both accidents happened as a result of natural forces. We just happened to be at the wrong place at the wrong time. Afterward, we were forced to adapt to the situation, adapt to the events that took place and it was that adaptation that allowed us to be successful, to put the first Canadians – Laurie Skreslet and Pat Morrow – on the summit of Mount Everest."

With the departure of the expedition cook as well, the restructured team welcomed the arrival of Colleen Campbell, who volunteered to cook for the Canadian climbers. Campbell, the girlfriend of expedition member Dwayne Congdon, one of the climbers who chose to continue with the climb, had been travelling solo in Kathmandu when she learned of the accidents.

Recalling her days at base camp spent baking scones to the delight of passing trekkers and those team members not higher on the mountain, Campbell, a grizzly bear researcher, says her own memories are positive ones.

"I think the outcomes of the expedition were really positive," Campbell says. "We did a really good job there. There was a lot of kindness and friendship in that camp. I think that expedition was really important to the mountaineering identity of Canada, and how perfect that a couple of unknown Canadian climbers got to the summit."

Still, the effort had cost four lives, and it was, and remains, a price some of the expedition members feel was too high.

"When I look back on it, I think, 'Why did I ever get involved in the first place? I should have seen it all coming,'" says James Blench, an internationally certified professional mountain guide. "It was a commercial trip, more dedicated to the goal of the sponsors than any mountaineering trip, and that's never been what my climbing was about. In the grand scheme of things, that trip didn't really have a big impact on my life. It was a negative experience, but I didn't really have any gems lingering from it."

Sharing similar views on the size and motivations of the expedition, Dave McNab and Jim Elzinga began planning a smaller expedition with Blench, who left the expedition with them, while they were still in Kathmandu. In 1986 all three, plus Skreslet, Congdon and Barry Blanchard, were part of a Canadian team of eleven climbers, a cook and a doctor who returned to climb Everest via the difficult west ridge and north face without Sherpa support. On May 20, 1986, Congdon reached the summit with Canmore's Sharon Wood, who became first North American woman to do so, by a new and still unrepeated route.

More than two decades after their experiences as members of the 1982 expedition, all of the Canmore-based members continue to climb, some recreationally and others as professional guides and safety experts, and all with varied feelings about the expedition.

"To be honest, I got involved because I didn't want to miss out, I wanted to be part of the show," Auger admits. "Deep down, I thought to myself, 'That isn't really why you're involved in climbing in the first place.' It was really disappointing to be part of something where there are a number of casualties and in all cases they were innocent bystanders.

You come face to face with the realization – one man's hobby – you smash people's families with it. In climbing, when you depend on other people to carry your loads, you're playing not with your lives, but with somebody else's. Accidents are mistakes, sometimes they're honest, but they're still mistakes. It really brought home the fact – look who paid the price. It wasn't the ambitious mountaineer who paid the price.

"Maybe we could have put our stamp on Everest in a kinder, gentler way."

May 29, 2003, marked the fiftieth anniversary of the first ascent of the world's highest peak, Mount Everest, or as it is known to the native people of Khumbu region, Chomolungma, a Tibetan word meaning "Mother Goddess of the World." Newspapers and magazines around the world published stories to mark the event. Writing for the Rocky Mountain Outlook *(a Banff–Canmore, Alberta, weekly newspaper), I chose to focus on Canmore residents who had been part of the 1982 expedition that placed the first Canadians on that summit. I asked Pat Morrow, John Amatt, Lloyd "Kiwi" Gallagher, Tim Auger, James Blench and Colleen Campbell how they viewed their own participation in the 1982 expedition, twenty-one years later.*

ON THE JOB

For those in this chapter, participating in adventures is an essential element of their profession. Here are stories of mountain guides, polar guides, physicians, educators and skilled technicians whose talents and expertise are invaluable to others in pursuit of adventure or in the course of scientific study in places that are remote, inaccessible and rife with adventure. These people facilitate the expedition, and they don't hesitate to sign up for duty.

HOLLYWOOD'S LEADING MOUNTAIN MAN (2000)

> Barry **Blanchard**

When Canadian mountain guide Barry Blanchard travelled to work in New Zealand in the spring of 1999, he wasn't hired to look after any of the country's millions of sheep. But he was asked to be a shepherd, of sorts.

In a steadily recurring role, Blanchard was hired to train a flock of Hollywood actors to look the part of mountain climbers.

Columbia Pictures' *Vertical Limit* is the fifth major motion picture forty-one-year-old Blanchard has worked on since his 1990 stint as a climbing double and member of the mountain rigging department for the feature film *K2*, parts of which were filmed in the Whistler, BC, area.

To land that plum job, Blanchard rode his motorcycle overnight all the way from Canmore, Alberta, to Vancouver – nearly 900 kilometres. Thoroughly knackered, he curled up beside the warmth of his bike's exhaust pipe and fell sound asleep in a ditch. Fortunately, he woke up just in time to make the audition – and get the job.

Since then, Blanchard has climbed a few rungs on the movie ladder. While working on *Vertical Limit*, he flew home to Canmore for Christmas holidays. The film's producer, Lloyd Phillips, said he chose Blanchard for the position after becoming familiar with his abilities when they worked together on *The Edge*, starring Anthony Hopkins, which was filmed in and around Canmore in 1996.

"Barry is a combination of being an extraordinary climber and also a gentle spirit, a gentle soul, but that's really a disguise for a very strong will," Phillips says from his Hollywood office. "No matter how big the ego of the actors, I knew they would respect this man and listen to him. I knew that even after ten months of shooting they would still be in awe of him."

As head of the talent/mountain safety department, Blanchard oversaw a staff of eight Kiwi and Canadian professional mountain guides, while his wife, Catherine, worked the administrative angle. Blanchard and his team bore the important task of making the actors look like experts as they travelled up glaciers with crampons on their feet, ice axes in their hands and danger all around them.

"Our department's job is to make the actors look like they know what they're doing. Most actors want to look believable," Blanchard says. No beginner at making climbing look believable on the big screen, Blanchard also made it look easy when he starred in the IMAX *Extreme* film, with Catherine sharing the rope.

In *Vertical Limit*, the actors included Chris O'Donnell, who is best known for playing Robin to George Clooney's Batman, Isabella Scorupco, who played the dazzling Bond girl Natalya in *Goldeneye*, and Scott Glenn, who rose to great heights in *The Right Stuff*.

"Barry knows how to take raw people and make them comfortable, with their gear, with their movements in the mountains," Phillips says. "The actors need to be pretty confident in themselves in that environment."

Blanchard and his crew spent a full month taking the actors rock climbing, ice climbing and alpine climbing, with helicopters, drivers and expense accounts at their disposal to make sure everyone was convincingly attired and equipped with all the right gear.

"We're relied on a lot to make everything look as it should," Blanchard explains. "Martin [Campbell, the director] relied on me to provide direction on breathing patterns at altitude, how to cough at altitude, on body movement at altitude. To the cast, I was the breathing guy. I had to provide input on the plot in regards to how the signs and symptoms of acute mountain sickness develop. Then the makeup people could make people look like they were dying of pulmonary edema."

A veteran of at least thirty expeditions to high-altitude peaks in Alaska, South America and the Himalayas, Blanchard is a credible authority on the difficulties of breathing above 7000 metres. He has seen clients and climbing partners suffer from the effects of acute altitude sickness; Blanchard himself experienced both cerebral and pulmonary edema while attempting the unclimbed northeast face of Mount Everest in 1988 with only one partner and no Sherpa support. That partner, Mark Twight, helped transport him safely down the mountain.

On the set, Phillips says, the work of Blanchard and his team is indispensable to the finished product. While spending long days in the mountains training for their roles as climbers, the actors confronted exhaustion and physical discomfort, which helped them understand what their characters were experiencing.

"In those extreme situations they performed like climbers; ice climbing, abseiling [rappelling], crossing a ridge, they were relying on harnesses and ropes. They wouldn't have done that without Barry and his team," Phillips says.

Modern moviegoers have higher expectations than those a few decades ago because they've seen so much on TV, he adds.

"I think we have the spirit of authenticity. However, it's not a movie about climbing. It's a movie about people," Phillips says.

Blanchard and the main body of the film crew, who at times numbered 300, spent ten months in and around Queenstown, a popular adventure destination on New Zealand's South Island. Much of the outdoor mountain footage was shot in the Mount Cook National Park area. The Kiwi mountains were meant to represent K2, in Pakistan's Karakoram Range, where the story takes place.

A sound stage was built in Queenstown, where indoor production days, not being weather dependent, could carry on for as long as eighteen hours. The crew also endured an entire month of night shooting. Blanchard's workweek averaged eighty hours in six days.

"I learn more about feature filmmaking all the time – how all the departments relate and how the physical process of making the film happens," he says. "On this production, if we shot a minute a day, that was pretty good."

Blanchard has also learned about the illusions so masterfully engineered by Hollywood filmmakers. In *Cliffhanger*, his feet doubled for Sylvester Stallone's. In various scenes of *Vertical Limit*, he doubled for Glenn, O'Donnell, Scorupco, Bill Paxton and Robin Tunney.

"It's fun seeing how enthusiastic the cast was about climbing," Blanchard says. "Probably the biggest enthusiasm came from Scott Glenn. If you have a couple of hours, just ask him what he thinks about ice climbing. He'll be coming to the Canadian Rockies next winter to go ice climbing."

No beginner in the world of climbing with the stars, during the filming of *The Edge*, Blanchard introduced Anthony Hopkins to the sport of rock climbing.

"He [Hopkins] is an astute man. He understood a lot of the appeal of climbing," Blanchard says. "He especially liked rappelling. He thought rappelling was the cat's ass. He liked the element of primal fear involved, of leaning back into thin air and trusting your partner and your gear. He recognized the feeling and knew he could perform it someplace."

Working on a big, $100 million production and carrying out his regular work as a mountain guide – where he is often working with only one or two clients – are two entirely different experiences, he adds.

"For sure, working on a movie is always a pretty interesting adventure," Blanchard says.

VICTIMS ARE ALIVE IN TEACHER'S LESSONS (2005)

> Ken **Wylie**

One sunny morning in February 2003, Ken Wylie was enjoying a day of backcountry ski touring in the Bonney Trees area of Rogers Pass in Glacier National Park, when he heard a helicopter. Pulling his radio from his pack, Wylie learned the helicopter was on its way to Connaught Creek, about five kilometres north, where some skiers had been buried in an avalanche. Without hesitation, he and his partner skied back to the trailhead and drove up the highway toward the site of the slide.

Wylie felt especially compelled to help in any way he could because, only ten days earlier, fellow skiers had rescued him when he was buried by an avalanche. Miraculously, after being trapped under a pile of heavy snow for about thirty-five minutes, Wylie survived. Of the thirteen people involved in the avalanche that swept down Tumbledown Mountain near Durrand Glacier, about fifty kilometres north of Revelstoke, BC, where Wylie had been working as an assistant ski guide, seven died, including world-renowned snowboarder Craig Kelly.

Wylie and fellow mountain guide Larry Dolecki soon arrived at the avalanche scene, where, despite the heroic efforts of other rescuers who had been first to respond, time simply ran out, and seven Calgary high-school students lost their lives.

"I was still numb from the first tragedy, working on adrenalin," Wylie says. "I couldn't believe this had happened. And I thought: I owe. I have to go. I felt a real need to assist the people caught in this accident."

Wylie, one of eight speakers sharing presentations with an audience of about 200 backcountry skiers, snowboarders, ice climbers and snowmobilers gathered at the Canadian Avalanche Centre's (CAC) 2005 "Outsmart the Dragon" avalanche workshop in Calgary, says living through those experiences affected him profoundly.

"When something like these events happens, it changes us," he says.

After each incident, Wylie says he asked himself what choices the skiers had made to arrive in those situations.

"Ski touring is really about moving from one place to another, and along the way we have things that happen to us," Wylie says. "Moving forward is an everyday process. It's the small things that happen that accumulate in the big events."

Everyone makes little mistakes in the mountains, Wylie says. The key, he continues, is to admit decision-making errors and to learn from them.

"How do we learn from the small events, not just the big ones?" Wylie asks. "We're not proud [of making mistakes], but we need to embrace it, let it become part of who we are. I came up with excuses why what happened on Durrand Glacier wasn't my fault. We want people to perceive us as competent, so we don't acknowledge responsibility. But if we sweep responsibility under the proverbial rug, we don't learn from what happened."

An internationally certified guide with the Association of Canadian Mountain Guides and a veteran educator who's instructed on Yamnuska Mountain Adventure's mountain skills semester course – an intensive three-month mountaineering program – Wylie is now a faculty member in the adventure guide program at Thompson Rivers University in Kamloops, BC. Soon after the two incidents, Wylie knew he would incorporate his experiences into his teaching.

"I was angry for about a month afterward," Wylie says. "Then I realized it could easily go somewhere ugly, so I knew I had to make it into something positive. It becomes part of you. You have to go forward with it."

The 2005 CAC workshops, one held in Vancouver and another in Calgary the following day, marked the first time Wylie had shared his experiences of the 2003 avalanches with the public.

In Calgary, he began his presentation by dedicating it to the fourteen skiers who died in the Durrand Glacier and Connaught Creek avalanches, showing all their names on the giant screen.

"They were just like us. They had a bowl of muesli for breakfast. They talked about how excited they were to go skiing as they put on their skins. They're our connection to the notion that this can happen to us," he says.

Drawing from the lessons he learned from his experiences, Wylie suggests all backcountry enthusiasts should approach each winter asking themselves, "What is the snowpack going to teach us this year?"

Responding to an audience member who asked if he trusted himself less after the avalanches, Wylie replied, "I think for a while, I did. But after thinking about it, and embracing it, now I trust myself more."

However, every time the snowpack settles, even on the flats and places where there is absolutely no danger of being caught in an avalanche, he admits, "It sends me right back."

When asked what he might have done differently at Tumbledown Mountain, Wylie pauses.

"Way too many things I can mention here," he replies. "I like to think they're alive, they're alive in the lessons I teach. And I'd like to stay there."

FROZEN MERINGUE AND TILTED MOGUL RUNS (2004)

> Denise **Martin**

Shortly after reaching the South Pole around noon Mountain Time, on December 28, 2004, Canadian polar guide Denise Martin used an Iridium phone to reach out and make some calls.

"We're just happy to get the skis off," Martin announced.

Martin and four clients reached the bottom of the earth after skiing across 600 nautical miles, or 1126 kilometres, of varied and frequently windy Antarctic terrain towing sixty-kilogram sleds. Martin said her team's time of fifty-three days was faster than most ski expeditions to the South Pole.

After setting out from the coast near Hercules Inlet in western Antarctica, the team resupplied twice, picking up food and cook-stove fuel at the halfway and three-quarter marks.

"It was freezing cold at the beginning," Martin says. "The temperature was −25 [°C] with forty-five-kilometre winds. In some places it was like skiing over a mogul run tilted sideways; in other places it was like skiing across frozen meringue."

Their pace slowed as they travelled farther south, and drier snow created a beach-like surface where their skis didn't have much ability to glide.

"The temperatures mostly ranged between −15 and −25, and when the wind wasn't out it was really quite pleasant," Martin says. "South Pole at Christmastime is the hot time."

North of their location, in the vicinity of 4897-metre Mount Vinson, Antarctica's highest point, Martin says temperatures can reach a balmy −5 during the austral summer. But, with the South Pole sitting at 2750 metres elevation, she adds, fifteen-kilometre winds often add a biting wind chill.

"Most of the time it was really windy and we were trying to work out that balance between staying warm and not sweating too much," she says.

Although the trip was a success, it wasn't entirely without mishaps. While undertaking a three-day training trip in Patriot Hills on

Antarctica's western coast, one of Martin's clients suffered frostbite and had to abandon her plans to participate in the adventure.

As well, during a storm the adventurers lost a camp, which forced them to share a single tent for three days.

"It blew away, quite literally, like a tumbleweed suddenly freed from a fence," Martin recalls.

On the same day, a guide with a second team of clients cut his hand so badly that he had to be evacuated. From that point on, Martin merged her clients with the other group and continued to the pole with four clients.

"It was more of a team expedition than a guided trip," Martin says. "Everyone was a strong skier with good navigational skills. All the members shared the responsibilities of navigating."

Not that Martin needed help navigating, as this was her second visit to the South Pole. But since she launched her first expedition from an inland starting point, the distance she travelled that time was considerably shorter. Starting her most recent South Pole journey from the edge of Antarctica's ice shelf made the trek – as judged by the small fraternity of true polar explorers – a legitimate South Pole ski.

As one of only a handful of women, and barely a dozen people overall, interested in leading such expeditions, Martin became the first Canadian woman to ski to the true North Pole in 1997, when she and American guide Matty McNair guided the first all women's team from Ward Hunt Island to the North Pole, which the team reached on Martin's thirty-first birthday.

A Saskatchewan native who discovered outdoor adventure through Katimavik, Martin started guiding Outward Bound trips at eighteen, eventually working her way up to running the winter program north of Thunder Bay and guiding dogsled and ski expeditions to destinations like Baffin Island. She has also guided in Norway, the European Alps, on South America's Mount Aconcagua and Denali in Alaska, and on camel trips in the Australian outback. While living in Yukon, she operated a guiding company with a partner, leading remote whitewater canoeing and dogsledding trips.

"I've always loved winter," admits Martin, whose Arctic experience began in 1990.

On this, her fourth Antarctic visit (she worked as a field guide and ski guide on previous trips), Martin says the biggest hazards included crevasses, storms carrying significant winds, cold injuries and monotony.

"The South Pole is really more of an endurance game, mentally and physically, than other trips I've been on," Martin says. "It's challenging keeping oneself happy, skiing into the wind and slogging it out. The scenery doesn't change much. For the most part, it's one big huge hard-packed lake. Wind, snow, ice in our faces."

As well, urging the body to work hard on a two-month diet of dehydrated food presents another challenge.

"It always becomes important to not overdo it, to have a good strategy," Martin says. "We had to be content every day with only going twelve to fifteen nautical miles."

When her clients – all experienced long-distance skiers who left jobs and mortgaged houses to come up with the $45,000 trip fee, and all of whom raised money for various charities – asked for training tips, she suggested they start eating ice cream and drinking beer to put on extra weight.

But that's only one bonus of polar ski expeditioning, she says.

"I really do love it. It just gets in your blood, being in the environment as raw as it is. It's such a beautiful place. And I love just getting there, getting into the plane and flying out onto the ice."

ANTARCTICA WEDGED IN ALBERTA MAN'S SOUL (2004)

> Alex **Taylor**

On Alex Taylor's first trip to Antarctica in 1992, he lived for months in a tent in the middle of a 200-kilometre-long, twenty-five-kilometre-wide glacier, while working as a polar guide for scientists conducting glacier studies with the British Antarctic Survey (BAS).

"We had a spectacular view of the Ellsworth Mountains, Antarctica's highest range," Taylor says. "Look in one direction and the horizon was dominated by huge peaks. Look in the other direction and it was flat and white – an endless polar prairie."

The scene would draw him back nine times, to a place where the landscape and low-latitude light combine to create a powerful and mystical site, which Taylor has attempted to capture on hundreds of rolls of film.

Unlike the North Pole region of the Arctic, which is comprised of frozen sea ice a few metres thick, Antarctica is a big continent covered in glacial ice. Because Antarctica's surface is constantly moving, the markers at the South Pole move five to ten metres annually and must be periodically relocated. Antarctica holds 90 per cent of the world's ice and 70 per cent of the world's fresh water, and it is home to several varieties of penguins, seals and birds that live around the edges of the continent, not very far inland. It is the only continent that belongs to no country and whose human inhabitants are limited to those pursuing scientific objectives. It is also the only place in the world you can see the Aurora Australis, or Southern Lights.

"With all its wildlife and snow and ice, it's pretty much unspoiled, and that makes it a really special place for me," Taylor says.

Ten trips have allowed Taylor to visit a large number of diverse places in an environment where the aesthetics and physics of a land dominated by snow and ice trigger a profound effect on the human experience.

On some trips Taylor worked with Fathom Expeditions, a Toronto-based adventure tourism operator. On others he worked with the US Antarctic Program. In 1999 and again in 2000 he worked in front of and behind the camera on the IMAX film *Shackleton's Antarctic Adventure*, filmed on location in the Weddell Sea and Antarctic Peninsula. During shooting, he and several others dressed in period costume to row lifeboats through the rough seas off Elephant Island.

"The waves were crashing on the rocks and we were rowing between small icebergs bobbing in the high sea swell amidst gusty winds and sleet," Taylor says. "For a fleeting moment we felt how it might have been for Shackleton and his men."

Taylor's love of the continent and its history led him to start his own company, Endurance Designs, which creates products that celebrate Frank Hurley's photographs from Shackleton's 1914 to 1916 expedition.

Taylor admits the first time he accepted a job in Antarctica he was curious whether the world's most remote continent would live up to its reputation as a land of spectacular beauty.

"The original reason was to visit a place that's otherwise difficult and expensive to visit," he says. "As with a lot of people, I got the bug and keep going back. It's such a special place; it's certainly lived up to its billings."

In October 2004 Taylor journeyed back to the bottom of the earth for his sixth stint working with the British Antarctic Survey. On that trip, he was stationed in West Antarctica for the first time since his earliest visit in 1992, also with the BAS. Working as a field technician, Taylor assisted scientists conducting a glaciology project on the Rutford ice stream, which runs parallel to the Ellsworth Mountains, in a region that is home to Antarctica's highest mountain, Vinson Massif, which soars to 4897 metres.

An ice stream, Taylor explained, is a river of ice that travels through slower moving continental ice. This particular ice stream is 200 kilometres long, thirty kilometres wide, about two kilometres deep, and moves about one kilometre a day until it reaches the coastal ice shelves, while the continental ice surrounding it moves only a few metres a year. As many as a dozen ice streams can feed into a single ice shelf – a mass of glacial ice that has flowed to the ocean from a landmass.

"An ice stream is basically a conduit of interior ice to the coast," Taylor explains. "You can walk faster than it flows. But in terms of glacial ice, that's very fast."

The scientists' main objective was to use a hot-water drill to penetrate the two kilometres of glacial ice to reach the bottom – sometimes consisting of bedrock and sometimes glacial till – then lower scientific instruments into the hole to gain a better idea of how ice streams flow.

The study aimed to decipher the relevance of ice streams to climate change. Scientists speculate that if ocean temperatures rise, the potential exists for ice shelves to disintegrate, causing ice stream flows to accelerate – and evidence is showing that they already are. If ice streams accelerate they could potentially dump massive amounts of ice into the ocean, causing sea levels around the world to rise, and ultimately causing flooding in low-lying countries such as Bangladesh and the Netherlands.

The $4 million project, funded largely by the British government, in partnership with scientific organizations, required five years of planning, and it took three of those years just to transport the necessary twenty tonnes of equipment to the remote inland sites where the project was carried out. The entire depot was buried by wind-driven snow when the team arrived, Taylor says, adding that part of his job was to dig it out.

"That's basically what I was, a professional hole-digger," Taylor jokes.

These studies represent the final pieces in the puzzle that will help determine how ice streams move, Taylor says, and marked the first time anyone had attempted to drill to the bottom of glacial ice in West Antarctica.

At its peak, the study included eight members from Britain and Iceland, an American scientist from NASA's Jet Propulsion Laboratory, and a robotics specialist, who piloted a specialized camera down to the bottom of the ice stream to examine the glacial layers and the bedding plane the stream slides on.

To reach the distant continent, Taylor flew from the Falkland Islands off Argentina to Rothera Base in northwestern Antarctica, where the plane landed on a runway from which lounging fur seals must be habitually shooed away. During the five-month expedition, Taylor spent three and a half months living in tents in the field with one or two others, far from the relative civilization of Rothera Base, which houses as many as 120.

"Rothera has all the comforts of home, with showers and great chefs and a cafeteria," Taylor says. "It even has a lounge and carpenters and plumbers. It becomes your home for a few weeks until you fly out to other places."

Taylor's home on the ice consisted of a double-walled, cone-shaped tent equipped with a makeshift eating/cooking bench that separates

two sleeping bags, and a vent to allow cooking inside while temperatures outside ranged from 5°C to –25°C. Other, more spacious tents
were furnished as living and working quarters for the eight-person
team, including laptops, radios and even a bread maker.

"As soon as the bread was ready, we'd have a break and some tea,"
Taylor says.

And for something completely different, throughout his Antarctic
stay Taylor maintained regular communication with some e-pals – the
Grade 6 students of teacher Sue Moleski's class at Banff Elementary
School, near Taylor's hometown of Canmore, Alberta.

Having Internet pen pals, Taylor says, turned out to be one of many
highlights of his Antarctic stay.

"I was surprised at how fun it was to correspond with the kids,"
Taylor says. "I didn't know what to expect. But then, in the isolation
and intensity of the camp, communicating with the kids was really
refreshing. Their intelligent questions really got me engaged in writing
back and communicating the experience I was having, and realizing
they were enjoying my letters and photographs added to the energy of
the correspondence. For me, experiencing their youthful enthusiasm
let me look at my experiences through their eyes, and that added a
whole new dimension to my being there."

The students wrote to Taylor in about fourteen separate e-mail
messages, setting up a list of volunteers who would send him a message
about once a week, to which he would reply about every second or third
week. They created a large poster from a collection of Taylor's printed
e-mail letters and their favourites pictures. After reading his messages,
they highlighted words they didn't know, or others they liked, and
compiled a vocabulary poster. They replied to his messages, asking what
certain words meant and what particular animals in photographs were
called. Sometimes they compared the weather, providing a great source
of amusement for the scientists when it was warmer in Antarctica than
in the Canadian Rockies. The class also shared Taylor's adventures
with the entire school during a general assembly, where very near the
top of the students' questions and concerns was how long had it been
since Taylor's last bath and exactly how stinky had he become.

And they also asked about the drill.

The scientists drilled for three days around the clock, because if they stopped, the drill would freeze up. During that time, team members slept in shifts for two to four hours, while the head driller didn't sleep at all.

"When things started to go wrong, fatigue became a factor and more could go wrong," Taylor says.

As they drilled the first hole, a storm moved in with winds up to sixty kilometres per hour, causing the scientific instruments to record "weird readings." It took the team about six hours to pull everything up out of the hole.

Then as they drilled the second hole, a hose broke apart at a coupling end.

"It spiralled down the hole; we couldn't recover it," Taylor says. "That hose will be locked in the ice for probably 800 years before it gets to the ocean."

The mishap marked the end of the project that had taken several years and a lot of money to prepare, Taylor says.

"We were pretty disappointed at the time," Taylor says. "Then we had a party."

After that, the team turned their attention to using available resources to drill shallow ice cores to carry on further research.

Then suddenly, after ninety-six days, it was over, Taylor says, and the team flew back to Rothera Base.

"It's a huge relief to get back to the base," he says. "You're exhausted, and you know you're going back to things like showers and friends and wildlife."

Back home in Canmore, Taylor, a long-time resident of the Alberta Rockies, who works as a prescribed-burn technician with the Parks Canada Lake Louise/Yoho/Kootenay field unit's fire management program during the summer, said he was already dreaming about returning.

"I am always scheming and dreaming of ways to get back south to Antarctica," he says.

"The Antarctic is a place that gets into your soul. If you get to go once, you become addicted, and you always want to go back to feed that addiction."

EASY TO FORGET EVEREST IS DANGEROUS (2007)

> Ola **Dunin-Bell**

On her first night at the Everest base camp medical clinic, where she had volunteered to treat patients for the 2007 two-month spring climbing season, Ontario physician Dr. Ola Dunin-Bell discovered her tent sat next to a major yak route.

She quickly realized how very challenging life at the clinic – consisting of a small two-person tent as her private sleeping quarters, a large tube-shaped tent housing the clinic, and a kitchen/ dining building with stacked rock walls and a blue tarp roof – would be. Over the next few weeks, Dr. Dunin-Bell and her colleague, Dr. Suzanne Boyle, an anaesthesiologist from Edinburgh, Scotland, moved their sleeping tents four times, while the kitchen walls repeatedly collapsed.

"We were right on the glacier, the mixed ice and rock flowing stream of the Khumbu Icefall," Dr. Dunin-Bell says. "At night, we heard avalanches or rockfall every hour. I learned to sleep through it. The ground underneath really crackles and pops, everything is constantly shifting and expanding. In the daytime, if I heard the start of an avalanche, I stopped sticking my head out to look."

The latrine consisted of blue barrels lined with plastic bags for solid waste only, since the charge for barrel removal is based on weight. Asthmatic, Dr. Dunin-Bell returned to Oakville with bronchitis and pneumonia.

"We were constantly dealing with weather and discomfort," she says. "The month of April was, in a word, cold. We lived in down jackets practically the whole time. It was so much physically tougher than I would have thought."

She is no newcomer to challenges. In 2003, after two decades as a general surgeon at Mississauga's Credit Valley Hospital, she left to teach at McMaster University and to work with Canadian Global Air Ambulance, flying international air evacuations of critically ill patients.

A Wilderness Medicine Society member, she was aware of the clinics operated by the non-profit Himalayan Rescue Association

(HRA) in Pheriche, which opened in 1973, and in Manang, which was launched in 1981. One day's walk south of Everest Base Camp, Pheriche is the last substantial village before heading up the eleven-kilometre long Khumbu Valley.

Situated west of Everest in the Annapurna–Dhaulagiri region of Nepal, the village of Manang sits on the northern edge of the popular 300-kilometre Annapurna Circuit trek, which circles a collection of mountains anchored by Annapurna I, which is usually climbed from the south, but which, unlike Everest, offers no straightforward route to its 8091-metre summit.

The HRA opened its Everest clinic in 2003, on the fiftieth anniversary of the mountain's first ascent, to serve trekkers, climbers and locals, with proceeds from treating Westerners financing care for Nepali and Sherpa patients.

In 2004 Dr. Dunin-Bell volunteered at the Manang clinic for over three months, living at 3500 metres and treating trekkers for HACE (high altitude cerebral edema), HAPE (high altitude pulmonary edema), acute mountain sickness and numerous blisters and foot problems.

Only two days after arriving in Kathmandu, Dr. Dunin-Bell, the first Canadian to work at the Everest clinic, began the trek to Everest.

The journey took eleven days, one more than usual, because the British Caudwell Everest Xtreme research team had hired every yak in Pheriche to ferry their mountain of equipment to base camp, which forced the clinic staff to wait to have their own gear transported up the valley.

With plans to study over 200 climbers and trekkers for physical reactions to altitude, the Everest Xtreme project ultimately aimed to conduct blood oxygen measurements on climbers at Everest's 8848-metre summit.

With about 250 climbing permits issued for Everest's south side for the spring season (plus more on the north), base camp swelled to 1,000 people, including Sherpas, cooks, support staff, climbers and trekkers. Over the following six weeks, the clinic treated over 200 Nepali and Western patients.

"Some days it was nothing more than Khumbu cough – a dry, hacking, irritating cough people get from the very cold, dry air – and sore throats," Dr. Dunin-Bell says. "But others would be snow blindness, HAPE, abdominal pain, retinal hemorrhage, just about anything. I never saw so much frostbite as I did at Everest."

Equipment was basic – stethoscopes (she brought her own), a BP cuff, thermometers (unreliable in the cold and altitude), ophthalmoscope, oxygen saturation monitor, dipsticks for urine testing. Neither the ProPac, for looking at cardiograms, nor the oxygen concentrator worked, so they relied on bottled oxygen. There was no facility for blood work or x-rays. Needles and IV bags were donated, "some good, some dreadful." The clinic's two beds were lawn chairs with foam mattresses. They built a desk of rocks.

Their camp also accommodated a Sherpa translator/helper, cooks, five climbers, a psychology research student, visiting trekkers and four BBC film crew members, who generously shared their computer after Dr. Dunin-Bell's crashed.

While the large commercial expeditions often get a bad rap, she says, they were very well organized and managed their waste well.

"There's a lot of negative things said about the big commercial teams, but one thing they have is a plan," Dr. Dunin-Bell says. "They have a backup plan, and a backup plan for their backup plan. They know what they're doing."

Some (not all) smaller, poorly organized teams were another story.

One team from Nepal's lowlands trekked to base camp in five dangerously speedy days, since their pace allowed them insufficient time to acclimatize. Determined to make a political statement, the poorly prepared group included a woman, Usha Bista, who would made international headlines after Western climbers saved her life.

The day before she started climbing, Dr. Boyle treated her for dehydration, nausea and diarrhea. "She was too sick to climb," Dr. Dunin-Bell says. "But she did not return for her follow-up."

A BBC member reported seeing her vomit as she left camp.

While descending from her own successful summit, Canadian Meagan McGrath discovered Bista alone at 8300 metres. Bista's oxygen had run out, so McGrath shared hers. Veteran American Everest guide Dave Hahn, also descending from the summit, executed an eleven-hour rescue with two fellow guides. An hour after he injected Bista with dexamethasone, her alertness improved. The rescuers packaged Bista in a sleeping bag strapped to a sled and lowered her down steep, difficult terrain until they reached Camp III at 7200 metres, where one of the Everest Xtreme doctors was able to provide advanced care, including an IV.

The following day, with help from half a dozen Westerners, Bista made her way down the mountain from Camp III to Camp II, where she remained for two nights under the care of another Everest Xtreme physician. Still unable to get down by herself, and with help from her own teammates not forthcoming, several climbers from a British Army team and a Western guide helped her down to base camp, as she was unable to unclip from the fixed ropes due to her frostbitten hands.

"I have nothing but admiration for Dave Hahn," Dr. Dunin-Bell says. "Somebody like [Bista] puts everybody else on the mountain at risk. I really did not expect people to be so laissez faire and casual that they expected others to pick up after them. I think with so many tents, so many Westerners, it's easy to forget the fact Everest is extremely dangerous. They think they can just snap their fingers and get rescued."

At base camp, the doctors dressed Bista's frostbite, administered appropriate medications and released her with instructions that included remaining on oxygen overnight and keeping her feet elevated. Everest Xtreme had arranged for a helicopter to evacuate one of their doctors the next morning and offered to transport Bista as well.

"I went to meet them at the helipad and she was still alert, awake and stable, but she had been picking at the dressings on her hands and they had partly come off," Dr. Dunin-Bell says. "She had nothing warm, just the dressings on her hands and feet; she did not have oxygen on and generally was not following any of the instructions she had been given. It was pretty frustrating."

As well, Dr. Dunin-Bell adds, evacuating anyone from Everest's base camp is a very tricky business.

"You need a clear, cold morning to get enough lift," she says. "The helicopter drops down the valley before it can gain enough lift to properly fly. That can't be taken casually. When you hit 5400 metres, the air is so much thinner it changes everything."

A recreational climber with experience in the Canadian Rockies and BC's Coast Mountains, Dr. Dunin-Bell says the array of people aiming to climb Everest amazed her, including some who had never worn crampons and couldn't tie a basic figure-eight knot.

"There's such a variety of reasons people had to climb the mountain," she says. "One woman said she needed it to pump up her résumé as a motivational speaker. Another had dreamed of it since he was a teenager. He was willing to do whatever it took."

That climber reached the summit in the dark at 3 a.m.

"But for him it was wonderful," Dr. Dunin-Bell says. "It seemed those who had climbed before had respect for the mountain itself. Those who were just checking off a tick list had not as much soul in their reason for doing it."

Capitalizing on a nine-day window of virtually windless weather, 514 climbers had summitted Everest by May 28 during the spring 2007 climbing season.

Dr. Dunin-Bell, however, is not interested in the climb.

"I have no desire to ever summit Everest, particularly after seeing the masses of people going up," she says. "But I met the challenge of living there for two months, and the boredom that can ensue if you are not climbing. I learned about physical and physiological responses at that altitude and enjoyed making a difference in the health of the climbers. I met some amazing people. And I think I have a better perspective on commercial climbing – Everest really is the ultimate. But from what I've seen, it takes three things to climb Everest: a body that is tolerant of altitude, sufficient motivation to put up with discomfort and trudging, and luck."

THE BIGGEST SKI (2006)

> Wally **Berg**, Kit **DesLauriers** and Maegan **Carney**

In his nine trips to Mount Everest – including the four times he's stood on its 8848-metre summit – Wally Berg admits his 2006 expedition was among his most gratifying.

And he never climbed above Camp II – 6300 metres.

Instead, on his fourth trip as expedition leader, Berg assumed a role he'd long wished for: coordinating his team from base camp (5360 metres), helping fourteen members to make the summit, and also helping three of them to ski down, including Kit DesLauriers, who claimed the title of the first woman to ski from the summit of Everest.

"I finally got to be the real expedition leader, rather than the leader slash climber slash guide," says Berg, fifty-one, chief guide and founder of Canmore, Alberta-based Berg Adventures International.

"I had no intentions of being on the summit. My role was important, for sure, but my intention was not to have anyone feel I needed to be high on the mountain. It was especially gratifying."

Berg's "hand-picked" team arrived at the mountain in late August, including DesLauriers, women's world free-skiing champion, her husband, Rob, and respected climbing photographer Jimmy Chin, all from Jackson Hole, Wyoming, and all of whom would ski from the summit.

Throughout the expedition, Berg's wife, Leila Silveira, who helps run Berg Adventures, led trekking groups up to base camp.

When Berg first met Silveira, she was a Canadian citizen living in Toronto who was born in Rio de Janeiro and had worked with the Brazilian Foreign Service. Berg was a mountain guide with two decades' experience leading international climbing expeditions, who worked winters as a pro ski patroller at Colorado's Copper Mountain.

After marrying, the couple moved to Canmore in 2001, choosing to be in Canada, and choosing to live in a small mountain town with easy access to an international airport (Calgary's is less than ninety minutes away).

Since then, Berg has parlayed his skills into a business that organizes expeditions to several Himalayan peaks, including 6857-metre Ama Dablam, as well as other climbing adventures in places such as Greenland, Bhutan and at Africa's highest peak, Kilimanjaro (with a safari option).

With three office employees, including Silveira, and several guides working on a contract basis, it's a business that keeps him on the move. Less than two weeks after returning to Canmore from Nepal,

Berg left home again to lead two clients up Antarctica's highest peak, 4897-metre Vinson Massif.

Under Berg's guidance, the 2006 Everest expedition not only made DesLauriers the first woman to ski from the summit of Everest – it made her the first person to ski from the highest summit of each continent, including Australia's 2228-metre Kosciuszko. While some mountaineers recognize Indonesia's 4884-metre Carstensz Pyramid as the highest point on the Australasian continent, Berg pointed out the distinction is irrelevant for skiers since Carstensz has no glacier or skiable snow slopes.

Adding to the accomplishment, their expedition marked the first time since 2002 that any climbers had summitted Everest in the post-monsoon autumn season, and the first time since 2000 that anyone had summitted in autumn via the standard South Col Route.

"This one left everyone with a good feeling," Berg says. "It was the biggest success on the south side of the mountain in the post-monsoon season that had been seen in some years."

While in springtime, he explained, Everest's base camp is populated by twenty or thirty teams of hopeful summitters, the mountain is a very different place in the fall.

"You hear lots of complaining about big lineups on summit days in May, and there's lots of discussion about questionable safety issues, but at the same time, many people are drawn to that, knowing if they get into a lineup of 120 people, thirty or forty will summit. There's a sense of security," Berg says.

Between 1986 and 1997, teams attempted the mountain's south side every fall, some years with nearly as many summits in fall as in spring.

But as he had encountered three years earlier, in 2006 Berg's team was alone on the mountain's Nepal side.

As the only team on the route, that meant members had to be experienced and capable of fixing all their own ropes, as they could not rely on any other teams for help.

"You don't have the luxury when you're the only team on the mountain," Berg says. "The successes are yours, but then so are the failures. This year, the mountain gods smiled on us favourably. The mountain defines what it will be every year."

Arriving earlier, highly skilled Sherpas began establishing the route, bridging gaping crevasses with aluminum ladders and fixing climbing ropes. The nine Sherpas who summitted included Danuru, a veteran of the 1982 Canadian expedition and Pemba Dorjee, Berg's friend since his first Everest trip in 1989, when he participated in a US medical research expedition.

On Everest, Berg maintained radio communication with thirty people, gathering weather, snow and avalanche reports from higher on the mountain and keeping in touch with trekking clients down the Khumbu Valley.

Long before arriving on the mountain, staff in Canmore and Nepal arranged climbing permits, liability insurance and equipment preparation, including oxygen systems – which Berg insists on, especially for Sherpas, some of whom perform well at altitude, while others don't.

"I want them to use a lot of oxygen; it's good for them," Berg says. "I've known many of them for many years, and their families. I want them to go home."

When assembling the expedition, Berg says he carefully weighed the personalities of potential participants.

"I wanted mellow people," Berg says. "That's hard on an Everest climb. But I wanted people who were experienced enough to know the mountain gets climbed one day at a time. Also, I have so much love and respect for the Sherpa people and their culture on the Khumbu side of the mountain, I wanted to have people on the climb who shared those values."

And, very often, his clients share similar perspectives.

"It means a lot to me to surround myself with people who believe in each other's potential," says Kit DesLauriers. "With such a lofty goal, it's not uncommon to come across people who see more possibilities of failure rather than focus on the probability of success. Wally has that positive outlook that is important to me."

Attitude, Berg agrees, makes a big difference when approaching a goal as monumental as climbing Everest.

"I never cease to be humbled by the big mountains," he says. "I believe if every foreign team came into Nepal as a group of people who already knew one another, and who agreed upon a common leadership model, there would be much less of a mess on Everest – less death, less disappointment, less theft, less confusion and, most importantly, more respect for the mountain."

After weeks of inching upward, the summit team left their South Col tents at 1:45 a.m. on the big day and were standing on the summit by 11 a.m. Starting from the top, the skiers made cautious turns until they came to the Hillary Step, which, bare of snow, was unskiable. A combination of dwindling oxygen, decreasing daylight and avalanche hazard prompted them to switch to crampons to reach their 7900-metre camp, where they decided to spend the night.

"It wasn't a difficulty of skiing decision," Berg explains. "It was a safety decision."

By 9 a.m. the next day, they started skiing the Lhotse Face – 1500 vertical metres of forty- to fifty-degree glaring blue ice.

"I think the really remarkable thing they did, after a miserable freezing night in frosty tents, was get up in the morning and ski the Lhotse Face," Berg says.

All were accustomed to skiing slopes where falling was unthinkable, but neither the ski poles they held in one hand nor the ice axes in the other could pierce the marble-hard surface. Consummate adventure photographer Chin declared he couldn't take photos.

"I think that's a remarkable statement of how difficult it was," Berg says. "It was the biggest ski any of them had ever done."

After two taxing hours, they safely reached the bergschrund (the highest crevasse on a glacier, where gravity has pulled the glacial ice away from the permanent mass of the mountain) and the end of the ski run of their lives. The trio, says Berg, was "whooping for joy."

While on Everest, DesLauriers says she was grateful for the encouragement of Canmore resident Maegan Carney, who in 2003 joined a Berg Adventures International expedition to Everest with her own hopes of becoming the first woman to ski the mountain.

A two-time world extreme skiing champion, Carney had made previous Himalayan ski descents, including 6440-metre Cholatse and

BARRY BLANCHARD CONSIDERS
HIS NEXT MOVE AT NUPTSE
NEPALI HIMALAYAS

DENISE MARTIN IS ALL SMILES AT THE SOUTH POLE, ANTARCTICA

KEN WYLIE IN HIS FAVOURITE CLASSROOM

**ALEX TAYLOR
LOVING THE COLD AND
THE SCENE IN ANTARCTICA**

OLA DUNIN-BELL TAKES A BREAK FROM
CLINIC DUTIES, MOUNT EVEREST IN THE
BACKGROUND, NEPALI HIMALAYAS.

WALLY BERG HIKING TO WORK IN THE NEPALI HIMALAYAS.

Ama Dablam. She was ready for Everest and reached Camp III twice (7200 metres) before high winds stopped her.

"The winds were so intense, I watched all my snow get blown away," Carney recalls. "It was heartbreaking for me. I hadn't even entertained the thought of not even being able to try."

Carney learned about DesLauriers through Berg, and following DesLauriers's progress via the Internet, Carney sent a message to base camp, which Berg relayed by radio.

"I knew they'd be headed to the summit, and I wanted to wish her good luck," Carney says. "I wanted her to have a chance at it, to get to the top and have a good shot. I wished her luck and calm winds."

High on Everest, DesLauriers was moved.

"I was touched," DesLauriers says. "Maegan's message was pure in her support for me and for our team. I was honoured, and also fired up to help carry her torch."

At first, Carney admits, news of their accomplishment was bittersweet.

"A part of me was just heartbroken," she says. "I thought, 'It's done.' But after going through the feelings of sadness, I came to this place of being so proud of her. I was able to feel the whole inspiration of what she'd done."

Although Carney notes DesLauriers didn't end up skiing the entire mountain, she acknowledges the skiers' wise decisions.

"Those were really good judgment calls," Carney says. "I think it's so easy for people to dismiss how incredibly deadly Everest is. It's a big scary mountain. Just because it's not significantly technical doesn't mean qualified people can't die on it."

Berg agrees, saying that although conditions forced them to abandon their plan of a "complete" ski descent, their accomplishment was not diminished.

"They came down safely. That's why it was successful – a good mountaineering accomplishment."

STORYTELLERS

The following stories are of people who pursue their adventures with the primary aim of capturing and recording a story for an audience, usually on film or in a book. Their chosen subjects – other people, themselves, pursuits or places – demand that in the act of recording the story, they must become participants in the adventure.

A VERTICAL GAME OF CHESS (2001)

❯ Richard **Else**, Dominique **Perret**, Steve **Robinson**,
Rob **Bruce and** Derek **Westerlund**

The rock face is wet; the rough surface glistens as a streak of sun-light touches the granite like a wand. A human hand thrusts into a cleft in the rock, skin scraping on stone. The climber's breath billows like smoke on the screen and people in the audience feel as though they are watching a magician's show, where sleight of hand and invisible wires have brought them within inches of the climber's elusive world.

For veteran mountain filmmaker Richard Else, director of UK-based Triple Echo Productions, capturing a climber on a new route presents ethical and technical, as well as physical, challenges.

"We don't want to affect the climb; I don't want to be in their line," Else explains. "I want the climbers to be able to carry on unhindered. I want the climbers to be able to experience the climb in the best and most natural way possible."

Depending on the location, his cameramen use a combination of techniques: rigging ropes on parallel lines, positioning them-selves on portaledges (small tents that are suspended from verti-cal walls by climbing anchors placed in the rock), or sometimes walking up the back of a cliff and rappelling down the face that's being climbed.

"It's like choreographing a ballet, like a vertical game of chess," Else says.

With his average shoot lasting seven or eight days, whatever the weather, Else says time is always of the essence.

"It brings tension to the filmmaking; some of that energy comes from having to get on with it," he says. "We've almost got an alpine style of filming."

Filmmaker Steve Robinson, producer of multi-sport documentaries for Britain's BBC, says his films are usually born of a dream his subject has cherished for years.

"We then try and make that come true," he says.

Weather, however, Robinson adds, pretty much dictates the execution of any project.

"Some projects you can virtually script like a drama and you know what will go where before you start," he explains. "The last BASE project we filmed (BASE jumping means parachuting from a fixed object such as a Building, Antenna, Span or Earth (e.g., a cliff) – hence the acronym), we were lucky enough to have a helicopter and five days of great weather and were able to film fifteen jumps to cut together into one sequence. But then you also have to be prepared to rip up your script and adapt to changing storylines beyond your control – usually weather."

On location, the adventure filmmaker's task is to capture the seed of a dream while the cameraman is in pursuit with the net, anticipating the flight of the butterfly. Very often, those cameramen have to fly alongside their subjects.

To capture the shot he wants, Swiss skier Dominique Perret, both star and producer of more than a dozen high-adrenalin ski films, selects a slope in collaboration with his cameramen, who also must be able to physically get to where the shot is.

"People want to dream," Perret says. "These guys can be on fifty-degree mountains, no problem. These guys are professionals; they're good mountaineers, great skiers and great cameramen."

California cameraman Rob Bruce is one of those professionals. Bar none, his most important ingredient is lighting, and once that's right, the more the subject skis where he wants to, the better the footage. Bruce just has to keep up.

"I think you will find that the top mountain cameramen are or were accomplished skiers or mountaineers," Bruce says. "It makes sense. The more you can move in the mountains, the more options you have for shots. The funny thing is that I almost always ski the same slopes as Dominique, but I have to leave the good snow for him. So there I am with this huge pack on a steep slope hating life in the sun-baked death crust or whatever. It can get pretty funny and/or scary."

More often than not, when it comes to equipment, the choice comes down to what fits the budget, Robinson says. Digital Betacam provides good quality and the equipment is easy to use. Different cameras are used for slow motion when filming sky diving, BASE jumping and surfing.

"We also use a lot of mini-DV for taping onto helmets, surfboards, paragliders, yacht masts and the like," Robinson adds. "Because they are comparatively cheap it doesn't matter if they get wrecked. They are light, small, easy to waterproof and so on. We get through quite a lot in a series."

Canadian Derek Westerlund, producer of envelope-pushing mountain bike films such as *New World Disorder*, uses old Second World War GSAP cameras, which were originally mounted on airplane wings to monitor the attack patterns of enemy aircraft.

"They break a lot on their own because they're old but we've actually never wrecked one," Westerlund says.

The cameras are bolted onto a lightweight bike helmet and counterweighted by their own batteries. The entire rig weighs about 7.5 kilograms.

"Capturing the speed of mountain biking has always been really hard," Westerlund admits. "Now we're using more Hollywood techniques with Steadicams, helicopters and cable cams."

No matter the equipment, however, a cameraman's experience counts for a lot.

"They know what the riders will do at a certain point on the trail, they know when the riders are going to move or change position," Westerlund says.

For Bruce, getting close to the action can only be done with a hand-held camera.

"When something is going by you at fifty miles per hour, just feet away, you'll have the most control hand-held," Bruce explains. "For Dominique's movies I use an Arriflex SR2. It is one of the most user-friendly cameras for sixteen millimetre."

But above the equipment, Bruce insists adventure filmmaking demands teamwork and mutual respect.

"I think it's irresponsible of many 'extreme sport' cameramen to ask athletes to take such risks over and over again, yet deliver subpar images," he says. "If an athlete is making that kind of effort for me I will do everything I can to match their efforts on film and on the job."

While terrain and activities dictate different filming techniques, all the filmmakers agree that safety is the priority.

"We carry out a rigorous risk assessment before deciding to do the project, which will look at how to film as safely as possible and also how to get people out quickly if something goes wrong," Robinson says. "Safety forms the biggest and hassle-iest part of my job."

For Westerlund, maintaining safety while shooting footage that aims to illustrate the progression of the sport presents an added challenge.

"We're always trying to up the ante but keep in mind the safety factor, while yet still taking the sport to a new level," Westerlund admits. "That always provides for a lot of challenge."

And despite taking every precaution possible, safety can never be absolutely guaranteed.

"There's always a possibility of an accident," Else adds. "You don't want to encourage any Kodachrome courage. I feel safety is more important than anything; often it dominates it."

Perret's team is small – with himself as skier, one cameraman, one still photographer and a professional mountain guide who oversees all safety aspects, including logistics, avalanches and helicopters, so the cameramen can concentrate on capturing the dream.

"They really get any shot the best way you can," Perret says. "And they get it every time."

I wrote this piece for the Banff Mountain Film Festival Magazine in 2001. While the techniques described haven't changed much in the years between, it's astounding how much technology has evolved over such a short period of time.

CAUGHT UP IN CLIMBING UNIVERSITY WALL (2006)

> Ivan **Hughes** and Tim **Auger**

To celebrate the fortieth anniversary of the first ascent of the University Wall Route on the Stawamus Chief Mountain, the massive 700-metre granite cliff that broods over Squamish, BC, Ivan Hughes shared a slide show with a hometown audience.

Not only did the crowd love the show, but a friend soon suggested to Hughes, a filmmaker who runs Fringe Filmworks with his wife and creative partner, producer Angela Heck, that the show might make a great film.

And after his initial doubts dissolved, Hughes began to imagine that it just might.

"It was never really intended to be a film," Hughes shrugs. "The show was thrown together really quickly."

The result, however, *University Wall*, is a delightful eleven-minute romp back to the mid-1960s when four University of British Columbia students spent months inching their way up University Wall, a 300-metre-long continuous crack system that extends up the towering rock face.

For Hughes, the project began at the turn of the millennium as he was recording interviews and collecting still photos and footage for another film project, the award-winning *In the Shadow of the Chief*, which celebrated the landmark 1961 first ascent of the Chief by Jim Baldwin and Ed Cooper. Among the climbers he interviewed was Tim Auger, a retired park warden who spent over twenty years at the helm of Banff National Park's public safety and mountain rescue service. In addition to succeeding on the University Wall first ascent, with ropemates Glenn Woodsworth, Dan Tate and Hamish Mutch, in 1964 Auger and Mutch also accomplished the second ascent of the Grand Wall Route, also on the Squamish Chief – all the more impressive since they were both still teenagers.

Starting on their University Wall project at the end of the 1965 summer, the four returned to the cliff the following spring, where for the better part of two months they toiled with pitons, slings, ropes and carabiners, methodically and determinedly working their way up beyond their previous high points and returning to the ground each night, until they finally reached the summit.

Since all of them devoted considerable time and energy to their project while they were supposed to be studying, they gave the wall an appropriate name, Auger says.

"It needed a name and we were all students," Auger explains. "We were all sneaking out there from school. We really got caught up in the climb."

And throughout that time, when they weren't inching their way up the granite wall above Squamish, those same four climbers were shinnying and scampering their way up the walls of the UBC campus buildings.

Incorporating black and white still photos of the climbers perched in spectacularly exposed positions on the sweeping granite cliff, and historical eight-millimetre film footage of them clambering up the brick and mortar walls of their school campus (none of which Hughes ended up using for *In the Shadow of the Chief*), *University Wall* captures a spirit of youthful expression, passion and innocent rebellion.

With a subtly psychedelic original soundtrack composed by a friend of Hughes's, the film focuses not on the mechanics of the historical climb but highlights the mood of an era.

"There's more of just trying to catch the flavour of the day," Hughes says. "They were just kids, trying to have fun."

For Auger, who continues to climb at a respectable level more than four decades later, climbing University Wall was a watershed experience.

"It was a big deal," Auger says. "I was just a teenager, and we were trying to bite into something that felt significantly over our heads. It was a total jazz that we could pull it off."

Regarding the climb, Auger, who acts as narrator in the film, admits, "I remember having nightmares. I had worked myself into a real lather. It was the scariest thing I've ever done in my life to this day."

Meanwhile, he admits the inspiration for their on-campus climbing came from a little book titled *Night Climbers of Cambridge*, which detailed the similar exploits of students at the staid British institution two or three decades earlier.

While the Cambridge climbers were vigorously prohibited from pursuing their recreational pastime on campus grounds, Auger says he and his UBC classmates carried on with theirs, as they accomplished first ascents of the library and chemistry buildings.

"We definitely didn't want to get caught," Auger says. "It wasn't as serious for us at it was for the climbers at Cambridge, but still, the campus cops wouldn't have understood anything like that. They'd probably take you to the office sort of thing."

The lofty tradition of buildering, Hughes remarks, continues at the UBC campus to this day.

TRAGEDY INFLUENCES FILMMAKER'S DIRECTION (2006)

> Dave **Mossop**

Through the winters of 1996 to 1998, I wrote a twice-monthly column about snowboarding for the Banff Crag & Canyon *weekly newspaper, which I called The Blind Side. At the time, snowboarding was still a young and often misunderstood sport. My columns spoke of the lifestyle priorities of young snowboarders and of the passion that drove the sport. Eight winters after I wrote the column below (and after my snow focus had evolved to backcountry ski touring), while attending an information evening at The Banff Centre organized by the Canadian Avalanche Centre, I met a young man who was working to produce an avalanche education DVD. I decided to interview him to learn more about his project, and in the process learned more than I had anticipated. That article follows this one.*

As Calgary high-school students in 1996, Dave Mossop and his buddies loved to duck under the Lake Louise ski hill boundary ropes to score some fresh powder lines on untracked backcountry slopes, such as Burnt Trees and Pipestone Bowl. They didn't wear avalanche

THE BLIND SIDE: SAFETY ON LOADED SLOPES, DECEMBER 1997

For the three winters that I've been writing this column, it has crossed my mind more than once that I might write about unprepared young boarders being buried by an avalanche. I sometimes feared it might be someone I knew and cared about. As it happens, I didn't know the four young people from Calgary who died in an avalanche just outside the Fortress Mountain ski area boundary on November 29, 1997. But that makes no difference to the parents, brothers, sisters, friends and classmates who did know and love them.

The most disappointing thing about the accident that claimed their lives is how preventable it was. Every newspaper article was full of comments about how smart the four of them were – how they all were great students and friends who loved the mountains; how they were full of enthusiasm for life and adventure and powder. Yet they ventured onto a snowy mountain slope without taking one single precaution to ensure their own safety. They carried no avalanche transceivers, no shovels, no probes; they travelled in close succession, ensuring they would all be trapped together in case of an avalanche. This also precluded any possibility of one rescuing another.

For the past two or three winters all the major snowboarding magazines have gone out of their way to inform their young and adventurous readers about lifesaving precautions necessary for those riding in avalanche-prone terrain. Many snowboard videos, too, make a point of informing their audiences that playing in the backcountry is a risky game that requires a whole lot of respect, learning and safeguards for those who want to be around to play again another day.

The facts are simple. It doesn't take a lot of snow to produce an avalanche capable of burying and suffocating a person or fatally breaking a body apart. Nobody should be fooled by our meagre snowfall so far this season – the danger still exists. Wind can transport snow into just the kind of gully that looks like it will give you the best turns of your life. Those turns could just as easily be your last.

The backcountry is every slope that is not regularly maintained by ski hill avalanche forecasters, whether you are five minutes or five hours from the area boundary. Just because you rode a particular slope last season, last week or even yesterday, doesn't guarantee it will be safe to ride today.

Any snowboarder or skier who values his/her own life and the lives of the buddies he/she rides with should be taking the responsibility to become informed through avalanche awareness courses such as those offered by the Alpine Club of Canada, through books such as Tony Daffern's *Avalanche Safety for Skiers and Climbers* and the practice of never travelling in the backcountry without safety gear and the knowledge of how to use it.

I like to believe that we are all here to learn in this life, from our own experiences and those of others. Those four youths from Calgary had their learning cut short, but their experience can be a gift to others willing to accept it. For anyone planning to scoop some freshies in the backcountry, remember that patience is a virtue, and tomorrow is another day (you hope). Take a minute to think about your family and friends and your powder partners, and do your homework before you dive in.

transceivers, didn't carry shovels or probes, didn't check on the current avalanche conditions and had no idea they were risking their lives every time they set out.

"We learned we could go duck the rope and ski Pipestone and walk out," Mossop says. "Nobody had a clue. We were pretty oblivious to the danger. We were fools, ambitious to explore. It was pretty sketchy in retrospect."

That carefree attitude was forever changed, however, when on November 29, 1997, Mossop and his riding buddies lost four of their closest friends in an avalanche at Fortress Mountain. They had gone in search of early season freshies at the not yet open ski hill. The bodies of the seventeen-year-olds – three boys and one girl – were found close together, buried under a metre of snow.

"The news came as an unbelievable shock," Mossop says. "It was absolutely life altering. And the amazing thing is how, from that, we formed this amazing bond of friendship that's been unbroken since. All these close friends from high school share this massive bond. We've all become part of this great labyrinth of friends."

Over time, their passion for the backcountry grew, with most following their interests deeper into the mountains and with many now working as professional ski patrollers and for backcountry lodge operators, including Banff-based Canadian Mountain Holidays helicopter skiing.

"In the end it turned out being a really positive experience," Mossop says. "We learned way more about our mountain surroundings and avalanches. It turned us into really keen backcountry skiers and into much more educated backcountry enthusiasts."

When Mossop, twenty-five, isn't backcountry skiing through the winter months, he pursues his passion for traditional big-wall rock climbing. A tree planter for the past seven summers, after graduating with honours from high school, Mossop studied film and anthropology at the University of Victoria. He graduated with distinction in 2004.

Now an award-winning filmmaker and published photographer in major North American ski magazines, including *Skier* and *Backcountry*, Mossop says his current project is very close to his heart – a comprehensive avalanche education DVD.

Designed to suit the needs of both recreational and curriculum distribution, the DVD will include an exhilarating snow-riding film that mixes glorious deep-powder footage with horrifying avalanche accidents in progress, followed by a series of five short training films. Covering the details, facts and practices integral to safe backcountry travel, the training films will contain much of the information learned in a beginner level avalanche course, including terrain evaluation, weather observation, understanding public avalanche bulletins, the fundamentals of snowpack analysis and stability testing and emergency equipment procedures.

Shot in the spectacular backcountry of Alberta and BC mountains, and employing real-life stories shared by avalanche survivors, the segments will re-enact different accident scenarios, highlighting the crucial mistakes leading up to the disaster being depicted.

"The capital objective of the project is to convince the viewer to take an introductory avalanche course," says Mossop, a graduate of the Canadian Avalanche Association's Level 1 Avalanche Safety for Ski Operations course. "Our youth need this information, and they need it in a language they can understand."

The DVD project, he says, has been in his mind since 1997.

"It was a dream ever since our friends died," Mossop says. "We've always been aware. Ever since our friends died, avalanches have been a big part of our lives. It's influenced my direction."

Along with friends, including Eric Crosland, owner and founder of Rocky Mountain Sherpa Productions, Mossop has been making films since 2001. The Sherpas made their first backcountry skiing film, *Deep Seeded Instability*, in 2003, inspired by an avalanche that claimed the lives of seven Calgary teenagers in the popular Rogers Pass area of BC's Glacier National Park.

Skiing in Rogers Pass the very same day as those teens, Mossop and his friends encountered the group of Strathcona Tweedsmuir School students at the Connaught Creek trailhead as they tested their transceivers, stepped into their ski bindings and hoisted their backpacks. They chatted with the teens, wished them a great day and began climbing up toward their own destination. Sometime later, Mossop and his friends noticed a giant snow cloud about three kilometres away and realized it was rising from the area where the students were likely to be.

"It was a moment of panic; we wondered if we could help," Mossop says.

He and his friends quickly surmised they were too far away to help save any lives. Later that day they learned what had happened.

"That was a pretty wild experience – again," Mossop says.

Motivated by the awareness that those teens contributed to a total of twenty-nine avalanche deaths in Alberta and BC over the 2002–2003 winter, *Deep Seeded Instability* is a thought-provoking montage of sensuous powder riding and stomach-flipping avalanche footage that captures the beauty and the lurking danger of winter backcountry travel, connected with a message of safety, awareness and education.

Accepted as a Banff Mountain Film Festival finalist and world tour entry in 2003, it also won Best Film and Best Editing at the 2004 Fernie Mountain Film Festival. Two more Rocky Mountain Sherpas films toured with the 2004 and 2005 festivals as well.

Although the Sherpas have benefited from some funding from safety gear manufacturer Backcountry Access, Sunshine Village and Biglines.com, Mossop admits more help would be appreciated.

"We're trying to spread awareness and save lives, to share with people both the joys of being in the backcountry and the dangers you need to be aware of to negotiate a great day safely," Mossop says.

"Backcountry skiing can be the richest, most happy, powerful, joyful, elating activity. At the same time, it can be so terrifying and so dark."

FOLLOWING IN THE KING OF THE MOUNTAINS' FOOTSTEPS (2007)

> Chic **Scott** and Hans **Gmoser**

Among the most memorable days mountain writer Chic Scott enjoyed while visiting Austria for three months during the summer of 2007 was an afternoon spent sitting at the base of Spitzmauer, a 2442-metre limestone pyramid in the eastern Alps.

Gazing up at the steep faces and sharp ridges from the Prielschutzhaus mountain hut with Scott was Franz Dopf, who six decades ago climbed the challenging north buttress route of the Spitzmauer with Hans Gmoser.

As one of the first climbing partners to share a rope with Gmoser, who after immigrating to Canada in 1951 pioneered climbing routes and ski traverses and launched an entire industry with his helicopter skiing business, Canadian Mountain Holidays, Dopf shared stories with Scott about Gmoser and their adventures as young men.

Among those stories was one about Gmoser's first experience using a piton, gaining knowledge that led him and fellow Austrian émigré Leo Grillmair to make the landmark first ascent of the south face of the Rockies' Mount Yamnuska in 1952, shortly after arriving in Canada.

"That was their Yamnuska," Scott says. "The rock on Spitzmauer is almost identical to Yam. Grey and yellow, moderately loose limestone. They were very at home on Yamnuska."

For the duration of his Austrian excursion, Scott based himself in Traun, an industrial suburb about fifteen kilometres from Linz, where Gmoser and Dopf grew up, and from where he spent his days compiling research for the biography he's writing on Gmoser, who died in a cycling accident not far from his home in Harvie Heights, Alberta, in July 2006.

"My favourite place came to be a park bench in front of the church where Hans was an altar boy, which is beside the school he attended," Scott says.

One day Scott cycled past the giant iron and steel works employing thousands of men, where Gmoser apprenticed to become an electrician. Another day he cycled along the Danube River to visit the town where Gmoser was born in 1932. During his stay, Scott was delighted to be welcomed as family at the house of Gmoser's brother, Walter, and his wife, Gretl.

Familiarizing himself with the mountains of Gmoser's youth, Scott climbed Austria's highest peak, 3798-metre Grossglockner, and the well known Hoher Dachstein, 2995 metres, in the northeastern corner of the European Alps.

IVAN HUGHES CARRIES THE TOOLS OF HIS TRADE.

DAVID LAVALLÉE DOES RESEARCH ON THE
COLUMBIA ICEFIELD, MOUNT ANDROMEDA
IN THE BACKGROUND, CANADIAN ROCKIES.

Among his stops was a visit to the very first hut Gmoser stayed in while on a holiday weekend with a community priest in January 1947, and where Gmoser experienced his first taste of the alpine, sparking his lifelong love of mountains. Although disappointed to find the long-neglected hut in disrepair, Scott savoured the moment, sitting alone on the deck, soaking in the sunshine and musing about Gmoser's experience sixty years ago.

The highlight of Scott's trip, however, was retracing a weeklong solo hike Gmoser made across the Totes Gebirge, a fifty-kilometre long plateau, the high point of which, the Grosser Priel, reaches 2515 metres.

"I hiked for a week across a small mountain range, going from hut to hut, just as Hans did in 1948," Scott says. "And I carried a copy of his journal with me, where he's being very eloquent, and falling in love with the mountains. I sat out and looked at the same views he did. You could say I was following in the footsteps of Hans Gmoser."

Scott began working on the biography shortly after Gmoser died, at the invitation of Gmoser's wife, Margaret, who handed him all of her husband's journals, correspondence and personal papers, including speeches and commentaries from skiing and climbing films Gmoser toured around North America with in the 1950s and 1960s to help promote his guiding business, Canadian Mountain Holidays (CMH).

Scott has scanned over 600 photographs, with subjects ranging from Gmoser at the age of two wearing a Tyrolean hat to climbing expeditions, and from heli-ski clients Ingemar Stenmark and Spanish King Juan Carlos to Gmoser as an accomplished gentleman receiving the Order of Canada from Governor General Jeanne Sauvé.

"I've got him just dishevelled and beat up and exhausted, and I've got him in tuxedos," Scott says.

A meticulous researcher, Scott has also conducted some forty interviews with people who were close to Gmoser, including Renata Belczyk, who worked as his first cook at his Little Yoho Valley ski camp in 1957, Rockies pioneer helicopter pilot Jim Davies, and ski clients Lloyd Nixon, Bob Sutherland and Dieter von Henning, who participated in the very first helicopter skiing week, in 1965 in BC's Bugaboo Mountains.

For his part, Scott recalled first meeting Gmoser in 1963, not long after discovering his own love for mountain adventure, as he and two friends were invited to help Gmoser and Grillmair haul a dismantled stove into the Alpine Club of Canada's Stanley Mitchell Hut in the Yoho Valley.

"Hans and Leo took turns carrying the frame on their backs; it had to weigh about 150 pounds," Scott says. "That night, when myself and Donnie Gardner and Gerry Walsh went to bed – we were seventeen, eighteen – we listened to Hans play the zither and Hans and Leo yodelling."

Later that year, Scott sat in the audience at a Calgary screening of Gmoser's *Skis Over McKinley*, a film capturing his epic expedition.

"Hans would come out to the foyer at intermission and socialize," Scott recalls. "By then he was king of the mountains. He was the first name you heard. And the biggest thrill was if he remembered your name. Little did he know that forty years later I would be writing his biography."

But first Scott had to make his own name in the mountains.

In 1960 Gmoser and five others made a much publicized attempt to ski the high alpine glacier route between Lake Louise and Jasper. Departing Kicking Horse Pass on April 2, the team laboured as far as Saskatchewan Glacier, where after enduring storms and avalanches, crevasse falls, lost food caches and group dissension, they were forced to abort their attempt.

"It was an absolute epic," Scott says. "And it was the greatest disappointment of Hans's life."

Within a few years, Gmoser was deeply involved with his helicopter skiing business, CMH, the world's first such operation and, with a dozen lodges, by far the largest. Only a month after the first heli-skiing week in 1965, Gmoser applied to build Bugaboo Lodge.

"Hans did everything the way he skied," Scott says. "Straight downhill."

Meanwhile, Scott teamed up with his Calgary buddies Charlie Locke, Don Gardner and Neil Liske to attempt the Great Divide Traverse.

"One of our great dreams was to complete what Hans had begun," Scott recalls.

After a magical three weeks of sunny skies and starry nights, the young local team was successful.

"We learned from all Hans's mistakes, from the size of their packs to the size of the team," Scott says.

Following the screening of their own slide show, Gmoser greeted the young adventurers with only one word.

"Congratulations."

For the next quarter century, the two men lived worlds apart.

"I was part of the Calgary Mountain Club – Brian Greenwood's team – and he was Hans and the Euro heli-ski team," Scott recalls. "We were rivals."

In 1988 Scott left a secure job at the University of Calgary to pursue guiding. In 1991 he published his first article for *explore* magazine on the history of mountain guiding. After failing his guide exam in 1993, Scott experienced his own taste of disappointment, a moment he now reflects upon as "the best thing that ever happened to me."

Scott devoted all his energies to his writing, including several backcountry skiing guidebooks, which culminated in the 440-page *Pushing the Limits*, a comprehensive history of Canadian mountaineering. Gmoser grew to be one of Scott's biggest fans.

"Hans was always supportive in every way," Scott says. "He liked my work; he supported it. We collaborated. He liked that I got my facts right, that I got the spelling right, and he liked that I got the stories right. Hans liked the fact I did a lot of digging. He had become a mentor, and we had become good friends."

And as the two men grew to know each other better over the years, Scott became keenly aware of Gmoser's honest and sometimes critical view of himself and his accomplishments.

"Hans was embarrassed by his own myth," Scott says. "He was honest with himself, and he knew himself better than anyone, how good he was and how bad he was. By the same token, when you got a compliment from Hans, you remembered it. He was sparing with his praise, so you probably deserved it."

Widely known and respected for placing his writing projects ahead of any financial aspirations, Scott admits being chosen to write Gmoser's only biography was an honour indeed.

"Although the book will probably do well, this is not primarily a commercial project," Scott says. "It's a tribute, a memorial to Hans. And it's the only one."

According to Gmoser's wishes, and those of his family, no other biography will be authorized, nor any mountains, backcountry huts or awards named for the man who opened so many doors and shared so much inspiration within Canada's mountain community.

"It's a great honour to be asked. It's a great responsibility, and I feel a great pressure to get it right," Scott says. "From my perspective, I want to write a book Hans would like, and his friends and family who knew him best – warts and all."

REAL EVEREST EXPEDITION IS A REAL PRIVILEGE (2006)

> Guy **Clarkson**

Every spring, hundreds of people travel to the Himalayas intent on climbing the highest mountain of all – Everest.

In March 2006 Banff filmmaker and mountain guide Guy Clarkson made the journey, not to climb the mountain, but to film a British Army team with its own hopes of reaching the summit.

Unlike those paying $80,000 to follow guides and fixed ropes up the South Col Route – by which over 2000 people have stood on the highest point on the planet – the British team had its sights set on the steeper, highly technical and never repeated West Ridge Route, climbed in 1986 by Canadians Dwayne Congdon and Sharon Wood, who in the process became the first North American woman to summit the peak.

"I knew this was going to be a real mountain expedition," Clarkson says. "Once I could see the route, I developed a great deal of respect for the '86 team. What a great accomplishment that was without any Sherpas. The fact that Sharon and Dwayne summitted and got back down – it's remarkable."

One of a dozen filmmakers with the requisite high-altitude experience, Clarkson flew to London, England, for two interviews before being selected for the job along with American Dave Rasmussen. Unlike Rasmussen, Clarkson had never been to the Everest region.

Clarkson admits he wasn't certain he wanted to be part of an Army expedition at all, at first – given customary rigid military protocol.

"At the interview I think I asked them as many questions as they asked me," Clarkson says. "But as soon as I met the commanding officers, there was absolutely none of that. They were just a bunch of people climbing together."

And climbing well, he adds.

"It was a fantastic team, everyone got along well and got down to the business of climbing the mountain," he says. "These weren't regular soldiers. They were very talented people accustomed to making life and death decisions. They work in teams all the time. It takes a lot of hard work to get one or two summit parties in place. In the end we were all tired, we worked hard and we came home better friends. It was a real privilege."

For Clarkson, that meant being up early, camera and gear ready to be in position to get the images, then staying up late to capture the climbers in their tents at night.

"They were long days, but cinematically it's very rewarding, the landscape is spectacular," he says.

While the harmonious group dynamics told a rather boring story compared to reality TV shows, the group's three-month expedition wasn't without drama.

While setting up six camps from base camp at 5490 metres, up to 8000 metres, sometimes breaking trail in waist-deep snow, they became acquainted with Swedish ski mountaineer Thomas Olsson and Norwegian Tormod Granheim. After they summitted with two Sherpas, Olsson was rappelling from a snow anchor when it failed. Granheim watched him cartwheel down the steep slope until he was out of sight, then he carefully downclimbed the same section without weighting his own anchor and skied down safely. Olsson's body was later recovered from a bergschrund at 6200 metres, and flown away by the Chinese Army.

"Thomas's death affected me personally, since I'd gotten to know him," Clarkson says. "One minute he was a young, healthy, strong, experienced skier who'd done a lot of extreme stuff. I interviewed him and had a few drinks with him. He was so bright and alive, a keen adventurer."

Suddenly he was gone.

"When his body was lying in front of me wrapped in canvas, I thought, 'I don't want to see any of our guys like this,'" Clarkson says.

Clarkson said he and his teammates were aware of about sixteen deaths on the mountain while they were there, mostly on the busy south side, where one climber reportedly died while sitting atop another dead body.

"You could see a line of tents, and climbers moving like ants up to the south col," Clarkson says. "Even the Northeast Ridge route is stitched up from bottom to top; people just clip into ascenders. They throw themselves at Everest like it's another Ironman. I'm not making a judgment, but many are not mountaineers. They are strong athletes, but they are out of their element. Above 8000 metres a lot of things can go sideways. When they get into trouble up there, they don't know what to do."

The north side of the mountain was, by contrast, a very magical place, he says. With twenty-two climbers and a seven-person film crew, the Scandinavian team was the only other group of people the British team saw.

"It was a real privilege to be alone, just our team," Clarkson says. "That was my main interest in going. If it had been on one of the commercial routes, I don't think I would have been interested."

Then, with a summit team poised at 8100 metres, and Clarkson and Calgary's Laurie Skreslet – who was aiming to return to the summit he was the first Canadian to reach in 1982 – ready to follow, the team leader made the difficult no-go decision. Hazardous avalanche conditions were not going to improve; continuing was unsafe.

"The mountain made it easy for us," Clarkson says. "There was no debate, no egos. But it was extremely disappointing. People were gutted. Three years of hard work and preparation. I'm sure there's a strong desire to go back and try again."

In the end, though, just being there was profound.

"The mountain had an enormous impact on all of us," Clarkson says. "It was spiritual. The northwest side is like a huge cathedral, with incredible ice towers. It's wild country; you work your way up through moving glaciers."

At the same time, some things were disturbing.

"Here's this holy mountain. It felt sacred to me," Clarkson says. "Lots of people don't share this mountain ethic. There's oxygen bottles, human waste, garbage. But I don't know if we were angelic there – Sherpas retrieved our waste from base camp – but it's not possible from the higher elevations."

Back in the Bow Valley, Clarkson says he's grown a new appreciation for his home.

"What an amazing place we live in," he says. "Tibet has no trees. Our water is clean; we can drink from the river. Living conditions over there are pretty challenging."

The locals, however, were a joy to meet.

"I really enjoyed meeting the Sherpas and the yak herders. I couldn't speak a word of Tibetan, they couldn't speak any English, but we had a few laughs just the same."

FILMMAKER BITES OFF A DOG GONE ADDICTION (2007)

> Becky **Bristow**

Standing on American Summit, a windswept, snowy mountaintop sparsely colonized by mangled, stunted, ice-plastered trees stuck in the frosty Alaskan air at 1043 metres, Becky Bristow panned the landscape with her video camera to capture the pastel mauves and pinks of the northern sunset.

From a distance she heard the jingling of dogsled harnesses and, as they drew closer, the panting of fourteen huskies and their musher's exerted shouts as they crossed over the cold, lonely summit en route from Fairbanks, Alaska, to Whitehorse, Yukon.

This was but one of thirty-one such teams that bounded from the start line of the Yukon Quest International Sled Dog Race – known as the toughest sled dog race in the world.

One thousand six hundred and ten kilometres of frigid northern wilderness. Three thousand and fifty metres of elevation gain. No substitution of dogs. If a racer kills a moose en route, they must salvage the meat before continuing. Fastest time the race has ever been won – ten days, seven hours. On average, one out of three racers doesn't finish. Some years it's half.

"On American Summit, the sun was setting and you could hear the dog teams coming from a long way away," Bristow recalls. "I watched the sun set for a long time; there was ice on the trees. It made me realize the beauty of the place they were seeing with their dog teams, and why they do it."

Why they do it was a question that drew Bristow to spend six cold weeks of the 2004 winter capturing the racers' journey on camera, to create her sixty-seven-minute adventure documentary *Dog Gone Addiction: Inspired by the Women of the Yukon Quest*.

The film features three women – seasoned veteran Kelley Griffin and rookie mushers Agatha Franczak and Michelle Phillips, who is cheered on by her four-year-old son Keegan – and their four-legged teammates who answer to such names as Ferdinand, Malachi, Daisy, Zippo and Denali.

The film also showcases the unfettered northern landscape, a frozen world of sturdy forests, bare willow bushes and icy riverbeds through which the sled teams pass, so tiny amidst that wilderness that when filmed from a helicopter the only clue to their presence comes with their movement against the still scenery.

"I wanted to make a movie about women who were inspiring – inspiring to other women and to other people," Bristow explains. "And I wanted to make a movie about the North. I keep getting drawn to the North. I was curious about the mushing community, about the race, and I was also really interested in where they got to go by dogsled – they got to see a lot."

Bristow too saw a lot, and her film bursts to life with dogs yelping and tugging at their harnesses with their pink tongues dangling, while a Bearfoot Bluegrass soundtrack augments the excitement like the fluffy powder snow kicked up behind the huskies' bootie-wrapped feet.

But it's in the quieter details that Bristow captures the remoteness, the devotion and the flavour of northern life – mushers gently massaging their dogs' paws in –50°C temperatures; mushers' swollen faces framed by frosty white hair and fur-trimmed parka hoods; Phillips hacking apart frozen salmon meat with an axe to feed her team; spirited Franczak recalling how as a child in Poland she told her skeptical mother she would grow up to live in a cabin in the woods with lots of dogs.

"I totally lucked into her," Bristow says of Franczak, the film's most colourful personality. "She's passionate and she's hilarious. She was really candid in front of the camera, just so herself. As a rookie, people can relate to her. No matter how many times I saw her on the screen during the editing, she still made me laugh."

Released in 2007, *Dog Gone Addiction* won Best Adventure Sport Film at the Taos Mountain Film Festival in October of that year and was runner up for the People's Choice Award at the Wanaka Mountain Film Festival in New Zealand. At the 2007 Whistler Film Festival, the film garnered a Special Jury Award for Mountain Culture.

"*Dog Gone Addiction* is adventure filmmaking at its very best," says Les Guthman, a New York–based producer of award-winning adventure documentaries. "It gives us poignant and sharp portraits of the mushers and their doggone addictions, along with majestic, bone-chilling coverage of what must be the coldest race on earth. In the lives of these three women, Becky shows us an essence of the raw human will to compete, and the drive to test oneself that transcends class and gender and adventure celebrity; for those who know not too much about sled dogs, the film is a revelation about a powerful will to compete that transcends species as well."

Growing up in Rocky Mountain House, Alberta, Bristow was an active 4-H member who jumped horses and showed cattle and steers. She loved embarking on multi-day canoeing trips with her dad and cherishes memories of a ten-day pack horse trip through the Canadian Rockies in celebration of her eleventh birthday.

After her second year of university – she graduated from the University of Calgary with a kinesiology degree in 1999 – Bristow spent the summer guiding for Blast, an inflatable-kayak tour operator running trips on the Red Deer, Sheep and Highwood rivers.

"It was more about being on the river, sharing my passion with people," Bristow, thirty-one, says. "I like teaching people how to do something they've never done before and watching them realize they can do it. It's pretty rewarding."

For her first multi-week road trip, she loaded up her camping and kayaking gear to paddle the Quesnel and Cariboo rivers in the Williams Lake, BC, area.

She's been exploring ever since.

In 2000 she travelled with friends for three months in Ecuador, climbing, backpacking, surfing and kayaking. Before long they had paddled all the known rivers, so a local acquaintance suggested they explore the river behind his papaya farm.

"There was a gorge that led to a forty-foot waterfall that led into another gorge," Bristow recalls. "I got to do the first descent of a forty-footer. We should have planned for two days, but we didn't, so we paddled the rest in the dark and camped on the rocks under a space blanket."

Smitten by expedition life, in 2003 she travelled to Bhutan for a month, a trip that remains her favourite.

"That country is so magical," Bristow says. "We got to do a first descent there, and we took some local Bhutanese with us. We hiked up and over three mountain passes. We took horses and carried boats for three and a half days to access the river. Then we paddled down some awesome whitewater. Some of the Bhutanese were quite talented. Just the hiking to get to the river was quite an experience."

A trip to Iran in 2005, however, via France, Greece and Turkey, was her scariest.

"It was the hottest climate I've ever been in, and we had to wear headscarves and long pants all the time," she says. "We had lots of stuff stolen, including film footage. We had to be really smart about where to camp and about things like whether to show our camera or not. But then we met people who were totally awesome, who were nice and giving and wanted to share."

Shortly after her Ecuador trip, Bristow encountered a Teton Gravity Research film crew while she was paddling in Revelstoke – which she now calls home after purchasing a small house there in 2006. The guys asked her for some local beta and then invited her to appear in their film.

"At first it was just a bunch of us boating, paddling together, and I was really excited to paddle with a solid crew," Bristow says of appearing in kayaking films. "Then it was cool trips to Norway, and it was neat to go to all these different countries and see all the different cultures – and I got to paddle awesome whitewater. I didn't really think about the camera aspect of it. There's a certain connection with people at that level of your sport, all amped up about paddling the next river together. It's great having a solid crew to go do first descents with."

While her determination and apparent lack of fear are impressive, says Jeff Croft, a long-time friend and paddling partner who worked with her on a BC forest firefighting crew, Bristow is a thorough planner and competent leader.

"Becky's sense of adventure, spirit and outdoor skills are truly legendary," Croft says. "She's a picture of determination, natural ability and infectious positive energy in all stages of planning a trip, whether it's for a day or many days. She's not overconfident or bragging but quietly confident setting up and running a drop and then exuberant afterwards. And she's a friend to everyone on the river, safety conscious and aware, very likeable and totally self-sufficient."

That same determination and self-sufficiency served Bristow well in Alaska and Yukon as she arranged helicopter flights to access remote locations and filmed Phillips on training runs from a sled speeding along trails winding through snowy bushes and in nighttime temperatures that dropped to −51°C.

"A lot of the race is at night; there's only six and a half hours of daylight," Bristow explains. "I met people at the start banquet weeks before the race and arranged Ski-doo and vehicle rides to wait with photographers for the mushers. I wanted to capture what they were going through. It [the cold] was fine until my camera crapped out one night. It got down to –51, and it started tweaking out; the audio wasn't working. It was really frustrating. It was right after Michelle had had an accident on the descent from Eagle Summit."

As soon as she had finished feeding and caring for her dogs, an excited Phillips took shelter inside the checkstop building to talk about her crash, but Bristow couldn't immediately follow her into the warm room with a camera that was solidly frozen.

The cold, however, was a challenge Bristow took in stride, one that only reaffirmed her love of the North. Although she hadn't been to Alaska in winter, Bristow's previous trips to Alaska to paddle world-class whitewater included starring in a Nissan TV commercial in October 2006.

"It was great; I got to go to Alaska. I hadn't been there in the fall or winter," Bristow comments. "When we got there, the waterfall they wanted me to drop was frozen, so I seal-launched off the canyon wall. They were pretty happy; the shot looked pretty dramatic with snow on the canyons walls.

"But I love going to Alaska for any reason. The proportion of wilderness to people – there's a lot of unexplored territory. It's so raw, the landscape, the ocean, the way people live. You feel like you're going back in time the farther north you get. Dogsledding is one example of that – people seem to still value the simple, beautiful things in life a lot more, like their relationship with their animals and the beauty of their surroundings and the natural world, over the newest computer gadget."

It was a trip to Russia in 2003 that started Bristow thinking about stepping behind the camera. When an uncle who trades with Russian businessmen was asked to suggest someone to assess rivers in the far northern Chukotka region for commercial whitewater potential, he recommended "just the right person."

Realizing "not everybody gets to go to Russia," Bristow captured her, and fellow paddler Dunbar Hardy's, experience.

The resulting film, *A Russian Wave*, which relates the alternately hilarious, heart-warming and thought-provoking ups and downs of their journey to remote Siberia at the invitation of aspiring Russian eco-tourism entrepreneurs, earned awards at several film festivals, including People's Choice for Short Films at the 2004 Whistler Film Festival.

The experience, she says, had a learning curve as sharp as dropping her first seventy-foot waterfall.

"I learned you can do a lot with a little bit of footage if you have the patience," Bristow says. "I learned that making a film is a tedious and time-consuming process, to create the story and the characters. And I learned it's a challenge to sit in front of the computer for long periods of time."

For *A Russian Wave*, Bristow edited eight hours of footage to produce a twenty-seven-minute film. For *Dog Gone Addiction*, she had sixty-two hours of footage. Editing the film took fourteen months.

Part of that time was spent living in Pemberton, BC, paddling the Callaghan, Ashlu and Cayoosh rivers, the rest sitting in front of her monitor. To help her complete the project, she received a Banff Centre grant. Prior to finishing *A Russian Wave* she had also participated in a Banff Centre filmmakers' workshop to hone her skills.

"It's probably one of the hardest things I've ever done," Bristow says of creating *Dog Gone Addiction*. "The story was there, it was a matter of how to tell it with what I had – and how to ditch sixty-one hours of footage that wasn't the best shot and didn't tell the story the best way. I stuck a lot of it in the special footage, things I still thought were important. Mostly, I was trying to learn patience and realizing it's not a quick process. But I like how it turned out – I've gotten e-mails from people who say they love it. The community does seem to appreciate that the story is told from their perspective."

Telling the story from the mushers' perspective was especially important to Bristow, who felt that was missing from her own appearances in kayaking films.

"It was just all about the images, about what I was doing in my kayak," Bristow says. "They didn't talk to us as athletes. I think I was inspired to make a film that did. My whole goal was to tell the story from their perspective."

Capturing the perspective of a musher who happened to be a mother was something Bristow also felt was important.

"I think a lot of women forget about their passions and their dreams and goals for themselves when they have kids," Bristow says. "I like the way Michelle shares her passion with her son and gets him excited about her wanting to be in the race and wanting to win. She's showing him you can still commit to yourself and your own goals and be a mom at the same time."

For musher Kelley Griffin, the film simply succeeded in capturing the nuances of the North and the mushing culture.

"I think it does an excellent job of capturing the essence of the Yukon Quest, and shows how different each musher's story and motivation are from another," Griffin says. "The humour of the sport and race is right on target, as is the respect and awe that mushers have for their dogs. I also like that she didn't put a feminist stamp on it. Becky simply films three women mushing dogs in an unforgiving and fantastic part of the world and touches on their stories, and I think the common thread of all of us is that we are living our lives and dreams and hopefully we can pass on inspiration to others."

THE LIQUID TRUTH (2008)

> David **Lavallée**

The light was flat as David Lavallée walked steadily along the gently inclining surface of the Columbia Icefield en route to Snow Dome. Amidst a seemingly borderless expanse of snow, he squinted through his sunglasses to see as far ahead as he could, on the lookout for slight depressions or folds in the monotone snow cover that would indicate the presence of a crevasse.

Then, suddenly, he was falling.

As he dropped into the chasm, he felt his body crash through a thin ice shelf as it collapsed under his weight. Then, with a jerk, he abruptly stopped falling, as the rope tied into his harness grew taut. His rescuers were on the job.

Free-hanging like a dead weight, he threaded an ice screw into the vertical wall and tied himself to it with a short sling to alleviate some of the pressure on his waist harness. Surveying his situation, he noticed he had come to a stop about ten metres into the hole, directly facing a much thicker, more substantial ice shelf than the one he'd crashed through.

"I looked across from me and realized that if I had landed on that ice shelf, I would have broken both legs. I felt really happy to land where I did," Lavallée recalls. "The crevasse was fairly well lit. I could see around, about forty feet below me it turned black, but I could tell it kept going a long way down. The wall was whitish, bluish, all these layers. I remember thinking, 'I wonder when these layers formed? Was Nixon president? Or was Cleopatra Queen?'"

Just forty minutes after falling into the crevasse, Lavallée's partners hauled him to the surface. Liberated from the cold, icy fissure and relieved to be standing on the solid glacier once again, Lavallée had but one thought:

"The shot! Did he get the shot?"

Travelling with Lavallée across the icefield – at 325 square kilometres the largest one in the Canadian Rockies – was professional guide Ken Bibby, his brother, Andrew, and their father, Alan Bibby, an award-winning documentary filmmaker. Rounding out the team were production assistant Scott Wilson and environmental scientist Nivea de Oliveira.

The group was attempting to climb to the 3456-metre summit of Snow Dome, not just to take in the spectacular high alpine view but to film the panorama visible from one of the most significant summits in the western hemisphere.

Located on the Continental Divide between the Athabasca and Dome glaciers, Snow Dome's summit is the hydrographic apex of North America, from where meltwater ultimately flows to three oceans – the Atlantic via the Saskatchewan and Nelson rivers; the Pacific via the Columbia River; and the Arctic via the Athabasca and Mackenzie rivers.

Just ten months earlier, in October 2006, Lavallée had participated in a field trip that was part of a conference focusing on the effects of climate change on alpine environments, which had been organized by the Alpine Club of Canada. Standing at the toe of Athabasca Glacier, he had looked up at Snow Dome's summit while conversing with University of Calgary glaciologist Dr. Shawn Marshall.

As Marshall outlined the prognosis for the Rockies' glaciers, including the Athabasca, in the face of a warming climate, the conversation flowed to the Athabasca River and the landscape it flows through, including Alberta's massive Fort McMurray oil sands developments, which use enormous quantities of water in producing oil through the extraction of bitumen – a heavy, black, viscous tar – from the sand.

Instantly, a light bulb sparked in Lavallée's head. "I thought, 'This is a film,'" he said.

His idea was to follow a single drop of water from the very genesis of the river at Snow Dome's summit all the way to where it drains 1538 kilometres downstream into the Peace–Athabasca Delta south of Fort Chipewyan in Alberta's northeast corner. Lavallée embarked on a journey – a physical journey that would include walking across glaciers, backpacking along a remote river valley and navigating sections of the Athabasca aboard an inflatable raft – in an effort to explore the watershed firsthand. But at the same time, he embarked on the creative journey of learning the art of documentary filmmaking.

He weathered the course of his trial-by-fire filmmaking apprenticeship solo for the first few months, and then, at a Banff World Television Festival reception in June 2007, Lavallée met veteran filmmaker Alan Bibby, who enthusiastically jumped on board as director and director of photography. By that point Lavallée had grown so committed to his project that he'd given up his position as a family counsellor and had turned to substitute teaching to supplement his part-time seasonal work as a hiking guide. Bibby's talent and experience were invaluable in creating a professional-grade product, and Lavallée pretty much started again at frame one.

"I met up with Alan and started all over again," Lavallée says. "He's a fantastic director. He brought the experience base that I needed to make my film real."

In an effort to gather as much footage as possible of the Athabasca River's true headwaters, in mid-August Lavallée, Bibby and their team hiked up the Saskatchewan Glacier to spend nine days on the Columbia Icefield, an expanse of glacial ice from which several glaciers flow to valley bottoms in several directions.

While on many days poor light kept them from exploring very far from their high camp set in the midst of the icefield, they did eventually climb to Snow Dome's summit on a bluebird day to capture significant footage. On another clear day, the team blew a sizeable chunk of their filming budget as Bibby captured the high-alpine landscape from a helicopter. Later, the entire group flew by helicopter to the west edge of Jasper National Park to begin a two-day wilderness hike following the early trickles of the Athabasca to its confluence with the Sunwapta River at Sunwapta Falls.

With the icefield and its crevasses behind them, the lessons the group learned from Lavallée's fall into the crevasse were valuable ones, he says.

"It was so obvious afterward," Lavallée says. "There had been a big melt, then some fresh snowfall on top of the crevasses, and we were travelling in bad light. Mother Nature's billboards were screaming at us, and we were speeding right on by. And when we thought about it, we said, 'Isn't this how we're acting as a society? Greenland, the Arctic, Antarctica, where the largest ice shelves are collapsing – they are Mother Nature's billboards and we're ignoring all those signs.'"

Farther downstream, however, Lavallée discovered the signs were impossible to ignore. Floating along a gently meandering stretch of the Athabasca for three days from Jasper to Hinton, Lavallée mused about the significance of the park boundary they crossed en route.

"We shot a scene of the park boundary, and we thought about how that river is no longer protected beyond that boundary," he says. "But then, if Parks' mandate is to preserve and protect, then Parks would have to speak out on external threats too if they were to really fulfill that mandate."

Ironically, he adds, Kinder Morgan, one of the largest pipeline transporters and terminal operators in North America, was in the process of twinning its pipeline, which runs right through Jasper and Mount Robson Provincial Park. Originally built in the early 1950s, the pipeline operates under an easement agreement, which from the beginning included a right of way through the parks, as well as a clause that contemplated twinning of the system as demand increased. Fifty years later, it is the only pipeline system to transports crude oil and refined products from Edmonton, Alberta, to marketing terminals and refineries in the Greater Vancouver area and Puget Sound in Washington State – and that pipeline capacity is being doubled to accommodate the growing volumes originating from Alberta's oil sands at Fort McMurray.

Lavallée recites the statistics:

> The oil sands operations cover a 65,000-square-kilometre chunk of Alberta – roughly the size of Florida.

> With over 170 billion barrels of recoverable oil, the region is second only to Saudi Arabia as an oil resource. The estimated 2.5 trillion barrels of bitumen make it possible to produce 2.5 million barrels of oil per day for 200 years. A push to increase production is scheduled to quadruple current output to four million barrels per day by 2020.

> The fifty-two separate projects operating in 2007 pumped out thirty megatonnes of greenhouse gases that year. If growth continues as planned, that number will rise to 100 megatonnes per year by 2020.

> It takes between three and six barrels of water to produce one barrel of oil.

> The tailings ponds created as a result of this process cover what used to be fifty square kilometres of forest and muskeg. Many of the ponds are as large as lakes in Ontario's cottage country. They are visible from space.

They contain polycyclic aromatic hydrocarbons, naphthenic acids, heavy metals, salts and bitumen.

And that's just the beginning.

"We're facing a perfect storm of water issues in Alberta," Lavallée says. "By 2010, this one industry will be using more water than the entire urban population of Alberta. Ninety per cent of this water is so poisoned by the steam injection and extraction process that it can never be returned to an ecosystem. Instead it ends up in poisonous tailings ponds that can be seen from space. Birds that land in these lakes do not fly away again.

"The volume of water that ends up in these ponds rivals waste production even in countries like China. One researcher calculated that if you were to drain Lake Erie, you could fill it with the sludge from the tailings ponds and it would fill that great lake to a depth of twenty centimetres."

Since the tailings ponds border the Athabasca River, he says, they present an enduring threat to one of Canada's largest watersheds. One dam alone, the Syncrude Tailings Dam, holds a fill volume exceeding that of China's Three Gorges Dam.

"One of the people we interviewed for our film, [renowned aquatics ecologist] Dr. David Schindler, said, 'If this dam were to burst, the world would forever forget about the Exxon Valdez,'" Lavallée says. "He's referring to the fact that if a tornado, earthquake or terrorist attack were to hit this area, this toxic sludge would, after poisoning the Athabasca, the Slave and the Mackenzie, end up in Inuvik and the Arctic Ocean."

For their part, most of the companies involved admit the process of extracting oil from bitumen does have a detrimental effect on the environment, but they partner such statements with declarations that they are taking measures to minimize those effects as much as possible, and that they adhere to current government-regulated standards.

In researching their story, Lavallée and Bibby participated in a flotilla on the Athabasca from Fort McMurray to Fort MacKay in early August 2007, which was organized by the Pembina Institute, an Alberta-based environmental think tank. Paddling alongside canoeists, environmentalists, Mikisew Cree First Nation members and politicians, they conducted several interviews, including one with Alberta Liberal environment critic Dr. David Swann, who in 2002 was fired from his position as medical officer of health for Alberta's Palliser region after he spoke publicly in favour of the Kyoto Accord. Although after much public outcry he was offered his job back, he declined in favour of focusing his work on the people of Iraq.

The flotilla and associated rally, Lavallée says, helped reassure him that his project was a film that needed to be made.

"What I saw was a broad-based coalition of Albertans getting together to protest what's going on," he says. "Albertans are not going to accept willy nilly what's going on up there. While government and industry are looking out for the economy, is anyone looking out for the river and the ecosystem it is part of? What's happening to the glaciers, and what's happening to our water supply? How are these resources being managed? Are our institutions on the job?"

From Fort MacKay, Lavallée, Bibby and de Oliveira continued paddling to Fort Chipewyan, where the river flows into Lake Athabasca. The settlement is inaccessible by road. Residents of Alberta's oldest community, which was once a hub of the fur trade, rely on seasonal trapping and fishing, as well as employment in Fort McMurray's oilsands industry.

Accompanying them in the capacity of river guide as they navigated a wide, open, meandering maze of channels, Lavallée says, was a Syncrude employee who preferred not to reveal his name.

"We saw pelicans, boreal forest, and pumping stations that are sucking water out of the Athabasca for oil sands development and threatening the water security of the 300,000 people who live along the watershed," Lavallée says. "We passed a First Nations fishing camp on the river. They said they'd been finding fish with tumours, even a beaver with its hair fallen out. They were super worried and concerned about the water."

But water isn't the only worry, Lavallée cautions.

One of those interviewed for the film, ecologist Kevin Timoney, described the findings of his study, the only independent one to date to examine sediments in the Peace–Athabasca region.

"He found an absolute witch's brew of heavy metals, mercury, arsenic and polycyclic aromatic hydrocarbons – PAHs," Lavallée says. "He attributed that leakage to the dams and smokestacks; they belch their stuff into the air and it comes down to earth again. The pollution settles into the sediment; people eat fish and moose meat; those fish and moose eat plants and sedges. Those who eat the most traditional diet, who follow the most traditional lifestyle, are the most at risk."

Those risks include leukemia, lymphomas, lupus, auto-immune diseases and rare cancers such as cholangiocarcinoma, or bile duct cancer, which are appearing in members of the Fort Chipewyan population at a rate so disproportionate that it caught the attention of the local medical examiner, Dr. John O'Connor, who also spoke at the rally in Fort MacKay. For his efforts, O'Connor found himself on the receiving end of a complaint registered by Health Canada.

With plans to have editing completed by spring 2008, thanks in part to a $5,000 Banff Centre for Mountain Culture grant, and with broadcast and distribution arrangements close to being secured, Lavallée says he feels like he's travelled farther than the length of a river since the birth of his film idea at the Columbia Icefield.

"I've learned a lot since that day at the Icefield," Lavallée says. "The problem is definitely far worse than I thought, not only for the river, but for Albertans. By 2010 this [oil sands] industry will be using more water than the entire urban population of Alberta. And huge quantities of natural gas."

Citing David Hughes of the Geological Survey of Canada, Lavallée says Alberta's natural gas supply peaked in 2001 and will be depleted by 2014.

"The oil sands are using enough natural gas to heat 3.2 million homes per day – with the expansion being contemplated, they will be using the equivalent of heating 15 million homes," he says. "The waste of natural gas is a double tragedy because natural gas holds great promise as a bridging fuel to the future, because it is the cleanest-burning of all the hydrocarbons. It can be the fuel to fight climate change. By 2010 the oil sands will be the largest single point source of greenhouse gases in the world. This is because of the energy intensity associated with separating the bitumen from the sand – which is a form of oil production that makes oil as carbon-intensive as coal. In terms of fighting climate change this is us going backwards in a big hurry. This is a doom machine. It's eating up all our natural resources – our water and our natural gas."

In addition to discovering a Pandora's box worth of facts about the impacts of climate change and oil sands production, Lavallée admits he's learned plenty about filmmaking, too.

"I learned it's a heck of a lot of work," Lavallée says. "You really have to stay open to ideas. It's like a scientific experiment. You start out working on a hypothesis, then your hypothesis gets challenged. You have to roll with the punches; you have to pursue different directions. Once your initial research is done you find you're not just scratching the surface – there's always more to learn, more layers to dig through. You keep learning there's more you don't know. You have to keep asking, 'What are you not telling me?'"

Answers to such questions led him to the film's title, he admits.

"Truth is a liquid because it slides through your fingers. It assumes no discernible shape," Lavallée says. "In this part of Alberta, the government and industry call it a win–win situation – others call this an ecological holocaust.

"We privilege certain facts and figures and statistics and ignore all others that don't fit with our preconceived plan to go ahead with this development regardless of the evidence we have that says we probably shouldn't. We turn the truth into a liquid; it takes whatever shape you wish it to."

ADVENTUREPRENEURS

Adventurepreneurs are "all of the above." They are fun seekers and explorers who tell their own stories but to the extent that they have made their adventures their professions, their livelihoods. They seek out sponsors; they write books and magazine articles; they sell their photographs; they produce films. They actively market their adventures to finance their next adventures and also to cover their daily costs of living. Adventure is their full-time profession; having fun is serious business, or, for some of these people, soon will be.

ADVENTURER FOLLOWS HIS OWN FOOTSTEPS
– TWENTY YEARS LATER (2004)

> Jerry **Kobalenko**

While it's not unusual for adventurers to follow their predecessors' footsteps or ski tracks, it's not as common for an adventurer to follow his own.

But that's exactly what Banff's Jerry Kobalenko did for nearly six weeks, skiing solo and towing a 130-kilogram sled across the windswept interior of Labrador following a route he pioneered twenty years earlier. And by the time he completed his 600-kilometre, thirty-nine-day trek on February 28, 2004, he was thrilled to realize he'd done so a full week faster than the first time.

"I assure you, it did not seem quick to me," Kobalenko declared from Nain, Labrador, before flying to Calgary to be enthusiastically greeted by his wife, Alexandra.

"It was like I was moving at the speed of light and time was stretched out to painful near infinity."

Starting out on January 21, Kobalenko says his journey from Churchill Falls to Nain was a little less difficult than his 1984 trip, which marked the debut of nearly two-dozen Arctic expeditions, involving more than 5600 kilometres of self-propelled travel. The first time, he recalls, his equipment wasn't as good and at times he was unsure if his intended route was even feasible.

"My first trip was slightly harder," he admits. "But this was a hard trip."

On his more recent trip, ferocious winds that wore his spirit created conditions ideal for towing his sled, as they scoured the landscape into a surface resembling cement, which allowed him to cover more mileage more quickly. While he averaged eight-and-a-half-hour days in 1984, he accomplished greater mileage in seven and a half hours on his second journey.

"You want the wind to blow, then to stop," he explains. "The wind is both your friend and bitter enemy."

Experience was also his friend, he admits.

"I knew when to walk and when to ski. On my first trip I never even thought to take my skis off."

Kobalenko travelled across high plateaus and small hills toward the increasingly bald northern region of Labrador, following barren frozen lakes and river systems. With any snow quickly blown away, there was no shelter from raging winds.

"It's a very harsh place; you get sudden storms with nowhere to hide," he says. "I kept my fingers crossed and raced against it."

He experienced only one significant snowfall, which kept him tent-bound for a day, but since he'd just travelled fourteen consecutive days, he welcomed the rest. By the next day, what snow hadn't been blown away was so hard his ski pole couldn't pierce it. In all he spent five of his thirty-nine days tent-bound.

Arctic travel may not produce the adrenalin of mountaineering, he says, but it's extremely challenging nonetheless.

"What you're dealing with is not being able to put up your tent in a storm. And it's cold, really cold. I saw winds I'd never seen before. Usually when it's forty below, it's calm. This time, it was forty below with fifty-knot winds. That's very, very cold. You throw a cup of boiling water in the air and it explodes into frost."

The coldest temperature he recorded during the trip was −54°C, which left his feet a little cool by morning but, he promised, no colder than if his foot had escaped the covers on his bed at home.

"I've learned how to sleep in fifty below," he says, adding the temperature inside his tent is on average five degrees warmer than whatever it is outside. His bulky sleeping system, including foam pads, a down bag constructed by a NASA engineer and a synthetic over-bag that absorbs moisture from inevitable frost buildup, weighs about five kilograms.

But while he kept warm at night, the howling winds took a toll in the daytime.

"My cheeks got frostbitten so many times, the slightest breath of wind was agony; it really hurt," he says.

Despite the fur ruff around Kobalenko's parka hood, the wind still managed to snake through little seams and edges between his goggles and facemask. With each bout of frostbite, the skin would scab up, fall off and expose a new layer of even more sensitive skin to the wind, resulting in more frostbite. While his hands and feet were in near constant pain on his 1984 journey, however, Kobalenko says wearing plastic bread bags from Banff's Keller Foods between thin socks and heavier oversocks worked as effective vapour barriers to keep his feet from freezing.

All the same, he found himself fantasizing about visiting the spa at the Banff Springs Hotel.

"It's a very ascetic, monk-like existence. You feel like man was born to suffer," Kobalenko says. "But then you fantasize about warm rocks between your toes."

As is his practice, Kobalenko carried no radio or satellite phone. Even though friends were advised of his route, things could change quickly should he become injured, particularly in the treed areas in the early part of the trip.

"It increases the pressure greatly," he says. "If you fell and hurt yourself, no-one would ever find you."

He carried a gun on the small chance he'd run into a polar bear – an experience recounted in his book, *The Horizontal Everest: Extreme Journeys on Ellesmere Island* – but saw only a few foxes, wolves and birds.

And why repeat the arduous journey he first undertook as a spry twenty-seven-year-old?

"I wondered, would the savvy veteran outperform the young whippersnapper?" he replies.

Was the first trip hard simply because it was a hard trip, because conditions made it difficult, or because he was inexperienced and had poor equipment?

"My Arctic career started in Labrador. I owe a lot to that trip; it certainly changed me," Kobalenko says. "It's one of those things you do for what you gain afterward. At the time, it's not a lot of fun; it's nothing but stress and hardship. Once you get back, you think of everything you've learned. The intensity is something you simply can't get in ordinary life."

And would he want to repeat the trip in another twenty years?

"I thought about that," he admits. "It was near enough my limits this time."

Twenty years from now, he jokes, he'd only do it if he felt he was a burden who should be set out on his final ice floe.

ALPINE PARAGLIDING ACROSS THE ANDES (2003)

> Will **Gadd**

Will Gadd is the first to admit that whenever he describes his upcoming adventures to people, the most common response is, "You're nuts!"

And after spending three weeks in South America waiting out howling winds, in hopes of becoming the first person to fly a paraglider across the Andes, Gadd says this time the naysayers were on to something.

"It was an interesting trip, a combination of alpine suffering and paragliding," Gadd says. "It blew the whole time; it was incredibly windy. The sailplane pilots said we were suicidal, the paragliders thought we were nuts. I'm getting used to it, everybody says what I want to do is nuts, but this time I think they were pretty much right."

But while the wind howled over towering peaks of the Andes, Gadd and his teammates, American pilots Othar Lawrence and Chris Santacroce, did manage to hook up with local pilots to fly along sections of the great range, on both the Chilean and Argentinean sides. They flew in the early mornings and evenings before the wind picked up, and on one flight an Andean condor flew with the paragliders, rising in the thermals alongside them. For the most part, however, bird sightings were minimal.

"It was so windy I think even the birds were hunkered down," Gadd says. "Every day it was blowing so hard that if we were in the air we would be killed. The few times we tried to push it at all we had pretty terrifying flights, even blown backwards. It was one of those trips where I could have done with a little less adventure."

Fortunately, apart from the standard bumps and bruises, the team suffered no injuries.

And after waiting out horrendous weather for days and days, they were finally rewarded. While hanging out at the Portillo,

Chile, ski resort, where the managers provided the team with a chalet to sleep in (the resort was closed for the summer), the wind finally subsided.

Gadd and Santacroce launched – Lawrence had given up and gone home – around 5:30 p.m., knowing sunset was four hours away. In the alpenglow they flew for two hours, soaring to heights of 4500 metres among 6000-metre peaks, over the Continental Divide, from Chile to Argentina, across the roof of the southern hemisphere.

"We flew over the heart of the Andes, the wildest, coolest part of the Andes," Gadd gushes. "That flight was the single best flight I've ever done. These were huge, huge mountains, like the Rockies on steroids. We were going from peak to peak to peak, asking ourselves, 'Is this real?' It was just amazing soaring up these huge peaks, flying in this beautiful alpenglow."

That flight was the reward for a tough trip, one which included hiking for nearly four days from Santiago, Chile, to Mendoza, Argentina, repeatedly climbing 2000 vertical metres over mountain passes, carrying twenty-kilogram packs loaded with paragliders, bivy sacs, sleeping bags and food, through stunning alpine terrain that sees few – if any – human visitors.

"We were the first people to hike paragliders across the entire Andes," Gadd laughs. "I guess your could call it alpine paragliding."

Throughout the journey, Gadd shot video footage – including while he was flying – as did filmmaker Pat Morrow from the ground, capturing the journey for a film called *Andes Adventure*, produced by Gadd.

And if the physical challenges weren't enough, the maps they relied on – tactical charts put out by the us military for jet pilots, the only type of pilots ever to fly the area – left something to be desired.

"The detail was lacking, so we often didn't really know where we were," Gadd says. "We got the best maps that were available. We actually had good maps of the Andes, but we were never in that part of the Andes. Nobody wants maps for where we were."

Some Chilean friends helped provide useful information, he says, while the improbability of their project generated considerable local support, including some from the Chilean and Argentinean air forces, as well as an avalanche of letters sent back and forth between Canadian, us and South American embassies, which allowed them to fly their route legally.

But exploration and adventure are exactly what he loves about flying, Gadd insists.

"You can never see the air. There are maps of what the ground looks like, but flying is exploration every time," he explains. "You never know what you're getting into. With flying you have to rely on your experience and your team and go exploring."

Gadd says he first thought about flying over the Andes when he climbed South America's highest peak, 6959-metre Aconcagua, about ten years earlier in beautiful conditions he thought were ideal for flying. He chose to go in December, he says, because, "somebody told me it was less windy in the Andes this time of year."

As a bonus, though, Gadd says he did see a lot of potential ice-climbing routes.

CLIMBER EXPLORES LOVE AND GRAVITY (2007)

> Steph **Davis**

It all started the day Steph Davis, an eighteen-year-old, non-athletic classical pianist and book-loving nerd, accepted an invitation to try rock climbing for the very first time. Fourteen years later, in October 2005, that same woman fulfilled her goal of being the first woman to free-climb the Salathe Wall, a 1000-metre route rated an extremely difficult 13b, which snakes its way up Yosemite's vertical to overhanging El Capitan.

The journey that transpired in the years between is what comprises the pages of her collection of personal essays, *High Infatuation: A Climber's Guide to Love and Gravity*, in which Davis describes the physical experiences of travelling to climb glaciated mountains and giant vertical walls in places as far-flung as Patagonia, Kyrgyzstan and Baffin Island.

But she also describes the journey that evolved in her head, and in her heart, as she embraced a life dedicated to climbing – a journey that culminated in the physical and mental struggles she battled throughout her marathon ten-day Salathe climb, the aftermath of which left her to face a personal crisis of belief and faith.

During that time of crisis, she thought about fear, she thought about attachment and she thought about death.

The crisis endured for nearly two years, until the start of the 2007 summer, when she decided there were two things she had to do: the first, free solo two classic routes on the Diamond, the 300-metre vertical east face of 4348-metre Longs Peak in Colorado's Rocky Mountain National Park; and the second, learn how to sky dive as a prerequisite toward BASE jumping.

And after only 150 skydives, thirty-four-year-old Davis leapt off a 155-metre bridge, an accomplishment she admits was slightly ahead of the average schedule.

"It's not normal to start skydiving and three months into it do your first BASE jump," Davis explains. "It's kind of accelerated."

Leaping into difficult challenges, however, is something Davis has trained herself to do ever since her very first day rock climbing, and it's what has become a key element of her persona. Insisting she was not born with any supernatural levels of talent, Davis has spent her adult life embracing the many and varied disciplines of what is a rather specialized sport to begin with. As a result, she has reached the highest levels of competence and skill on short but intense bouldering problems a metre or two from the ground, climbing complex aid routes and sleeping on portaledges suspended a thousand metres up Yosemite's vertical rock walls, hunkering down in snow caves for days on end with only the barest of essentials to escape howling blizzards in high-altitude snow and ice terrain, and climbing solo without ropes on sheer rock faces – the culmination of which has placed Davis among an elite few worldwide and among an even smaller group of female climbing peers.

Despite the potential appearance of a person engaged in a continual battle, however, Davis embraces a philosophy of maintaining balance between tackling the next crux and flowing seamlessly through challenges like a river through a placid countryside.

So, when she found herself consumed by doubt after reaching what, at the time, was a pinnacle of accomplishment, through a process that was nothing short of gruelling, Davis knew she had to find her way back to that balance.

The only way to handle her fears, she concluded, would be to embrace the act of letting go – and free-falling from an airplane, then from the much more committing height of a bridge, and climbing technically challenging vertical rock routes without any safety ropes were, for Davis, the undisputable solutions.

Through the course of her 150 skydives – for which she relocated to Boulder, Colorado, for the summer – Davis says she was immediately captured with a desire to improve her skills and technique, the same way she always has with climbing.

"Skydiving gives you a really engaging two minutes of flight," she says. "It's very technical, the body positions. And you're thinking how can I correct my body position to fly longer?"

Climbing the routes on the Diamond, solo and without a rope or any other safety equipment, was simply another one of those challenges she felt she had to embrace.

"The Diamond – I knew it was just the right thing," Davis says. "It's a personality type thing. I get really captured by stuff. I think of a challenge, something that interests me, and the more I do it, the more things unfold. It's an obsessive quality. You see people all the time, how they find that one thing that just fits for them."

Her very first climb on the Diamond, she explains, was a pivotal experience.

Four years after she started climbing, Davis explored her first route on the Diamond at the age of twenty-two. Until then, her rock climbing experiences had been limited to simpler and shorter climbs at popular crags.

"It was my first time exposed to anything beyond typical rock climbing," she says. "It was an alpiney environment, a whole different style of climbing from what I was used to. The Diamond is where I developed skills I expanded to the big mountains. It was a turning point and a special place as a young climber. The idea of going back and free soloing it this summer was really appealing."

Recalling the sheer angst and both physical and mental struggles she endured to accomplish her Salathe climb – which included recruiting a stranger to belay her for the ten-day epic effort – Davis approached her Diamond climbs differently. Although her ultimate goal was to climb the routes unroped, she climbed them first with partners to familiarize herself with the moves and the course of the climbs.

"After I did it, I didn't really want to have such a thing in my life as consuming as Salathe," Davis says. "I was proud of myself, but I fought tooth and nail. I wondered, 'Should things be like that, or should they flow?' So with the Diamond, it was super calculated. I was analytical. I spent lots of time with friends, but I found someone for whom it was a good thing, too. I found people who really wanted to climb each of those routes roped. It was fun; it was part of the plan. Then when I was alone, it felt really good, it felt right. Everything felt great, and everything went well."

Free soloing, like BASE jumping, she says, requires a full commitment to letting go of everything that has the potential to hold a person back.

"With BASE, you can't screw up. You have only a few seconds to do what you have to do," she explains.

And with climbing, Davis says she craves an experience that heightens all her awareness as she explores nature's playground.

"Climbing lets me be outdoors, in nature," she says. "But climbing gives you time to contemplate. I love that element of risk that makes it urgent and deep. That really captures me. I need it to be deep, serious, life-threatening, intense – that clicks me in a little harder. It makes me focus. I like that directed effort. I love being exhausted and having to maintain technique; that's the kind of climbing I love. I do love all kinds of climbing, but the thing that calls to me the most is maintaining technique while I'm exhausted."

All the while insisting she's a private person, Davis took one of her biggest risks ever when she shared some of her most personal thoughts, doubts and fears in the pages of her book, a collection of essays that had been published in magazines over a period of several years.

"I totally struggled with that," Davis admits. "I've always been a writer; I've kept journals since I was twenty. I've always written [climbing magazine] articles, but they force you to be blow by blow about the technicalities of the climb. When I wrote the book, it was super personal.

"But when I read other people's stories, I'm only interested in what's inside this person. I was super nervous just before it was published, but I figured that's who I am, that's the book, that's it. And I got great feedback. It's been amazing. I was really happy that I hadn't backed off and made it sterile. Everybody's thinking these things – this was really hard, this was really scary, and I had to work very hard to do it. Everybody works hard, everybody gets scared, and it's not easy for anybody."

SONNIE TROTTER'S GOLD MEDAL CLIMB (2007)

> Sonnie **Trotter**

Growing up in Newmarket, Ontario, Sonnie Trotter played hockey and competed in gymnastics. At sixteen, he tried climbing on an indoor wall at the Canadian National Exhibition and instantly fell in love with the creativity and freedom of movement. He's been pursing that freedom on some of the hardest rock climbs all over the world ever since, becoming recognized as Canada's most accomplished free-climber.

In June 2006, after three years of effort, Trotter successfully climbed Cobra Crack at Squamish, BC's Cirque of the Uncrackables wall, at the time the hardest traditional rock climb anywhere, rated at 5.14a/b. After years in Squamish, Trotter, twenty-seven, lives in Canmore, Alberta.

Where did you go on your first climbing road trip?
My girlfriend at the time and I went to Rifle in Colorado during the summer of 1998 on a shoestring budget. We were very, very poor and

highly thrifty, and we took this tiny little Toyota Tercel that couldn't go faster than 100 kilometres. We slept in a tent in this free camping area called the Dirt Pile. Apparently it is highly radioactive land with a fairly high level of uranium in the soil, and after a month we were questioning if we should pay for camping and for better quality of living. In the end, we decided we couldn't afford it and stayed the rest of the trip. I recall living on mostly ramen noodles, peanut butter and cereal – I even remember eating cereal for a week without milk, just water.

I don't think I've been home for more than three or four months since that first trip. I've spent countless months traversing the lower forty-eight from Texas to California. In 2002 I made a successful five-month coast-to-coast trip across Canada. My goal was to spend as little money as possible while I visited every significant climbing area and small town along the way, from Halifax to Victoria.

One thing I've come to realize through climbing and exploring is that fear is an illusion. No matter where we go, there will always be good people around a warm fire, there will always be a friend to share a cold beer with and there will always be a new adventure lurking somewhere over them there hills.

What was your first international climbing trip like?

I went to Austria to climb at the Junior World Cup in 1997. I remember being extremely overwhelmed by the level of professionalism. The kids over there had pro trainers and dietitians and massage therapists. We had some team sweaters and that was about it. It was rather intimidating. But the landscape was beautiful. I was awestruck by the quality of rock in Europe, and I fell in love with the chocolate, the bread and the cheese. And I learned that I have many vices and don't have the discipline or the passion for world championship climbing.

What's been your favourite climbing trip?

I really loved our 2005 trip, when we went to Malta. We did three weeks of deep-water soloing over the Mediterranean. No ropes, everything was climbed up from a kayak that we paddled around. We made some outrageous first ascents – more than I could have imagined.

But in terms of productivity, it was a trip I did to Spain with Tommy Caldwell and friends in 2001. We managed a high volume of climbs at a very high level of climbing. That trip taught me much about hard climbing and what it takes to be really good and comfortable on stone. It launched me into a new level.

What attracts you to rock climbing? Do you interpret different kinds of rock differently – granite, quartzite, limestone, sandstone?

I must say, I rarely find stone that I don't enjoy climbing on. It's all good. Every rock is different. I switch from one to the other all the time, and I think, by mixing it up frequently, one makes me climb better on the other. And I'm attracted to beautiful movements. If a climb flows really well, then that's what matters the most to me. I try to pick out a beautiful line, like a skier choosing a descent route. I pick a line that is striking in nature, challenging – sometimes on the verge of my ability – and that glides from one handhold to another. Some pretty ugly climbs get a lot of attention, though, and when I finally get to see them I lose interest. I'd rather climb a 5.6 that was fun and beautiful than climb a 5.14 that was ugly, painful and awkward.

What do you look for in new routes?

I don't look for anything in particular; most of the time a new route will jump out at me. They say you can't choose who you love, and sometimes climbing is the same way – routes choose me. Sometimes it's the way the light hits a certain wall, or the colour or the angle. I'm very flexible, very open-minded and I feel that I have a fairly big appetite for beauty, so I will climb anything that moves me. I suppose I'm in a different position, where if I do seek out a new climb, I want it to be hard and very challenging, which to me is fun. It's rare, but those gems are out there and I live for them and the experience they offer me.

What inspired you to climb Cobra Crack?

I'd heard rumours of an unclimbable crack. I'd heard stories of legends who failed on the climb and some experts who declared it impossible. It was these stories and the lure of trying to do something nobody else can do that piqued my interest. It was a challenge – a challenge with no guaranteed outcome. It was very exciting.

I was inspired to try it because of its aesthetics. You don't need to be an expert climber to understand or appreciate the beauty of the Crack. It's shaped like a giant 100-foot wave – clean, flawless – and without the crack that slithers down the centre of this magnificent wall, it would otherwise be blank and, without question, impossible. So we in the climbing community see it as a gift. It's very special.

And as much as I wanted to do it for myself and my own experience, I think somewhere deep down inside I also wanted to climb it to represent Canada. I feel Canadian climbers are overlooked on the world scale. We just don't have the season or the rock or the support that other countries have, so in a way the Cobra Crack was a way for me to climb one of the world's hardest routes, by a Canadian on Canadian soil. It's sort of like my gold medal.

Why do you write your Summit Secrets column in Gripped *magazine?*

I write it because I enjoy it, truly. I think writing is fun, and I thought that *Gripped* was lacking in the department where pros can give tips to beginners, which is who the column is designed for. It's a great way for people to connect and we have fun with it. The money I get is marginal, but I keep putting gas in my car and every little bit helps.

Have you taken Barry Blanchard up on the suggestion he made when you interviewed him: that you should go alpine climbing?

No! If the end of the world was coming along and the only way to survive was to climb up into the mountains, I would follow Barry to the ends of the earth and trust his every command, for he is without question one of the funniest, strongest and most experienced climbers I can think of. But until that day comes, I will stick to the rock, not the mountains. The truth is I hate being cold. Hate it. I enjoy medium-sized alpine adventures. I will cross a glacier if it will get me to good rock climbing – but I have very little interest in going so high up a mountain that I need to wear full down and use ice tools – those things are sharp and the climbing is often quite miserable.

How do you support yourself?

I realized that I love travel and climbing so much that I wanted to do it for the rest of my life. I can't think of a better way to kill time on this planet than by running around in the world's grandest playgrounds. I chase the sun, the surf. I surround myself with people who smile a lot. I knew that it was going to be hard and challenging to get paid to have fun, so I've joined forces with some of the great companies of our sport to help sponsor me. I write articles; I make short videos – this year Cobra Crack won the Banff [Mountain] Film Festival for Best Short Film – I take photographs and I teach lessons. I make a living from various different sources and it all comes together to help pay the rent and keep me chasing my dream.

What is your dream trip?

A sunny day, a gentle breeze, in a warm, beautiful place where wildflowers grow. It would need to be close to the ocean with world-class limestone. My girlfriend would be there, practising yoga on a flat rock, and some great friends to climb with who have a sense of humour. A place where we can watch the sunset and enjoy a bottle of wine.

Why did you choose to go climbing in Australia in 2007?

The place is legendary. It just has all this amazing history and the climbing is the best sandstone found in the world. It's bullet hard and it moves very three dimensional; climbers are always putting our bodies into strange and awkward positions, which to me is very interesting. It's a constant puzzle, like a game of vertical twister. I am always on the rock in some contorted posture thinking to myself, "Now how the hell am I going to get out of this one?" It keeps me on my toes. And, I always wanted to see the country and find out what it's all about. I will say, kangaroo tastes great.

What's your favourite thing to do when you're not climbing?

I love to spend time with my girlfriend, Lydia. We just hang out together, laughing and enjoying each other's company; she is extraordinary and a pleasure to be with. We joke a lot. Also, living in

Canmore, I go snowboarding quite often, but it's expensive and I need to watch my financial diet. Yoga is also a fun activity, good for the long-term health of our bodies, and I try to take it fairly seriously. But usually I'm climbing, thinking about climbing or writing about climbing. I don't know why it consumes so much of my life and I don't think about why anymore. I just go with it – I just love it.

DARING CLIMBERS SCALE BOBBING ICEBERGS (2005)

> Ben **Firth** and Will **Gadd**

The first free-floating iceberg Ben Firth chose to tackle off the coast of northern Labrador reminded him of all the ice on the vertical, football-field-sized Weeping Wall in Jasper National Park being compacted into a giant lump and tossed into the ocean, its contents pressurized into a fifty-metre-high, solid mass of brittle ice floating in the sea.

And as the Atlantic Ocean rose and fell, so did the iceberg.

"The big ones take the swells, small ones definitely move around a lot," Firth says. "The boat is bobbing five feet at a time, and you've got to time it just perfect to swing in. Then as soon as you're on, the boat pulls away and you're hanging there. It was like being on a big eggshell. You'd throw your tool in there and hear this blood-curdling Crack! – like taking an ice cube and throwing warm water on it."

Attempting to time his first leap perfectly, Firth's crampon-clad feet skittered on the fibreglass boat deck and he suddenly found himself hanging over the cold, deep Atlantic by a single ice axe hooked into the swaying ice wall.

"I just pulled it together and started climbing. It was awesome!" Firth says. "After that it was like any type of climbing: once you're engaged it's not too bad. It's the precursor that gets to you mentally."

For Firth and Canmore, Alberta-based adventurer Will Gadd, there was plenty of time to imagine climbing icebergs. The duo started planning the trip in 2003, but the adventure finally became a financial reality two years later, after Gadd approached energy drink manufacturer Red Bull for sponsorship.

Working to produce a Fox TV special, the crew, which included Firth, Gadd, Canmore-based mountain photographer Andrew Querner and videographer Pat Morrow, originally planned to climb among hundreds of icebergs that float south from Greenland in late spring and early summer past the Newfoundland coast, where iceberg watching is a tourism mainstay that lures visitors from around the world. Discovering a scarcity of bergs during the June 2005 season, the group flew another six hours north to Makkovik – population 350 – in northern Labrador.

"Even then, we only had three bergs in a week we could get on," Morrow says. "It was hard work finding them; then it was exciting as all hell for the guys to climb them."

From the local population of Innu and Inuit subsistence crab fishermen, the team hired a family to ferry them the daily six-hour return trip to the floating icebergs.

"They were ocean people, well familiar with the properties and behaviour of the bergs," Morrow says. "They told Will how dangerous it was; they were quite concerned, and also for themselves, getting so close to the bergs."

Before attempting to climb any of the bergs, the crew would fire upon the floating sculptures with a shotgun or .303 rifle to test its tensile strength. Some broke apart instantly and fell over with a great splash. A mere ten minutes after he got off one iceberg, Firth says, it rolled right over.

"It was fun to experiment, but I don't think I'd be doing it again," Firth says. "It's too dangerous. You never know if it's going to snap in half or roll."

For the most part, Firth says climbing floating icebergs required that he and Gadd continuously adapt to new and changing situations.

"Just getting away from the usual ice mediums in the mountains – we thought about what other frozen water mediums exist," Firth explains. "Icebergs are always cool formations, plus being out at sea, it's a new form of deep-water soloing [where ropeless climbers scale sea-bound rock cliffs to heights of fifteen metres or more before falling into the water], but not using the water as a crash pad."

Although Gadd and Firth did wear full dry suits and life jackets, neither really wanted to test their safety equipment.

"There was no guarantee they could be fished out by a rescue boat," Morrow says.

"You don't want to be attached, so you're soloing the whole time," Firth says. "Then you have to downclimb what you just climbed up and you have to think about that. The cracks aren't as loud when you go down – only then you have to get into that damn bobbing boat."

PARTNERSHIPS EASIER IN THE WILDERNESS THAN THE LIVING ROOM (2006)

> Pat and Baiba **Morrow**, Will **Gadd** and Kim **Csizmazia**, Karsten **Heuer** and Leanne **Allison**

Being partners in the middle of the wilderness is often easier than being partners in the living room.

That was one common thread shared by three couples who comprised a panel titled Dynamic Duos at the 2006 Banff Mountain Film Festival.

"We travel really well together, that's easy," says internationally ranked ice climber and paraglider Will Gadd of himself and live-in partner Kim Csizmazia, former women's world ice climbing champion. "Then when we're home, we have to deal with real life. Real life is really annoying."

In a climbing or similar adventure situation, partners have to work together for reasons of safety and success of the endeavour, Gadd says, regardless of their personal relationship.

"Some of the things that are important in an adventure relationship are the same as any adventure partnership," Gadd says.

At the same time, however, knowing each other more intimately as live-in partners can often affect decision-making in stressful situations, adds Baiba Morrow, who has shared a home and adventures to remote corners of the world with husband Pat for more than two decades.

"Decisions may not be the same when you have all these other emotional elements involved," Baiba says.

Some stressful situations might even produce unexpected reactions.

Gadd once grew so furious with a competition judge that he wanted to slug him. Knowing that would result in ejection from the competition, he held back, but infuriated with the treatment of her partner and overcome by a protective urge, Csizmazia hit the judge.

Travelling together for long periods of time in challenging situations can generate a deeper bond between couples by virtue of a shared memory bank, says Karsten Heuer, who spent five months following the Porcupine caribou herd across the remote Yukon tundra with his wife, Leanne Allison – as their honeymoon.

"You end up with this bank of incredibly intense moments and memories, and a bank of experiences where you've overcome really big challenges in the past," Heuer says.

At times, he says, communication between him and Allison in such a focused, intense world transcended the verbal.

"It's almost something chemical, communication that transcends regular communication," Heuer says. "Then coming back and trying to relearn how to function using regular communication cuts like a knife. We call it the re-entry process."

While some people have asked him how he and Allison managed to be together all day, every day for five months with no other people around, Heuer turned the question around. "How do you guys get up in the morning, see each other for forty-five minutes, then go off to separate jobs and meet up at the end of the day while you're getting the kids off to hockey? How do you connect?"

At the start of a big expedition, Allison says she and Heuer experience a period of adjustment to being away from the comforts of home and friends and to the weight of a heavy backpack.

"There's a tendency in that environment to blame absolutely everything on your partner," Allison says. "We're finding a similar adjustment with parenting."

Now raising two-year-old son Zev, both admit to missing the intensity of long wilderness trips and express their hope to incorporate their exploring lifestyle into their family life while their son is still in his formative years and guided by his natural internal rhythms. But those trips would have to be scaled back in terms of intensity and potential dangers.

"We're hoping this adventuring duo becomes an adventuring trio," Heuer says. "We're willing to take risks with him, maybe some that are not acceptable to conventional society, but not as great risks as when it was just the two of us."

"But I'm still of the mind that driving on icy highways and things we do in everyday life are just as risky as what we do in the mountains," Allison adds.

Lifestyles of adventure, however, are all about choices, says Baiba Morrow.

"If we had chosen to have kids, that would have totally changed everything. It was a conscious decision not to," she says.

While adding a child to the home and the adventures requires adjustment, so does a change in individual focus, Gadd adds.

Retired from competitive climbing and pursuing a master's degree in creative writing, Csizmazia comments she'd gone from "one bum lifestyle to the next."

For her and Gadd, Csizmazia explains, living a lifestyle dedicated to adventure pursuits means "living richly below a certain level of income."

"If I have a container of beans, a case of chips and a jar of salsa, I'm pretty much good to go," Gadd admits. "I'm still full-on obsessed with climbing rocks and icicles, and Kim is getting her creative writing degree. There's some adjustment, but I'm cool with that."

At home or in the wilderness, what it comes down to, Baiba Morrow says, is that partnerships are about working together.

"For any partnership to work you have to acknowledge what each does well," she says..

In the end, all agree their relationships are based on the fact they enjoy each other as individuals.

"It's about the relationship, not about the adventure," Csizmazia says. "In the end, we really enjoy being together, whether we're talking about avalanche conditions or paying the bills."

THE PATH (2007)

> Sonnie **Trotter**

Whenever Sonnie Trotter goes rock climbing at a new crag, he scopes out the walls in search of the most difficult climb.

"I get teased that whenever I go to a new crag, I always want to do the hardest route," Trotter admits.

True to form, one tranquil summer day in 2005, Trotter followed the busy tourist trail to the vertical, multicoloured quartzite cliffs at the far end of Lake Louise, and before the day was over he'd found his line.

"I saw the line a couple of years ago, and right away I said, 'I want to do that!'" Trotter recalls. "I'm always attracted to the most beautiful, and the hardest. It looked like the hardest."

So on August 21, after about ten days of effort, Trotter did just that, accomplishing the first ascent of a route he christened The Path.

Considered by many to be Canada's top rock climber, Trotter, twenty-seven, has been featured on covers and inside pages of international climbing magazines for two of his previous free-climbing accomplishments – establishing new routes at the highest end of the difficulty scale, using only his hands and feet to progress up the wall. And, in Trotter's case, climbing those routes in traditional style, placing removable nuts and camming devices in natural cracks for protection in case of a fall, rather than relying on bolts permanently drilled into the rock.

One of those routes, Cobra Crack, rated 5.14b/c, which follows a single, continuous crack up an otherwise featureless thirty-metre overhanging granite wall in Squamish, BC, is currently the most difficult traditional climb in all of Canada – and one of only a handful of that difficulty worldwide.

The Path, Trotter says, deserves equal respect and attention.

"It is one of my hardest, most memorable creations," Trotter says. "After climbing Cobra Crack last summer, and then making fast progress but not redpointing Rhapsody [a route in Scotland], the world's other hardest trad climb, in May, I feel it's safe to say that this climb ranks among the world's most difficult. I can't compare the three, as they all climb so differently, but I feel that it's solid 5.14 trad, and I am stoked that climbs of this nature are becoming more and more feasible."

Before beginning his project, Trotter learned his intended route, which continues on an overhanging wall above a route called Wicked Gravity, rated 5.11a, had been fitted with permanent bolts about twenty-five years ago, at a time when it would have been the most difficult climb of that genre and when no local climbers possessed the skills to climb it.

"It's gorgeous, the colour – it's jaw dropping," Trotter says. "It's intimidating because it looks blank upon first glance. It's just as special and magical as Cobra Crack, in a different way. It's a daunting-looking overhang. I like the thought of the impossible. I was almost hoping it would be harder, that it would take me three years."

On his first two reconnaissance trips up the wall, he climbed the line, clipping his rope into the fixed bolts for protection. On his third trip, he brought a rack of gear, to ascertain it could be climbed using natural gear for protection, rather than the fixed bolts. Climbing an easier route on an adjacent wall, he was able to rappel the length of the route from a bolted anchor at the top, coincidentally placed so as to be accessible to both routes. From that vantage point, he decided his route should follow a natural weakness in the rock to the left, whereas the bolts led to the right.

"I just wanted to make certain the climb would go free," Trotter explains. "And I realized the whole thing would go on natural gear."

Overall, he made about ten attempts on the climb, every four or five days spread over several weeks. Then, after warming up on Wicked Gravity, he made the redpoint – climbing the route he had rehearsed, without falling or hanging on the rope, from bottom to top, placing his gear on lead.

The climb, he says, took about thirty minutes, with the most difficult move consisting of a five-foot sideways lunge with pencil-width ledges for his fingers to land on.

"You really only get one shot at that move. I call it an iron cross move," Trotter says. "When you think about what you're hanging on to, thirty minutes seems like a long time."

Before making the climb, however, Trotter made the potentially controversial decision to permanently chop the bolts from the rock, dictating that anyone repeating the climb should do so in the same trad style in which he climbed it, and increasing its level of difficulty and danger in case of a fall.

"I've created what it is now," Trotter says. "It's a very distinct line. Maybe I uphold my own certain style of ethics, but so far, I've had great feedback, not one negative comment."

By having its bolts removed, he says, the climb offers the same challenges for anyone attempting to repeat it as it did for him on first ascent.

"Why does everything have to be easier for everyone?" Trotter asks. "Should you pave the trail to the Back of the Lake just to make it easier? The challenge is the same for me as for anyone else. [Chopping the bolts] just changes the style. For me, style is everything. I felt I was able to climb the route in a style I felt good about. I like the way the rock dictates the way you climb it, rather than by the bolts someone placed. Maybe my actions will influence the next generation in a positive way."

While he admits there are several more difficult "sport" routes in Canada fixed with drilled bolts, The Path is at the top of those without.

"There are definitely harder climbs in Canada, but not in this style," Trotter says. "Along with Cobra Crack, this is one opportunity for rock climbing in Canada to get its fifteen minutes of fame. People are out there doing it every day, pushing hard, then all the recognition they get is to go have a beer. This is like my gold medal for Canada, as a Canadian who can climb on the world stage."

A self-admitted part explorer, part perfectionist, Trotter says, with this project completed, he looks forward to his next, including a return to Scotland, hopefully to make the second ever ascent of Rhapsody.

"It's done now. I have to think of something else to do," Trotter says. "I have a lot of energy; it seems like I always need to be working on something. I like to find things that haven't been done. I put all my energy into it and master it till it's done. Then I move on."

UNDERGROUND ICE CLIMBING LIKE A SCENE FROM *ALIEN* (2007)

> Will **Gadd**

Throughout his years of devotion to the sport, Will Gadd has explored a wide variety of climbing media – from fat and solid vertical waterfalls to thinly glazed gymnastic mixed climbs, from steep dangling giant icicles to dome-like ice cave roofs, and even free-floating icebergs.

A former world champion whose first memory of climbing a frozen waterfall dates back to when he was ten or eleven years old, he's won every major competition in existence and has dozens of new routes of ever-increasing difficulty to his credit.

But nothing, he states, compared to the ice inside Sweden after he spent half of April 2007 exploring a virtual ice wonderland – underground in abandoned mine shafts.

"These mines are everywhere in central and western Sweden; the country is just riddled with them," he says. "There's more ice hiding under the surface of Sweden. There's a lot of ice!"

The mines represent something of a Swedish historical treasure, he says, from where miners extracted gold, silver and iron for hundreds of years. Long abandoned, some of them were among the most productive iron mines in the world.

But while no longer fruitful as mining sites, the caves offered an enormous wealth of climbing opportunities for Gadd, who just turned forty, and his expedition mates, including Swedish–Norwegian climber Andreas Spak, us photographer Christian Pondella and local Swedish climber Daniel Karlsson.

"The mines are a labyrinth. They're insanely complicated, and they go on for miles," Gadd says. "We only got to about one tenth of the places he [Karlsson] thought we should check out. That's what he spends his weekends doing. It's just bizarre. You drive out there and there's no ice on the surface, the land is flat. Then you rappel seventy metres into a hole in the ground and you're surrounded by ice."

JERRY KOBALENKO STOPS FOR A SELF-PORTRAIT IN LABRADOR, THEN AND NOW.

WILL GADD SOARS INTO THE SUNSET OVER THE ANDES, CHILE/ARGENTINA BORDER.

BEN FIRTH STICKS HIS TOOLS INTO AN ICEBERG OFF THE LABRADOR COAST.

BAIBA AND PAT MORROW.

LOGAN GRAYLING TAKES A
BIG PLUNGE ON THE SECOND
DESCENT OF JOHNSTON FALLS,
CANADIAN ROCKIES.

SONNIE TROTTER WORKS
OUT THE MOVES ON THE
PATH, BACK OF THE LAKE,
CANADIAN ROCKIES.

WARREN MACDONALD CLIMBS MOUNT KILIMANJARO, TANZANIA.

COLIN ANGUS AND JULIE WAFAEI (ANGUS) WORK THE OARS ON THEIR JOURNEY ACROSS THE ATLANTIC OCEAN.

On the surface, the climbers were comfortable in T-shirts in 20°C temperatures. It was an unusually warm winter for the far northern country. Minutes later, they'd be in winter – and in the dark.

"It's kind of like rappelling into a giant cooler. The ice forms like stalactites and stalagmites," Gadd says. "It looks surreal; it forms drip by drip by drip. There's actually a lot of colour in the ice: there's iron ore leeching out of the walls, and then there's blues and whites and greens. The features are just insane, and there's no wind. I've climbed all over the world and I've never seen ice like this. It was like a movie set, where you expect to see an alien come slithering out."

While he said he expected the site would become popular based on its sheer magnitude, climbers would also likely be attracted by the assurance of consistently good-quality ice.

"It's always the same temperature. It's not affected by global warming in any way," Gadd explains. "It's almost constant. I don't know if it's bad luck, but I've had so many problems finding ice on other trips – in Norway and Nepal and Europe. It's nice to find ice that will always be there."

Gadd first learned about the mines some four years earlier, when he was presenting a slide show in Norway and one of the audience members showed him some photos.

"He said, 'You've really got to try this,' and it took me four years, but I'll definitely go back," Gadd says. "There is a world of ice to be climbed."

Filming the adventure in the underground vertical landscape, however, presented challenges for the pair of British filmmakers producing a show for the *Jeep World of Adventure Sports* series, which will air on the US network NBC. As well, Gadd says, they planned to create a DVD version and another film version to be entered in the Banff Mountain Film Festival competition.

"It was just so different," Gadd says. "We'd go down and scout it out with just our headlamps. In some places there was a bit of light coming in from the surface, but mostly it was dark. Then we'd fire up the big film lights and get a sense of the space. We got down to about 300 metres in one hole, and later we talked to one of the owners of the mine – he said that one went down to about 500 metres."

The climbers had to secure themselves to the vertical shafts at all times, since a fall on a casual five-degree slope could send them plummeting hundreds of metres into darkness.

"You don't see the danger; you're only worried about what you can see in your headlight," Gadd says. "We'd be casually walking on an ice shelf, and we'd have another 300 metres below us. It was like big-wall cave ice climbing. We thought we'd drop down a shaft and then be standing on a big hockey rink, but it was never like that. We'd be 200 metres below the surface and sometimes it was pretty exposed. It was pretty tricky. There were a lot of moments on this trip where we said, uhm . . ."

One day the team experienced a heart-stopping fright when a giant chunk of falling ice exploded to pieces dangerously close to the camera crew.

"We did a bunch of cleaning to get rid of some ice lingering in the spring sun near the top of a shaft," Gadd explains. "The camera crew was positioned in what we'd decided was a safe place lower in the shaft, but they'd moved out to capture a better shot, and when the giant block fell about 100 metres, it blew up not too far from them. It shook the camera crew up, and me too, but in the end the only damage was a little piece of flash equipment that got broken. If that's all that got broken on a trip like this, that's cool!"

During a trip such as this one, which lasted two weeks, experience and solid thinking are essential, he says.

"On any given day, there's lots of things on a trip like this that could kill you," Gadd says. "That's a big thing, keeping each other safe, and yourself. We had a strong crew, and that makes a big difference. I'm lucky; I have really competent people I work with."

As with all his adventures, Gadd says meeting the locals was a treat, particularly former mine workers.

"We kept meeting up with people who used to work in the mines," Gadd says. "They're really proud of their mines and the work they did in them. It was great to get the history from the older locals. We'd hear all about the mines, and they'd tell us about all their near misses, and we'd tell them about the near misses we had."

Surprisingly, the locals were approving and encouraging of the climbers' exploits, he adds. And as a bonus, Gadd points out Sweden is a thoroughly modern country to visit, and although expensive against the Canadian dollar, not as prohibitively expensive as its Scandinavian neighbours, Iceland and Norway.

Practicalities aside, Gadd admits the uniqueness of the ice mines made for a genuinely memorable – and challenging – trip.

"I think it was a big stretch for everyone on this trip," Gadd says. "It was a hard trip. Accessing stuff was always difficult. We always had to be tied in, there were no floors. It's one of the harder trips I've ever done. It was a tough trip, but it was very rewarding."

LOGAN'S LAUNCH (2007)

> Logan **Grayling**

Letting go, he says, was the hardest part.

Long before he did so, Logan Grayling knew that the moment he released his hand grip from a slab of rock on the bank of Johnston Creek, the kayak he was sitting in would immediately be swept into the surging current. He also knew that as the powerful flow plunged 30.5 metres off the barely boat-wide lip of Upper Johnston Falls, his kayak – with him in it – would go with it.

And he knew there would be no changing his mind.

"It went by so fast," Logan admits. "Pushing off that rock was definitely one of the scariest parts."

While there wasn't much time to think while he dropped through the air, suspended amidst the frothing torrent for a few long seconds, before his boat pierced the bubbling pool at the base of the falls, Logan had thought about the task for a long time before he hiked up the popular tourist trail on June 13, 2007.

Already an accomplished snowboarder, gymnast and surfer, the nineteen-year-old Canmore, Alberta, native took up kayaking when he was fifteen. Since then he has chased whitewater and first waterfall descents in Africa, Norway, Switzerland, Ecuador, California, Oregon, Vietnam and western Canada.

Logan started thinking about running Johnston Falls about two years into his kayaking career, but he was away travelling when the water level was at its highest and most optimum.

In the spring of 2007, he decided to think seriously about making his mark in his own backyard, at the site of a previous world record.

"It's in my backyard. I figured it was time a local did it," Logan says. "And it's a big one. Only one other person has ever done it."

That happened in 1999, when Washington State native Tao Berman ran the falls, setting a world record for the longest vertical drop in a kayak. At the time, the waterfall was measured at 30.04 metres. On the day Logan dropped off the lip, a high seasonal runoff had pushed the height of the falls to an even 30.5 metres. The current world record was 32.18 metres, set by Ed Lucero on Hay River's Alexandra Falls in the Northwest Territories in 2004.

But for Logan, dropping the falls wasn't about setting records or beating anyone else's – it was about testing his own abilities at the highest possible standard.

Prior to Johnston Canyon, the biggest waterfall Logan had kayaked was twenty metres, in Vietnam. To prepare for Johnston Falls, he hiked up the paved tourist trail to study the falls – the lip, the trajectory, the pool at its base – four times, in different seasons over several years.

One of the key things about a runnable waterfall, he explains, is that it offers a safe landing, with no rocks to crash into.

"You need a good amount of water, with a good volume, good line and definitely a nice lip," Logan says. "This one rolls off nicely at the lip."

Any waterfall with a wave curling at its lip would likely cause a kayak to flip back on itself, resulting in the kayaker landing on his head or on his back. Had Logan landed flat at the base of a waterfall of this calibre, the resulting injury would likely have been serious, or worse.

"I would have shattered every disc in my back," he states. "You'd either die or be a quadriplegic."

To help ensure he didn't land flat, Logan poured about six litres of water in the nose of his boat, a technique employed by Berman as well. Two days before his big drop, he hiked up to study the falls again.

"I wanted to figure out where I'm going, figure out my line, where the dangers are," he says.

Together with his paddling buddies he discussed the safety aspects of the drop – where he might get hurt and how, and from which locations downstream his two fellow paddlers should spot him. They also decided on the best perches from which to capture still and video images. On Monday evening, Logan made some phone calls to line up all the hands he needed for safety and video, including local kayaker Chris McTaggart; Nelson, BC, paddler Mikkel Duncan; outdoor adventure photographer Ryan Creary; and Banff filmmaker and long-time friend Andrew Hardingham, who would shoot video.

Then Logan tried not to think about his big plan. He and McTaggart went out for a few beers, eventually heading home around 2 a.m.

"I was trying to think of everything but kayaking," Logan says. "The more you think about it, you can psych yourself out. You think about what can go wrong before, you set up your safety. Then don't think about what can go wrong. It's better to know you can do it, and then just go do it."

When the crew walked up the pathway to the falls on Wednesday morning, the summer tourists were already there. As the team prepared themselves by setting up their tripods and paddling their kayaks into their safety positions, the tourists began to ask questions.

"People kept asking me if I was going to do it and my reaction was, 'No way! What, do you think I'm crazy?'" Logan recalls. "But when people realized I was actually going to, they gathered to watch."

While the tourists wondered about Logan's plans, his father, Christo, working in Banff only twenty kilometres away, had plenty of his own thinking to do.

"I'd known about it for years," Christo admits. "It was something that was always in his plans; it was one of his dreams. I never had any doubt that he wanted to. I just didn't know if the stars would line up. Sometimes you hope it's just talk, but that's rare; normally it's backed up."

When Logan returned from a creek-paddling festival in Montana on the Sunday night, he told his dad he was going to check out Johnston Falls the following day.

"When he came home on Monday night, he said, 'It's on,'" Christo said. "It was a pretty clear statement."

By the following day, Christo realized he had to work at controlling his own emotions. He was worried his son might be seriously injured or even killed. He was well aware that on his son's first trip to Africa, a good friend of Logan's had drowned in the White Nile only six metres away from Logan, on the same section they had been running day after day. When Logan was in Norway, a paddler with a faulty helmet had been sucked underwater and never emerged. Christo knew the stakes were high, but he also knew he had to turn his own thinking around.

"I could keep being Mr. Worrywart, asking way too many questions – which I am well known for," Christo says. "But I had to really put it in perspective. I had little influence over anything. I'm mostly okay with that. I totally trusted him, and he didn't need any negative energy. I'm also not stupid enough to know things can't fuck up. But I had a pretty high level of confidence in him, especially when he's planned something. I've always respected his solidness."

Throughout their childhoods, Logan and his younger brother, Luke, were enthusiastically encouraged to participate in any sport or activity that interested them, and the family travelled together to far-off places to surf and pursue adventure. Both sons responded by excelling at many sports, particularly gymnastics and snowboarding. When at seventeen Logan headed off to Ecuador for his first international kayaking expedition, Christo – who at eighteen had travelled to India and the Himalayas on his first international adventure – was proud and supportive. So was Logan's mom, Barb Hertell, who had left Toronto at the age of eighteen to go climbing in the Canadian Rockies.

Knowing his family supported him as he prepared to drop off Johnston Falls meant a lot to him, too, Logan says, as did having his brother on site relaying communications by radio.

"Luke wanted to come. He got out of school for the day. I was happy he was there, for support. He helped me stay calm before the drop," Logan says. "My mom wanted nothing to do with it; she wanted to hear none of it. My dad knew I'd made the right decision."

And as he let go of his grip from the rock at the creekbank, Logan was confident he'd made the right decision, too. Keeping his position in the centre of the boat and his line off the lip straight, off he plunged into bubble-filled air. About eighty feet down he tucked his body forward, staying centred until he landed in the churning pool. Taking care the force of his landing didn't cause him to hit himself with his paddle, he did graze the rock wall with his head and paddle just before he landed.

"Everyone got into position; everything felt right. I threw my gear on, and I was in the water pretty much right away. There was no eddy. As soon as I was in my boat, I was going," Logan recalls. "I made sure I was on my line, came to the lip, held my boat straight, leaned forward enough to not land flat. I barely felt the landing. There was so much water going off, it was really soft. I was stoked on that! And everyone there was super stoked when I came out at the bottom all good."

For Christo, a corporate leadership consultant, the waiting was definitely the hardest part. Working with a client group that day in Banff, he was distracted. Familiar with the flight patterns of helicopters called to rescue missions in Canada's most visited national park, he didn't dare look to the sky for helicopter traffic.

"That was a big day," Christo says. "I was working with a group, and I needed to be present. I anticipated it [the drop] would be over a lot sooner. I was waiting for a phone call for a long time. It finally came five minutes before I met with my group."

As parents of a serious adventurer, Christo Grayling and Barb Hertell are aware their son is measuring risky decisions any time he's travelling far away in foreign countries. This time, however, knowing he was taking such a big risk close to home left a deeper impact, Christo says.

"We know when he's far off in Vietnam or Africa or Norway, that they're doing big things," Christo says. "We send e-mails back and forth and we can tell when something's building up. When I can't sleep at night – but then I'll admit I'm naturally wired – I'll be checking for e-mails. A lot of time, we'll hear about adventures after them. But there was something about it being so close to home. That waterfall is frickin' gnarly."

Barb says she too relies on her trust of her son's judgment, explaining that she felt her best role would be to stand back as the plans took shape and have faith that all would be fine.

"I really do trust him, and I do trust life, that things do work out," Barb says. "With Johnston Falls I knew all the other guys who were there with him, and I knew he couldn't have it any better. They're all great kids. As a mom, though, I didn't feel it would be right to be in heavy nurturing role. I felt like I had to sit back, trust and listen to what was going on. Of course, as parents, we were just pacing that whole day, waiting for Luke to call and tell us it was over, waiting to hear how it went. And when it was over, I was relieved. I'd just been so tense, my shoulders, my neck, my teeth. It was an emotional relief for both of us – complete with tears."

The family had embarked on some river trips when the boys were younger, but Barb says she feels proud that Logan has developed his deep passion for kayaking on his own, adding that she felt it helped that she and Christo shared an affinity for water sports.

"We know a lot about water, and about its wonders and its hazards, and I'm not sure if that's in our favour or not," Barb says. "But we do really understand water; we love water; we appreciate what Logan's doing. He's always liked adventure, he likes being on the edge, and we're really excited about what he's doing."

"I'm incredibly proud of both kids, of what they've accomplished, how they live life," Christo adds. "And I'm also pretty nervous. I'm not trying to be blasé about it; it scares the shit out of me. But I wouldn't want it any other way. Logan certainly is his own person."

With the drop behind him, Logan was heading back to northern Alberta to his job as roughneck – the toughest, lowest on the ladder of oil rig jobs – where spends his work days dreaming about blowing his paycheques on his next paddling expedition, and how he hopes to attract more sponsors so he won't always have to work on the rigs to support his kayaking adventures.

"Working on the rigs, I'm thinking about my paycheque. Survive the day, don't get killed," Logan says. "I'd like to see kayaking be a little more mainstream; right now there's no money in it, and no girls.

But I love it – I love the adventure, mostly. It's great travelling. The feeling going over big waterfalls or getting into big canyons where the only way out is to run all the rapids is such a great feeling. Being able to push yourself physically and mentally, getting into situations where you're not comfortable, and see what you can do. It's good to push myself, see how far I can go."

Having dropped one of the biggest waterfalls ever run in a kayak, Logan knows he's on the path to opening doors and attracting more sponsors, and seeing just how far he might go. But first, he plans to let his big drop soak in and bask in the realization of a dream.

"I was scared, yes," Logan admits. "Then after, it felt great! Amazing! I knew I could do it. I wasn't thinking about much that day. It was time to get it done; it had been eight years since the last time. After, I was super stoked to be down, and excited that I don't have to think about it anymore.

"When you do stuff like this, having faith in the guys who are there, your friends, in case something goes wrong, and who know how to deal with it, is huge. You can have all the confidence in the world in yourself, but it means nothing till you have confidence in the guys you're paddling with. I've had a few close calls, but when it happens it makes you appreciate everything. It makes you want to live your life, not walk through it. Makes you want to get something done."

CONDITIONS TOO RISKY FOR POINTS ON A SCOREBOARD (2007)

> Will **Gadd**

With back-to-back top-level competitions scheduled in the same area, Will Gadd was keen to spend a whole month in Australia, flying alongside the world's best paragliders.

In the end, however, Gadd says he was simply happy to return to his home in Canmore, Alberta, even if he didn't have any trophies to show for his efforts – and particularly in the wake of a serious accident that took the life of one pilot and saw another barely escape with hers.

The Manilla Open xc competition launched in mid-February 2007, with pilots competing to fly the longest possible distance each day. Immediately following that competition, the tenth FAI Paragliding World Championships would attract 150 of the world's top pilots.

No stranger to high-level competition, Gadd, thirty-nine, is a former world champion ice climber who holds the distance record for paragliding, in addition to having accomplished several firsts, including flights across the Andes and the Grand Canyon.

"I was pretty fired up to see Australia," Gadd admits. "We had fantastic conditions for the xc. I was flying with a lot of the best pilots in the world, and I came eighth. I flew over 1000 kilometres in about forty hours in a week. The cloud base was relatively high, the lift was strong and we flew 100 to 200 kilometres every day. Competitions always have different vibes, and the vibe was really good. It was just insanely good conditions for the week and I ended up with a good result. It felt really good to fly with the top pilots in the world and do well."

That good feeling, however, was shaken when two of the competing pilots flew into a volatile storm cloud, and only one emerged alive.

"Well, that was an interesting day," Gadd says. "There were about forty pilots flying in that area, and I flew right by that storm early. But at that point it wasn't a menace. When it started to be a menace, I went and landed, and so did a lot of others. If we were flying in the Rockies and saw a storm like that, you'd land pretty quickly, it's not something you toy with. At some point you realize it's not a good time to be in the sky."

Among those pilots who didn't land quickly, was German Ewa Wisnierska, thirty-five. She was sucked into the storm cell and made international headlines by surviving the "hell" of an ascent to a height of almost 9946 metres – 1000 metres higher than the summit of Mount Everest. Apart from likening her survival to a miracle equal to winning ten lotteries in a row, doctors credited her emerging alive to the simple good fortune of losing consciousness, which slowed down her heart and other body functions.

While Wisnierska's mishap made newspaper headlines around the world, what was not as enthusiastically reported was the fact that forty-two-year-old Zhongpin He, a member of the Chinese paragliding team, died in that same storm cloud, likely of a lightning strike. His body was retrieved the following day, seventy-five kilometres from where he'd taken off.

"All the media attention focused on Ewa surviving, but a Chinese guy died, and I think that's the story," Gadd says. "It showed how ridiculous it was to be flying in those conditions."

During high-level competitions, he explains, it's human nature for athletes to push themselves past points they would normally consider acceptable.

"Unfortunately, Mr. He had to die to make that point," Gadd says. "But even though it's a competition, you still have to watch out for your own safety. Cross-country is not a defined course, it's more like an adventure race. If you fall in a hole in the ground, it's your own fault."

In the wake of the accident, which prompted "intense philosophical discussion about what pilots will do if left to their own devices, and what the organizers should do for safety for the pilots," Gadd ended up being chosen as a member of the protest committee assigned to create guidelines to deal with the human-nature element of the competition. The committee eventually decided organizers would look at the weather forecast for the day and set course guidelines pilots would be expected to fly within, while the organizers would monitor the conditions.

As it happened, the area never experienced the same intensity of weather buildup through the remainder of the competition.

Gadd shared his thoughts on the incident on his blog, and he later learned passages were being translated into German and French magazines.

At the start of the world championships a week later, what the Australians had been calling a 100-year drought came to an abrupt end. With an inch of water on the ground, flying conditions quickly deteriorated from fantastic to grim, as the sun's energy was spent evaporating the water rather than creating strong thermals.

"It was kind of like showing up at a surfing contest and there were only six-inch waves," Gadd says. "The lift was so weak a lot of people would be flying in the same small thermals. There were a lot of mid-air collisions. It was not the type of flying I felt comfortable with. I've taken a lot of risks in my life, but I don't enjoy that much risk for a result on the scoreboard."

Nonetheless, after all was said and done, Gadd says he was happy with his flying, and his judgment.

"The last day, I ended up seventh for the day – any time you crack the top ten in a Worlds task, you're feeling pretty good," he says. "I've won a lot of competitions. I'm there to do well for myself. I would like to represent Canada better, but if conditions aren't something I feel comfortable with – ah, to hell with it. Maybe I'm a wuss, maybe I made the right call. I'm okay either way. The whole event was a lot of fun. One of the best parts of paragliding is landing in all sorts of weird places and meeting the locals. And I had lots of opportunity to do that."

WARREN MACDONALD'S UNFATHOMABLE POTENTIAL (2004)

> Warren **Macdonald**

When amputee adventurer Warren Macdonald wheeled onto the main dining room stage at the Banff Mountain Book Festival in November 2004, it marked his third consecutive year attending North America's premier adventure book and film competition – but his first as a guest presenter.

Macdonald made his debut in 2002 when his film *The Second Step* captured audiences' hearts and imaginations – and also the festival's Grand Prize. He related how he lost both legs above the knee after he was pinned for forty-six hours in a running creek by a table-sized boulder in hauntingly remote Hinchinbrook Island off Australia's north Queensland coast. And his film details his down-to-the-wire rescue, gruelling rehabilitation and ultimate return to climbing, culminating in his tenacious twenty-eight-day journey through rugged wilderness to the summit of technically challenging Federation Peak.

The following year, Macdonald returned to the festival as the star of adventurer Will Gadd's first filmmaking effort, *Part Animal, Part Machine*. The lively film captures Macdonald making his second ever waterfall ice climb – up the 180-metre central pillar of the Canadian Rockies' Weeping Wall, a vertical parking lot of ice bordering the Icefields Parkway in Banff National Park.

On centre stage as the star attraction of the noon-hour presentation, Macdonald furrowed his brow mid-sentence. Reading a passage from his book *A Test of Will: One Man's Extraordinary Story of Survival*, he was sharing how, after he had endured excruciating pain, heart-numbing loneliness, the intense fear of rising water, and swarming, biting ants, a helicopter and rescue crew had finally freed him from under the rock and delivered him to hospital in Cairns.

As he began to read how the surgeon explained to him that, having escaped with his life, he must now sign the permission form for his legs to be amputated, Macdonald paused.

"I thought this would get easier after all this time," he said, staring at the page. Lifting his gaze, he faced the audience and stated in his thick Aussie twang:

"It hasn't."

Previously published under the title *One Step Beyond* in Australia in 1999, *A Test of Will* was released in North America in 2004 by Greystone Books.

"I didn't set out to write a book, I just wanted to write it down," Macdonald says. "It's a hell of a story, a hell of a thing to go through. It just turned into a book."

Now making a living as an inspirational speaker based in Vancouver, BC – all the while planning his next adventures – he lives with his partner, Canadian ice climber Margo Talbot, whom he met at the 2002 Banff festival.

While his book takes the reader on a journey, Macdonald says it's through his public presentations that he aims to make the biggest impact on his audience.

"One of the main things I set out to do is, basically, I want to stop people in their tracks and get them to think about what they're doing in their lives," Macdonald says. "I want them to think about whether they're reaching their goals or their full potential. That's pretty much what people are going to get out of the book – a kick in the pants."

At the time of his accident in 1997, Macdonald was a thirty-one-year-old experienced traveller who favoured the not-so-posh destinations. He had hitchhiked from London to Istanbul, then continued to Africa, where he hung onto a pile of cargo in an open transport truck for three days travelling between villages in Zaire. A lifelong appreciation for the natural environment prompted him to become a passionate and determined environmental activist, which led to his being arrested while attempting to halt road construction through a pristine wilderness in Tasmania. The charge was later dropped.

After a two-and-a-half-year walkabout, he returned to his native Australia and began working toward becoming an accredited wilderness guide. When a back injury forced him to take a break from his guiding pursuits, he took a painting job at a five-star resort. Upon completing a phase of his contract, he decided he needed a mini-vacation and settled on Hinchinbrook Island, with plans to climb Mount Bowen, the island's highest peak. Along the way he hooked up with a Dutch tourist and neophyte bush walker, Geert van Keulen. When a stroll in the dark just metres from their camp to relieve himself left Macdonald pinned by the one-tonne boulder, van Keulen hiked for an exhausting day and a half until he met up with a boatman who radioed for help, setting in motion the chain of actions that would save Macdonald's life.

After surviving not just the accident but numerous infections and months of arduous rehab, Macdonald slowly began to reclaim his life. Just ten months after losing his legs, with the help of friends, Macdonald climbed to the top of Tasmania's Cradle Mountain, relying on a modified wheelchair and his indomitable will. A year later he spent four weeks travelling through some of Australia's most rugged terrain to climb Federation Peak, a technical ascent that had intimidated him when he had two good legs.

In February 2003 he upped the ante, and in the company of Hamisi Lugonda, a nineteen-year-old Tanzanian farmer born with no arms, Macdonald became the first double above-the-knee amputee to reach the summit of Africa's highest peak, 5963-metre Mount Kilimanjaro, in an effort that took eighteen days.

On a roll, that March, using specially designed "crampon feet," he made an ascent of the Canadian Rockies' landmark Weeping Wall with Talbot and Michael O'Donnell. Eight months later, in an astounding effort that required him to execute more than 2800 pull-ups over four days, with Colorado speed climber Timmy O'Neill, Macdonald accomplished his first Yosemite big-wall climb on the 580-metre El Capitan route called Tangerine Trip.

Relying on three different sets of wheelchair wheels (street, knobby and three-spoke carbon-fibre), four sets of legs (full-length; Vibram-soled short hiking legs; Stealth-rubber rock-climbing feet; and crampon-equipped ice feet), and the custom, carbon-fibre socket to which his prostheses attach, Macdonald said he's grateful that his input is welcome at Hanger Prosthetics' design table.

"If I have a foot fall off halfway up El Cap," he says, "I'm the one who's going to have to figure it out."

When asked about his future plans, Macdonald says a dream trip would be to travel to Antarctica and climb a mountain that has never been climbed.

"It would be pretty cool to go climb something that hasn't been climbed before, and not just climb it as a person with no legs," he says.

While he admits to having succumbed to some dark moments after his accident, Macdonald explains that he learned he had a talent for not staying there.

"From early on, I looked at my situation from the perspective that this is a huge adventure. Everything is totally new – the potential is unfathomable."

AROUND THE WORLD IN 720 DAYS (2006)

> Colin **Angus** and Julie **Wafaei (Angus)**

Seven hundred and twenty days. Forty-three thousand kilometres. Four thousand chocolate bars, 259 kilograms of freeze-dried foods, seventy-two inner tubes. Zero emissions.

On May 20, 2006, Colin Angus and Julie Wafaei cycled up to Vancouver's Kitsilano Beach landmark totem pole, and with one final spin of their bicycle tires marked the end of their landmark journey, which earned Angus the title of first person to circumnavigate the globe propelled entirely by human power.

Angus, who makes his home on Vancouver Island, left Vancouver in June 2004, cycling with adventure journalist Tim Harvey and with Wafaei, who accompanied them as far as Alaska. Over the following two years, Angus and Harvey became the first people to cross the North Bering Sea by rowboat, and they crossed 5000 kilometres of roadless Siberia in the dead of winter by foot, ski and bicycle. After Harvey and Angus parted ways, Angus continued with Wafaei, cycling from Moscow to Portugal, rowing across the Atlantic Ocean for 145 days and then cycling again from Costa Rica through Central and North America, right up to Vancouver.

Unwinding at his mother's house on Vancouver Island days after wrapping up the expedition, Angus says that, at first, completing the journey didn't feel real.

"It was two years non-stop," Angus says. "It was an amazing trip, an amazing way of experiencing the world, but at the same time, it was a gruel. Touching the totem pole at Kitsilano seemed a little surreal at first; it was hard to imagine the trip was actually over. It was part of our lives for so long, getting up at five in the morning to row or ride our bikes day after day."

Ironically, after surviving a powerful storm on the Bering Sea, brain-numbing cold crossing Siberia, dodging freighters close enough to touch and getting through one of the worst hurricane seasons ever recorded while crossing the Atlantic, Angus says it was the long-distance cycling that felt most dangerous, particularly through parts of Eastern Europe and Central America, where roads were narrow and drivers aggressive.

"You couldn't help but worry about being hit by a truck or a bus," Angus says. "Especially after coming so far for so long and being so close to the end. Until you actually get there, you're always a bit nervous."

With such a long journey, explains Angus – whose previous expeditions include sailing solo across the Pacific Ocean as a nineteen-year-old and, with partners, rafting the Amazon River from the Andes to the Atlantic, and the Yenisey River from Mongolia to the Arctic Ocean – staying motivated is a constant challenge.

"You have to break it down into smaller goals – just have to get across the Bering Sea, just have to cycle to Moscow, have to ride to Lisbon. When we docked in Costa Rica it was 'Okay, we just have to cycle to Vancouver.'"

Throughout the trip, challenges – and wonders – lurked around every corner. Pedalling heavily laden bikes over steep mountain passes in blistering heat along central BC's Gold Rush Trail and the partially paved Cassiar Highway, they cycled past grizzly bears, hawks, beavers and moose for more than 2500 kilometres.

"After the first few days, we were overwhelmed," Angus says. "Our bikes were really heavy, and it was my first time using this mode of transportation. I was thinking, 'We've still got 43,000 kilometres to go, and this is the easy part – we're on paved roads!'"

Arriving in Whitehorse as out-of-control forest fires raged throughout the Yukon, Angus and Harvey cycled on, with flames on both sides of the road reducing visibility to thirty metres, to say nothing of their breathing capacity. With only a brief window for attempting their crossing of the North Bering Sea, they abandoned their plan to pedal to Fairbanks and instead bought and patched a $200 canoe, which they took turns paddling non-stop for 1600 kilometres along the Yukon River – where a closed order was "unenforceable" – as flames leapt from tree to tree on opposite banks.

"It was the fiery roads of hell," Angus says. "But we decided to take our chances with the fire rather than be caught on the sea in deadly storms."

Cooking, eating and sleeping in the canoe amidst 320 kilograms of gear, and paddling through strong headwinds, the pair finally reached Fairbanks. There, they loaded everything they needed for five months into the rowboat, including their bikes, since no shipping companies service the northeast coast of Siberia.

"A trip like this has so many bureaucratic hurdles," Angus comments. "Physically, you're doing the work of a marathon every day, then you stop at a gas station pay phone to call a shipping company."

Situated at about 64.5 degrees north, the distance across the Bering Sea from Nome, Alaska, to Siberia is about 400 kilometres of shallow open water, where constantly shifting winds produce waves bigger than those on the Atlantic.

With dying winds signalling calm weather on the evening of August 4, they launched the six-metre-long *Bering Charger*, a sailboat they'd purchased on eBay for $2,400 and converted to a rowboat by removing the mast, installing a hatch, sealing the boat and rigging it with oars. By the following afternoon, waves rose to over a metre, gale force winds were forecast and a small-craft warning was in effect. Having decided to seek shelter in a small port 180 kilometres from their launching point, Angus and Harvey were within four kilometres of the port when shifting winds made reaching shore impossible. Hammered by waves that broke over the top of the boat, the two relied on survival suits as they kept the boat on course.

By the next day they were within thirty kilometres of St. Lawrence Island when the winds sent them farther out to sea and they turned their course to Nome, 200 kilometres away.

"It was the scenic route," Angus jokes.

With the rudder cracked and the hatch broken, the pair decided entering the Nome harbour would be impossible. As they turned toward a small island with the intention of taking shelter behind it, an enormous Russian research vessel appeared through the fog. Already alerted to the rowboat's predicament, the R/V *Professor Khromov* dropped a rope, which the Canadians used to tether their craft to the larger vessel and ride out the storm.

After repairing their rowboat for several days in Nome – including the hatch, which had locked them out from the inside during the turbulent seas – Angus and Harvey began rowing once more toward Siberia. With only forty kilometres to go, thirty-knot northerly winds blew for three days. Manning the oars in two- to five-hour shifts around the clock for days on end, they used their sea anchor to slow their travel in unwanted directions. Finally they managed to reach St. Lawrence Island, a mere dot of lichen-covered volcanic rock with no trees or bushes, that, although a part of Alaska, sits in the Bering Sea only fifty-eight kilometres from the Siberian coast, and is home to about 1300 local Yup'ik, who lead a traditional, subsistence lifestyle hunting walrus, whale, seal, reindeer and fish.

"It was cold up there," Angus recalls. "We were waiting to have some winds in our favour. But it doesn't get calm there; the wind is always blowing one way or another."

After waiting out bad weather for a week, they set out from their sheltered cove, and hugging the island's northern coast they made a final dash and rowed sixty kilometres to Siberia. When they finally reached the port of Providenya, they tied up their rowboat and collapsed, utterly exhausted, only to be roused from their deep sleep by a boatload of Russians bearing breakfast and vodka.

With winter bearing down, the adventurers abandoned their original plan to row along the coastline to reach Anadyr, the administrative centre of Russia's remote Chukotka region, and instead set off overland on foot. Carrying homemade backpacks, they were joined by their translator, a sturdy, twenty-something Russian woman named Yulya. Five weeks and 650 kilometres into their gruelling trek across a trailless landscape of drifting snowbanks and partially frozen rivers that made crossing a tenuous exercise, and complete with a nerve-wracking encounter with an agitated bear, they reached the port town of Egvekinot, where Angus came to the disheartening conclusion that he was seriously ill. After a brief and dicey stay in a Siberian hospital, he hastily arranged to return to Vancouver for critical surgery to treat an acute urethral stricture brought on by a dual kidney infection and infected bladder. The detour was less than straightforward.

"From Egvekinot I caught an icebreaker to Anadyr," Angus recalls. "The airport in Anadyr is across a river, and in summer there's a ferry. In winter people drive across the frozen ice. But it was shoulder season, so I boarded this giant Soviet thirty-passenger transport helicopter, flew a domestic Russian airline to Moscow, then Aeroflot to Seattle. Then I rode a bus to Vancouver. When I returned to Anadyr, we rented this tank without a turret to make the overland trip to Egvekinot. It wasn't human power, but when there are emergencies ..."

Carrying on, Angus, Harvey and Yulya crossed 5000 roadless kilometres of the coldest inhabited region of the planet during the dead of winter.

Along the way, due to incompatible travel paces and mindsets, Angus became stranded alone in a Siberian blizzard, where, relying on survival tips he admitted to picking up from TV, he scraped out a makeshift snow cave with his pocket knife. By April, despite surviving encounters with polar bears, −45°C temperatures accompanied by sixty-five-kilometre winds and sharing the delights of brief, yet rich encounters with colourful characters in remote outposts who graciously shared fermented mare's milk, raw fish and reindeer meat, Angus and Harvey had disbanded.

"Tim and I were incompatible as teammates and were unable to continue together – that was it," Angus says.

With Harvey and Yulya – who had become lovers less than a week into their acquaintance – pursuing their own adventure, Angus cycled solo for 9400 kilometres to Moscow, persevering through a bottomless, bike-sucking mud bog, savouring the home cooking of a grizzled grandmother in a roadside shack in the middle of absolute nowhere, curling up in his sleeping bag next to human waste in an abandoned Russian factory after losing his tent, and fearing for his own life after witnessing a possible murder involving Russian mafia who were dangling a man by his ankles over a highway overpass.

With only 23,000 kilometres to go, Wafaei joined Angus in Moscow for the second half of the journey. An experienced marathon runner and backcountry skier, Wafaei took time out from her job as a market research analyst for a pharmaceutical company to serve as expedition manager and website designer for Angus and Harvey, organizing logistics and sorting through Russian red tape.

Embarking on what many jokingly referred to as "the ultimate litmus test," the couple cycled along the narrow streets and through the pastoral countryside of Russia, Ukraine, Hungary, Austria, Germany, Switzerland, France and Spain, en route to Portugal to rendezvous with their eight-metre rowboat.

"The people in Russia were so friendly. They were so interested in what we were doing," Wafaei says. "They were really happy we were there, that we wanted to visit their land. People would stop and give us gifts, usually food, but whatever they had, one guy gave us a bottle with half a sports drink. They don't have much; it really came from the heart."

Throughout their ride, while savouring the aroma of roadside shishkebab stands from miles away, enjoying the freedom of carrying all they needed in their panniers, and camping in farmers' fields, they planned for the big adventure – their five-month ocean row.

Specially designed, their craft had two small cabins, one at each end of the boat, with a rowing station in the centre. It was equipped with a water desalinator and fishing gear, and, just in case, one of their sponsors supplied them with a life raft and an emergency locator beacon. With little room for extras among their four-month, 5000-calorie-per-day freeze-dried food supply, Wafaei tucked a few tiny treats on board to celebrate Christmas and their birthdays: her thirty-first and his thirty-third.

"Getting it from second-hand boat to seaworthy craft was a huge amount of work, especially in a foreign country where you don't have all the tools you have at home. And there's the language barrier," Wafaei says. "When we finally put it in the water fully loaded, it was very exciting."

Anxious to avoid the hurricane season, the couple departed Lisbon in September in the overloaded and theoretically self-righting craft, in which Angus likens cooking dinner to "trying to juggle while on a mechanical bull."

"It was very small," Wafaei says. "It was stuffed with gear to the extent that we couldn't sleep lying flat; one person had to lie on their side. But it was a wonderful feeling to know we had everything we needed to survive for however long it would take to cross the ocean."

Attracting excitement like a bull's eye, however, they dodged three hurricanes and a couple of freighters.

"About a week out, we were almost hit by a tanker," she recalls. "I looked out and the tanker was about a metre away from us. All I could see was this massive wall of steel. Lucky for us, the bow wave pushed us to the side. That was extremely frightening. The whole thing was over in less than a minute."

The fear that came with the hurricanes was longer lived, as they learned via radio from the US National Hurricane Center in Miami that Vince was headed their way – the most northeasterly hurricane ever recorded. Trying to prepare themselves, they observed unusual cloud formations, watched as the ocean currents switched direction and noted the presence of insects, including moths and house flies, more than 600 kilometres from the African Coast.

"The only way they could be there was to have been blown by the wind," Wafaei says. "That whole period, with the growing seas, never knowing how bad it would get, that was terrifying. The anticipation was worse than being in it."

They rode out the storm, complete with 100-kilometre winds and waves five storeys high. And they would relive the experience twice more.

Balancing the excitement, they delighted in intimate encounters with a pilot whale, dolphins and a six-metre great white shark, as Wafaei rowed her way into history as the first woman to cross the Atlantic from mainland to mainland, and as the first Canadian woman to row across any ocean.

"I loved the marine life, especially the whales," Wafaei says. "You could smell them first, this huge burst with an overpowering fishiness. They were very curious. They would swim next to us for a few minutes; they're huge creatures. We could see the gentle slope of their back, but we never had any worry that they would bump us."

After 121 consecutive days on the water, the couple enjoyed a well-deserved 12-day pit stop in St. Lucia, where they gorged themselves on fresh fruit and tried to adapt their sea legs to dry land. Unaccustomed to being off the rocking ocean, Wafaei experienced motion sickness on land and was forced to return to the boat to settle her stomach. Their send off from St. Lucia, Angus says, complete with a flotilla of sailboats and power yachts blowing air horns, was bittersweet, as they embarked on the last leg of their Atlantic crossing.

Then finally, after three and a half more weeks of rowing – five months and 10,000 kilometres after launching their little rowboat – they reached Costa Rica's Puerto Limón, having crossed the entire Atlantic Ocean by human power.

"The food was really good in Costa Rica," Angus says. "It's a great blend of Latin American and Caribbean. We were thinking about food all the way across the Atlantic."

Of their 145 days of rowing, Angus says it was the final two weeks that were the most challenging, as they battled a fierce storm that pummelled their craft with 165-kilometre winds and ten-metre waves.

"We'd been through some rough seas, but nothing like that," Angus says. "It was intense. And really scary."

When the storm finally abated, they encountered their next obstacle – a countercurrent so strong that if they stopped rowing for two hours they would lose an entire day's progress. At times even when they rowed at full force the boat was pushed backward.

"We were trying to come in and the currents were coming out, trying to push us back out to sea," Angus says. "We were exhausted."

The duo resorted to double rowing for twelve hours, single rowing for the other half of the day, which meant rowing eighteen hours per day each, with only six hours each to sleep and eat. With neither the time nor the energy to cook, they lived on cold food from cans, powdered milk and Truestar nutritional supplements supplied by one of their sponsors. In the soggy aftermath of the storm that repeatedly shoved the boat onto its side, wet blankets would not dry and clothing mildewed, while food began to rot.

Nearing land, as soon as the water was shallow enough they dropped anchor and collapsed, utterly spent. Once they mustered the strength to disembark, a restaurant owner invited them for a free dinner.

Still, Angus says, despite moments of sheer terror, there was plenty of natural beauty to discover during their twenty-four-day passage from St. Lucia. Shallower than the deep-blue mid-Atlantic, the Caribbean waters displayed a greenish hue. Schools of flying fish skimmed above the waves to escape predators below, and one day a five-metre shark swam parallel to the boat for several hundred metres, its thin, sickle-shaped fin slicing through the water's surface like a knife. The couple also spotted a pair of pilot whales, a species that visits the area to breed every February.

With their ocean crossing behind them, Angus and Wafaei prepared their gear for the final leg of their human-powered journey, cycling 8300 kilometres through Nicaragua, Honduras, Mexico and the western US toward Vancouver.

While the cycling was often the most dangerous aspect of the journey, Angus says rowing across the Atlantic was at once the most challenging and the most enjoyable part.

"What made it the hardest was the psychological aspect of the two of us being alone for five months and the physical aspect of rowing and rowing and the monotonous food that doesn't change," Angus says.

Not to mention ships that couldn't see their tiny rowboat and churning hurricanes passing close by. While Angus had previously sailed solo across the Pacific, travel in the much slower rowboat provided an entirely different experience.

"We had this whole ecosystem going on under our boat," he says. "First barnacles grew on the boat and that attracted small fish, which attracted bigger fish like the dorado – which we caught and ate. Then there were the dolphins and turtles and sharks. You could always look over the side and see a nature documentary going on. We learned so much."

Now that they are home, Angus and Wafaei have a film about their adventure to produce and books to write. Since he's reached his mid-thirties, Angus figures he chose exactly the right time in his life to make the journey.

"I think I'm becoming more cautious," he admits. "I feel like I've got the right combination of skills with the right balance of the fear factor."

After two years of making his way around the globe with a purpose, Angus says what impressed him most was the weather.

"It's given me a greater appreciation of the world around us and how fragile it is," he says. "We experienced so many weather disasters: forest fires in the Yukon and Alaska brought on by drought, German villages on the Danube being flooded, drought in Portugal and more forest fires, and then the worst hurricane season ever.

"Hurricanes are driven by warm water, and one element of our journey was to promote travelling by low emissions and awareness of climate change, and it really was worrisome seeing all over the world the fingers of man reaching into the wilderness. People live six blocks away from where they work and they want to drive their big suvs. We travelled from Vancouver to Moscow using our arms and legs, until one day we were home again."

WALK THE WALK

The people who star in the following stories may be fun-seekers, explorers, storytellers, adventurepreneurs – or a combination of any of these – but an essential component of their adventures is that they seek to educate or inform, or to attract attention to a place or an issue greater than themselves. Their adventures are carried out in part in the service of others – humans, other animals or the natural environment. Their adventures are a means to a larger goal, often part of a genuine desire to make the world a better place.

WISDOM'S TRAIL (2002)

> Lynn **Martel**, Bob **Sandford**, Greg **Horne**, Ed **Struzik**,
Darro Stinson **and** Ron **Hooper**

"This would be a bad place to fall," Ed Struzik commented casually as Dillon, the horse he was riding, followed close on the hooves of Wisdom, upon whose broad back I was seated.

He was right. The narrow track wound gradually up a steep and rocky side slope with an especially deep, turbulent braid of the Whirlpool River flowing about ten metres below us to the right.

Struzik was teasing me, because just a few hours earlier, while Greg Horne, a Jasper National Park backcountry warden, had adjusted the stirrups on Wisdom's saddle to fit the legs of my five-foot-four frame, Wisdom had thrust up her head, kicked her forelegs into the air, stepped backward and the next thing I knew I saw stars, felt pain as I hit the ground, and more pain as Wisdom landed on my leg.

"It happened so fast," I sputtered.

"Looked like a good six seconds to me," Darro Stinson had joked. "If you had just stayed on two seconds longer…"

A former national park superintendent, Stinson was a competent and commanding horseman. He walked, leading Wisdom with me aboard her, around the campsite, offering a few valuable pointers. Gently pull on the left rein to turn left, likewise on the right, back to stop, not up.

"Power steering," Stinson said. "That's all, power steering."

For the next few hours, our train of ten pack horses and nine saddle horses had crossed river flats, charged up steep banks and sauntered down roller-coaster hills on rock-strewn, muddy sections of the moss-covered forest. I'd become quite comfortable with Wisdom's gait and liked the way she chose her steps carefully on the rutted, rooty trail. Given an option, she'd choose the high line with steady footing while the other horses slipped on rocks and sloshed through gooey mud.

But now we were on the most exposed and dangerous section of the trail and it happened. Wisdom slipped. First her front hooves clacked in desperation to gain purchase on a smooth, tilted limestone slab. She lurched forward, her back legs in frantic motion as we pitched to the left, then to the right above the freezing, fast-moving water. If Wisdom were to fall on me on the way down this steep, rocky bank it would be very bad for both of us.

Then it was over. As quickly as she'd lost her footing, she regained it, and we nonchalantly continued up the narrow trail away from the surging river, both of us breathing a sigh of relief.

The expedition began at the Moab Lake trailhead, in Jasper National Park, our group of eleven people and nineteen horses following the Whirlpool for two days and forty-one kilometres to Kane Meadows. Named after the nineteenth-century painter Paul Kane, the campsite served as base while four of us set off to climb Mount Brown, a glaciated mountain rising to 2799 metres on the west side of Athabasca Pass.

It was no ordinary climbing trip.

Organized by United Nations International Year of Mountains (IYM) coordinator for Canadian Celebrations Bob Sandford, the entourage included Jasper National Park superintendent Ron Hooper, Jasper backcountry manager Gord Antoniuk, Jasper Yellowhead Museum manager Glenn Charron, Jasper National Park wrangler Sean Elliott, Edmonton journalist Ed Struzik, Alberta section head for the Alpine Club of Canada (ACC) Dave Pors, Headwaters Outfitting cook Liz Norwell, Darro Stinson, Greg Horne, and me.

Our six-day trip in late August was planned as part of the 2002 IYM Canadian Celebrations. The IYM was declared at the 1992 Earth Summit in Rio de Janeiro, where it was recognized that mountain regions worldwide were important planetary water towers and repositories of biodiversity and cultural heritage. At the summit it was also recognized that mountain ecosystems worldwide face challenges as important as desertification, climate change and tropical deforestation. While many of Canada's most cherished mountain areas may appear to be well protected by national and provincial park designations, their ecosystems face many of the same threats as mountain regions in less developed countries. Pressures due to heavy visitation and urban growth in areas bordering protected lands affect the capacity to manage those sensitive regions. Canada's protected lands may not be as well protected as we think.

Our trip to Athabasca Pass was designed to help draw attention to the importance of Canada's mountain areas with the hope that the more people become aware of the unique, fragile and valuable resources found in our mountains, the more people will care about preserving them.

For forty years after David Thompson's first recorded crossing in 1811, Athabasca Pass remained the main fur trade route through the Canadian Rockies. In May 1827, while travelling with Hudson's Bay Company traders and voyageurs, a young Scottish botanist named David Douglas tightened his snowshoe laces and ascended the glaciated slopes of the peak west of the pass and, reaching the summit, inadvertently became North America's first mountaineer. Pleased with his endeavour, he named the peak after an illustrious British botanist named Robert Brown and attributed heights of 4900 metres and 5200 metres respectively to Brown and nearby Mount Hooker, claiming they were the highest in North America.

Douglas, however, was a botanist, not a surveyor, and famously poor-sighted to boot. While travelling some 16,000 kilometres through the remote western Canadian mountain landscape, however, he identified 880 species of plants, 200 of which were new to science, including his namesake Douglas fir. The heights assigned to Brown and Hooker were outrageously generous, but it is possible Douglas believed Athabasca Pass rested at 3355 metres, based on an earlier, incorrect map.

The prospect of climbing such colossal mountains in the Canadian wilderness lured many accomplished mountaineers for decades afterward. While Brown and Hooker were eventually proven – in August 1893, by A.P. Coleman, a Canadian professor of geology from the University of Toronto – to reach a disappointing 2801 and 3307 metres, much had been accomplished in the exploration and mapping of the uncharted Canadian Rockies in pursuit of the mystery peaks.

Sitting atop Wisdom, rocking gently with the movement of her body as we splashed through smoky-blue braids of the Whirlpool, Wisdom feeling out the slippery riverbed rocks in fast-moving, silty water rising to her thighs, it was clear to me that little of the remote and rugged mountain landscape had changed in the past two centuries. While glaciers tumbling from mounts Kane and Scott have retreated high above treeline, fresh wolf, moose and bear tracks appeared frequently in the mud. The only other people we encountered in six days were five Americans in a group, coincidentally also following Douglas's travels.

Other than the luxury of established trails, the physical labour of a horse trip hasn't changed much either. With the help of Stinson, Horne, Antoniuk and Hooper, Elliot looked after nineteen horses, replacing horseshoes, securing loads, checking their legs for injuries and hobble burn and riding bareback in the pre-dawn light to round up the spirited steeds after a night's grazing in lush meadows before saddling them all up for another day's travel. At mealtime Norwell made sure we feasted on pasta and salad, cornbread and roast beef, all cooked over open fires.

On the third day, all eleven of us hiked to a pair of jewel-tone lakes at the crest of Athabasca Pass. Marking the divide between the Pacific and Arctic watersheds, one of the lakes, now known as the Committee's Punchbowl, was where fur traders would stop and drink a toast to the officers of the Hudson's Bay Company. We stopped to toast the committee, and also Douglas, with some rum and enjoyed a refreshing dip before Horne, Pors, Elliot and I embarked on our climb.

No doubt equipped with better clothing and footwear than Douglas, the four of us made our way up through meadows and rocky benches, crunching over scree and through rock bands and short cliffs, finally following a snow ramp until we found the perfect high camp. With a 270-degree view, and protected by a low rock wall, our strategic location would allow us quick access to the summit the following morning and also shelter from the wind that accompanied booming thunder and lightning flashes that evening.

Shortly before 11 a.m. on August 30, we reached the summit cairn, sitting quietly amidst a dozen perfectly round craters, each about half a metre across and half that deep, punched into the rock-strewn plateau. Inside a plastic tube we found the soggy register notebook that had last been signed by Glen Boles, Rollie Reader and Mike Budd in 1993, testimony to the relative present-day obscurity of a mountain that had once been sought after by the world's best mountaineers. On that day, the summit view coveted by all mountaineers was not to be ours, and we descended through cloud and fog along the sometimes technical northeast ridge. Lower down we endured a section of bushwhacking much like Douglas may have encountered, and we feasted on a profusion of ripe blueberries that prevented the steep descent through thick, rain-slick alders from being entirely heinous.

Back at the campfire that night we celebrated our climb, Douglas's ascent, the serendipity of his great mistake and the splendour of the Canadian Rockies.

In the spirit of fun and historical re-enactment, an inquiry was staged. Wearing a saddle cinch over his head to resemble (just barely) a magistrate's wig, Hooper presided over the campfire court as Justice. Charron sat quietly on a tree stump in the role of Douglas, accused of lying about his ascent and exaggerating the heights of mounts Brown and Hooker for his own personal gain. Struzik took to his role as prosecutor like a starving dog to a T-bone; Stinson filled the defence's shoes with off-the-cuff aplomb. One by one the four climbers were called to the stand as witnesses to the validity of Douglas's reported ascent and descent times, his recordings of plant life above treeline and the possibilities that much higher glaciation levels would have allowed Douglas to climb a very different Mount Brown than we did in 2002. With a noose lying unceremoniously on the ground, anyone stumbling upon this evening scene two days from the nearest road may have headed quickly for faraway hills. In the end, Hooper found Douglas innocent on both charges, although he chastised the acquitted for his poor altitude estimating abilities.

Despite its imperfections, Douglas's ascent of Mount Brown is considered the birth of North American mountaineering. Our expedition marked one in a series of commemorative climbs in 2002 celebrating the IYM. In May, national park wardens climbed an unnamed peak in Auyuittuq National Park Reserve on Baffin Island, unfurling an IYM flag on the summit to celebrate more than fifty years of organized rescue services in Canada's national parks. Another group of wardens participating in regular training camps in June climbed two 3050-metre peaks in the front ranges of Yukon's St. Elias Mountains. They restored a maple leaf constructed of white rocks on a slope above their camp that was first built by participants of the ACC's 1967 centennial camp in the Steele Valley, where a dozen peaks first climbed that year were named after deceased ACC presidents.

In July the centennial of the first ascent of 3747-metre Mount Columbia, Alberta's highest peak and the second highest in the Canadian Rockies, was celebrated. Two separate teams participated, one comprised of park wardens on a training exercise, the other a party of three clients led by a Yamnuska Mountain Adventures guide, Mike Olsthoorn.

As I crawled into my sleeping bag on the last night of our trip, I felt completely intoxicated by my surroundings and the pleasure of my companions' acquaintance. Travelling by horse train provided an enchanting richness that I had not experienced on any other kind of mountain trip. I felt transported through time; I felt I had become part of the landscape so that I was not simply moving through it but I was participating in its existence: the landscape and I had merged. Time also had merged. I felt bad for unwilling women who had been forced by their husbands to endure the hardships of mountain travel, all the while expected to raise children in a physically and spiritually challenging landscape.

But then I felt camaraderie with those women who came here early in the twentieth century, educated and independent women who found their spirits in these mountains and chose not to return to their former, urban homes.

I was lulled into a land of sweet, earthy dreams by the faint and distant tinkling of the horses' bells as they munched contentedly in the riverside pasture, and in that moment I understood fully the allure that drew Douglas and many others before and since to explore the unique and miraculous landscapes of the Canadian Rockies.

Y2SKI (2000)

> Karsten **Heuer**, Leanne **Allison** and Jay **Honeyman**

The first snowmobiler to whiz by them didn't even register the presence of Karsten Heuer, Leanne Allison and Jay Honeyman as they skied steadily toward a tree-rimmed clearing at Kakwa Lake, BC, just beyond the northern tip of the Canadian Rockies.

After two weeks of skiing by day and camping in snow-blanketed wilderness under star-splattered skies by night, the trio emerged from the forest into a virtual outdoor showroom of motorized snow recreation vehicles. Midway through a 450-kilometre, twenty-eight-day ski tour they'd launched from Jasper, Alberta, the trio were headed to Monkman Provincial Park, in northeastern BC.

The surprised snowmobilers, numbering over 100, were gathered for an Easter weekend celebration. Exhibiting true northern hospitality toward the skiers, they generously shared moose steak sandwiches wrapped in white Wonder Bread slices. They would also end up being the only people Heuer, Allison and Honeyman would encounter during their entire trip.

The first people ever to ski the route, the trio travelled for four weeks over remote and unspoiled Rockies passes following a course that, at its closest, was a three-day ski away from the nearest plowed road.

More than a journey for its own sake, however, the ski tour would mark only the second leg of a 3400-kilometre journey for thirty-year-old Heuer, a Banff National Park warden and wildlife biologist. Starting out on June 16, 1998, from Yellowstone National Park in Wyoming,

Heuer eventually hiked, snowshoed, skied, canoed and bushwhacked for a total of 188 days in three separate sections over several seasons and sometimes solo, concluding his expedition at Watson Lake, Yukon, on September 3, 1999. Dubbed the Y2Y Hike, Heuer's odyssey was a dedicated personal initiative aimed at increasing awareness of the Yellowstone to Yukon (Y2Y) Conservation Initiative.

First conceived in 1993 by Calgary lawyer and conservationist Harvey Locke, Y2Y has grown to encompass a network of over 200 conservation organizations, wildlife scientists and economists working together at a grassroots level in both Canada and the us to establish and maintain a system of core protected wildlife reserves that are linked together by wildlife movement corridors. The idea developed from growing scientific evidence that reveals North America's current system of national parks, which forces animals into island-like protected areas, overlooks the fact that larger species, such as wolves, wolverines and grizzlies, require a much larger roaming area to avoid inbreeding and the challenges presented by natural disturbances, such as fires, food shortages and disease. At a combined 20,238 square kilometres, the Canadian Rockies' Banff, Jasper, Yoho and Kootenay national parks comprise only one sixth the area required to sustain 2000 grizzly bears – the minimum number of individuals needed to maintain any one species.

When Heuer first learned of Y2Y in 1994, he wondered how possible it might actually be for an animal to travel the migration routes in their current state along the length of the Y2Y corridor. The question evolved into a quest, one that led him to decide to travel the entire route himself, following one of several most likely large-mammal migration routes. While resting his weary body after his summer 1998 journey, during which he had walked 2000 kilometres of rugged, mountainous terrain from Yellowstone to Jasper over eighty-six days, Heuer spent much of the ensuing winter poring over maps, making phone calls and delivering food caches. Travelling by ski, snowshoe and Ski-doo, he made several forays to deliver his precious cargo, tightly secured in large steel paint cans clamped shut with wire levers to deter crafty scavengers.

Throughout his journey, friends, journalists and photographers joined Heuer for sections of his trek. But it was his childhood friend, Leanne Allison, who became his main partner, accompanying him for several weeks during the summer 1998 Yellowstone to Jasper segment, again with third member Honeyman for the month-long ski tour, and then for the entire summer 1999 segment, when she, Heuer and his border collie, Webster, travelled through BC's largest unroaded area, across uninhabited, rough terrain with few trails and raging, unbridged rivers. Twice the hikers were stalked by aggressive black bears, but they managed to carry on physically unharmed, albeit unnerved.

Although bears were asleep during the ski portion of the journey, the winter leg presented its own challenges, as high alpine passes descended into dense valley-bottom bush during the final third of the ski traverse. For the last ten days their progress was reduced to less than one kilometre per hour from three to four kilometres per hour, forcing the skiers to navigate the thick and tangled forest by compass.

"We did things on skis I didn't know were even possible!" laughs Allison. An experienced mountaineer and backcountry skier, she is no newcomer to adventure: in 1993 she was a member of the first all-woman team to summit Canada's highest peak, 5959-metre Mount Logan.

"A lot of the terrain we crossed on skis is very wet and marshy, so it made more sense to travel it in winter," Heuer explains. "But winter is also a very interesting time to travel in terms of wildlife sign; you can see two or three days' worth in the snow."

While Heuer studied wildlife sign throughout his journey, with the aim of learning more about how best to preserve the animals' natural habitat, when it came to route-finding through gorges blocked by vertical frozen waterfalls, it was the wildlife who repeatedly came to the humans' rescue.

"In some cases the wolverines showed us the best routes through canyon areas," Allison recalls.

Throughout the expedition, Heuer also stopped to visit communities in Wyoming, Montana, Alberta, BC and Yukon to present talks and slide shows and to share the Y2Y vision with the very people who live within the region's boundaries. To sometimes skeptical audiences, which included those making a living off the land through forestry and mining and by operating remote hunting and fishing lodges, Heuer carefully explained how Y2Y hopes to draw up individual regional plans that include limited resource extraction and municipal growth plans, as well as tourism and recreation, all the while seeking ways in which wildlife and human populations can co-exist throughout the Rocky Mountains from the greater Yellowstone ecosystem all the way north to Yukon's Mackenzie Mountains.

By the end of his travels, Heuer says he was pleased to find himself left with a feeling of optimism, since he had seen signs of grizzly bear or wolverine activity on all but thirty-one of the 188 days.

"As a biologist, when I first learned of Y2Y, I thought it was a pipedream," he says. "But now, after covering the distance on foot, I'm pleased to learn that it is one small possible route already pretty much in place."

Perhaps ironically, one area with the highest level of disturbance, he learned, is the Bow Valley in the Alberta Rockies, which includes the towns of Banff and Canmore – and Heuer's own home and the Y2Y head office. With Banff situated within Banff National Park, and Canmore just east of the park boundary, human development in the region has created a bottleneck in a place where the natural geography of a narrow valley bordered by high mountains already severely restricts mobility for animals.

For the Y2Y administrators, however, Heuer's efforts – which include a book, *Walking the Big Wild*, published by McClelland & Stewart – have been invaluable in raising awareness of Y2Y and the reasons why such an initiative is necessary.

"Karsten has turned out to be a tremendously effective presenter as he talked to people about the fate of these great wilderness icons, like the grizzlies," says Bart Robinson, Y2Y network coordinator. "He's been so dedicated and committed to involving people and communities as he's moved across the landscape."

While for Heuer the journey, including the ski tour, was obviously a labour of passion, he admits to experiencing a few wistful moments when he might have liked to lighten his purpose.

"We passed through incredible ski touring terrain, passes that linked one beautiful bowl after another," he recalls. "It would have been nice to be able to take off our packs and make some turns."

BIG BOW FLOAT REACHES ITS FINAL DOCK (2005)

> Danielle **Droitsch**

It was an enormous and challenging project, and she wouldn't have missed it for the world.

That's how Danielle Droitsch says she felt after paddling the entire 657-kilometre length of Alberta's Bow River with her canoeing partner, retired biology teacher and dedicated environmentalist Jim Kievit and his dog, Rocco.

Droitsch's journey began in June 2005 with a trip to the Canadian Rockies' Wapta Icefields, from where glacial meltwater flows into Bow Lake, marking the river's headwaters, and ended when they took their boat out of the water for the last time on August 2 at Grand Forks, where the Bow and Oldman rivers meet.

"It was a huge undertaking, much bigger than I expected," Droitsch says. "It's hard to convey how much work this was. But I'm so glad I did it. I wouldn't trade it for the world."

The journey involved four months of planning, five weeks on the river and a lot of time spent organizing, maintaining a website, communicating with the media and coordinating with other groups representing river users and stewards, including anglers, canoeists, farmers and First Nations representatives. Droitsch says she especially appreciated the contributions of Kievit and expedition leader Don van Hout, both of whom volunteered their time.

A native of Washington, DC, Droitsch moved to Canmore, Alberta, in 2004 to take the helm of the Bow Riverkeeper organization. One of only nine such groups in Canada, the Bow Riverkeeper is a member of the Waterkeeper Alliance advocacy organization, which boasts Robert Kennedy Jr. as president and over 130 grassroots member organizations in such countries as Australia, Colombia, Czech Republic, Mexico, India and the United Kingdom.

As Bow Riverkeeper director, Droitsch serves as the public advocate working as the full-time eyes, ears and voice of the Bow River. She is assigned to protect and restore the Bow watershed.

And as a relative newcomer to the region, Droitsch says she viewed spending the bulk of her summer paddling the entire length of the river she's assigned to protect as a "rather involved on-the-job training."

Through the journey, she learned how important it was to see the river from the perspective of a canoe.

"The diversity is extraordinary, in terms of personality of the river," Droitsch says. "I knew it was glacially fed from the mountains to the prairies, but to actually see that diversity – the geography, topography, the ecology, the wildlife, how much water is in the river, how fast it moves, its size – you wouldn't know it's the same river from one end to the other."

People tend to think of the river in terms of individual segments, she says, when in reality it is a single entity.

"The river is so segmented, but really it's a continuum," Droitsch says. "When you see the transition zones, you watch it slowly become a prairie river. It makes you appreciate how, collectively, this one river system provides and sustains so much of the landscape."

Launching the trip by spending a few days exploring the Wapta Icefield, Droitsch and a few friends based themselves from the Alpine Club of Canada's Bow Hut. Walking on the very icefield from which the river originates, Droitsch says she discovered three distinct elements of the river's character.

The first, she explains, is the glacier and snow character of the river in solid form, which she witnessed for the first time by climbing the slopes of mounts Olive and Nicholas with internationally certified mountain guide Kirsten Knechtel.

Even though conditions prevented the group from reaching either summit, Droitsch admits she was awed and humbled by the expanse of snow below her, stretching in every direction over rounded and jagged mountaintops, into deep valleys and over high saddles leading to the next snow-covered peaks and valleys. Resting on those slopes, Droitsch realized she was sitting in the very nucleus of a watershed.

"There is a tremendous amount of water stored up," Droitsch says. "I wish that everybody had the opportunity to see how beautiful and how critical it is. That ocean of snow – to make a connection to how important it is to have a healthy snowpack and intact glaciers. I think most people don't feel connected or affected by climate change. We need to be concerned with the impact of climate change, decreased snowpacks and drought. All of us need to be concerned with water conservation."

A fistful of snow scooped up from the Wapta Icefield, she pointed out, is quite literally part of the water supply for all communities downstream, as, once melted, the snow flows through Calgary and Alberta's ranch and farmland.

After descending from the icefield, Droitsch and Kievit, a Bow Riverkeeper volunteer and veteran canoeing instructor with four decades of experience paddling the Bow and other rivers, launched their canoe into Bow Lake's luminous turquoise waters and paddled to the narrow outlet creek that forms the beginnings of the Bow. Here the river reveals an entirely different character.

"For about nine kilometres the river is an absolutely beautiful whitewater river, like Bow Falls – only not as big – over and over and over," Droitsch says.

Because of the unnavigable character of that section, Droitsch and several companions hiked and bushwhacked along the riverbank before launching the canoe again at Mosquito Lake. Droitsch and Kievit then paddled to a point just above Lake Louise, skipping one section of serious Class IV and V whitewater, which some volunteer participants later navigated in kayaks.

Near Lake Louise several Siksika First Nation members on a raft joined the canoeists. The Siksika, who have made a formal claim to land at Castle Mountain in Banff National Park – and the section of the Bow flowing through there – joined the paddlers again when they passed through the Siksika reserve downstream from Calgary.

Beyond Lake Louise, the river changes in character again, Droitsch says, becoming a broader, fast-paced river of glacier water meandering through the Bow Valley, periodically branching off to create islands and habitat for water birds and other wildlife.

"The river really is home for so many animals," Droitsch says. "There is such tremendous diversity in the different types of river we have. And that flow is critical in the summertime; that's when the river needs the water the most."

In summer, glacier melt can make up as much as 50 per cent of the river's flow, at a time when human demand for water from the river is at its highest for residential, recreational and agricultural uses.

Despite its increased value during summer months, however, glacial meltwater represents only 2.5 per cent of the annual flow of the Bow River. While precipitation that falls in the form of rain runs almost immediately downstream, moisture that falls as snow is naturally stored for later use.

"In terms of volume, reduced snowpack is a real problem," Droitsch says. "We have to plan. Canadians are some of the highest per capita users of water anywhere in the world. The whole purpose of this trip is to talk about the value of the water in this river."

While early summer flooding throughout southern Alberta destroyed property and attracted a great deal of public attention, Droitsch says the issue of water conservation remains as real as ever for those who live in Alberta's southern regions.

"Early in our trip the public's attention was understandably distracted by the flooding," Droitsch says. "But it didn't detract as much as I though it would have."

In the lower reaches of the Bow, she says, water use – much of it for irrigation – leaves water levels 75 to 90 per cent lower than they would be if left natural.

At Bassano the flood chart showed the three flood spikes in late June, during which the river was flowing at 1000 cubic metres per second. By the time Droitsch and Kievit reached that section in early August, flow was down to fifty cubic metres per second, or one quarter of the river's natural level. A full 75 per cent of the river's water is diverted for municipal, agricultural, industrial and other uses. Droitsch says that by the time they reached the end of their journey, temperatures were in the thirties and lawns were drying up in an area where cactus grows.

While water is available in reliable abundance in the upper reaches of the Bow River, communities downstream don't have the same luxury.

"We in the Bow Valley need to think about water management," Droitsch says. "There's not much thinking about how to allocate, conserve water here – but that's all they think about in the lower reaches. The ones who spend the most time worrying about it are the ones who receive the last bits."

As with land boundaries for wildlife, Droitsch says, a river cannot be divided neatly into sections.

"No ecological issue is that simple," she says. "Our role is to help make people aware of that."

A key issue, she adds, is that of in-stream flow needs – the flow needed in the river to provide for recreational uses and also to protect the river's natural environment after water allocated for consumption is drawn out.

"The question is: Where is the line for how much water we can continue to take out of the Bow?" Droitsch says. "We think it's a good idea to set water conservation objectives. We don't have a water problem today, but that doesn't mean we won't five or ten years from now."

FUNDRAISING FOR AFRICANS HELPS SOLO HIKER PERSEVERE (2007)

> Paul Žižka

Not long after Paul Žižka got dropped off by jet boat at the south-westernmost tip of New Zealand's South Island, he shook his head and asked himself, "Why did I come here?"

With no trail, Žižka plunged into the thick bush of Fiordland, a landscape of steep rock faces, deep valleys and a forest floor smothered in a tangle of rotting branches and lichen-wrapped tree trunks.

"Once I got dropped off, there was nowhere to go, I just had to start walking and remind myself I'd come here for a good reason," Žižka recalls.

That reason was not just to become the first person to hike between the two farthest points of New Zealand's South Island – 1488 kilometres from Gates Harbour, the island's most southwest point, to Cape Jackson at its northeast tip.

Having christened his project *arokä*, the Maori word for awareness, Žižka, twenty-seven, hoped by doing something that hadn't been done before he'd capture and then shift people's attention to his larger purpose – to raise awareness and funds for victims of the AIDS/HIV crisis in Africa.

A Quebec City native, Žižka graduated from earth and ocean sciences at the University of Victoria. As a great lover of the natural environment, he also harboured a long-time desire to become active in fundraising initiatives. But it wasn't until he travelled to Peru, Bolivia, Chile and Argentina that he started thinking about social issues.

"It was the first time I was exposed to people who have a quality of life lower than we have in Canada," Žižka says.

Then his friends Meghan Ward and Rachel Slater, both keen international development students in their mid-twenties, began telling Žižka about the efforts of UN special envoy for AIDS in Africa, Canadian Stephen Lewis. Žižka decided his first foray into fundraising would be a campaign to benefit AIDS sufferers in Africa.

"The guy is amazing," Žižka says of Lewis. "It seems like a lot of people who are already stuck with it [AIDS] are left out. The Stephen Lewis Foundation focuses on those people who are stigmatized, and helps ease their pain."

To learn more about AIDS in Africa first hand, Žižka travelled to Ethiopia in 2006 and spent three weeks with NGO Goh Ethiopia, a group helping AIDS orphans in an area hit particularly hard by HIV/AIDS and malaria.

"It was really overwhelming, but it also gave me a big boost, seeing their faces, knowing the people you're doing it for," Žižka says. "Three weeks is not a lot of time, but now I know more than I did."

At the same time, however, he realized the best way Westerners could help was simply by giving money.

"I was overwhelmed by how useless you feel and how you feel you could never do much that would really help," he says. "There's only a very small minority of people who, if they want to help, should actually go there. I think really the best thing 99 per cent of people can do is send money there and make sure it goes to an organization that does good things with it."

So the following summer, while he was serving tables at Num Ti Jah Lodge on the shores of Bow Lake in the Canadian Rockies, Žižka teamed up with Ward and with other co-workers and university students to found the Mountain Movement, his own grassroots organization dedicated to raising money for Africa's AIDS/HIV victims, with the Stephen Lewis Foundation as its beneficiary. By summer's end, the campaign had raised nearly $14,000 through a variety of initiatives, including AIDS Climbing Weeks and Servers Against AIDS events, through which serving staff at several Canadian Rockies dining rooms donated substantial portions of their tip money and collected additional funds from willing customers. The money was then turned over to the Stephen Lewis Foundation.

Once the summer season ended, Žižka spent the next few months planning in earnest for his New Zealand trek, corresponding with New Zealand tramping clubs and alpine club members to gain as much information about his route as he could.

Then in mid-January 2007, he flew to Christchurch from Quebec, where he had based himself at his parents' home in Alma to organize his trip. From Christchurch he travelled to Invercargill and on to Tutapere, where a boat driver had offered to ferry him to his starting point.

"Gates Harbour is as far southwest as you can go," Žižka says. "It's not on many maps – you need one with a pretty good scale to find it."

Remembering his purpose, he says, helped him persevere through the toughest hours of his forty-four-day solo trek, which he completed on March 6, 2007.

"The first three days were harder than I thought they would be," Žižka admits. "Fiordland was really good exercise for sure! I got really soaked the first couple of days. I've never been in bush that thick before, bushwhacking less than one kilometre an hour. I wasn't used to rivers swelling so much after it rains, and waiting for the rivers to go down so I could cross. I was definitely asking myself, 'Why did I come here?'"

After three days Žižka finally reached a faint track, and the following day he encountered his first fellow trekker. From then on, he saw people regularly.

"It was a lot more challenging than I expected," Žižka says. "It rained a lot, the bush was thick and the sandflies were awful. Navigating was difficult. You have that green wall around you all the time. There's not a lot that's on your side. You feel like the first person who's been in that area. It's pretty harsh terrain to travel in."

To navigate, Žižka used a GPS, and for safety he carried a personal locator beacon. Through the Fiordland section he also carried a New Zealand mountain radio, part of a national program that encourages trekkers and climbers to rent the units, which they set up to receive daily weather forecasts at 8 p.m. for all regions, and to check in with their own positions.

"You have to set up eighty metres of wire as straight as possible for it to work, so I had to get started early," Žižka says. "When you set it up successfully and you start receiving, it's very satisfying."

Travelling from south to north, in reverse to what most other trekkers he met were doing, Žižka camped and spent nights in about thirty huts, usually alone. The New Zealand hut system was "really nice and really convenient," he comments.

On nights when he did have company, he handed out business cards and shared information about the purpose of his trek. General reaction was very similar to that of most Canadians, he says – people had heard about the issue but weren't aware of its magnitude.

"There's a kind of numbness. People hear so much about it and then it slips off the radar," Žižka says. "A lot of people were surprised when I started talking about the numbers. They weren't aware that the level was so catastrophic in terms of the numbers of lives that have been lost in Africa."

Once north of Fiordland, Žižka felt fortunate to experience a nearly unbroken spell of highly unusual pleasant weather.

"Fiordland. I'll never forget that for sure," Žižka laughs. "But after that, I got really good weather. The locals were saying it was really unusual, the driest year in about ninety years. I crossed over Haast Pass and never saw a drop, and I got to see Mount Aspiring National Park at its best. It was a real treat and really different to walk up the west coast and be standing on a beach looking up at 3000-metre peaks, the ocean on my left and peaks on my right."

Throughout his trek, Žižka was continuously amazed and delighted with New Zealand's famously diverse landscape, a virtual kaleidoscope of sand beaches, rocky seashores, rainforests, snow slopes, boulder fields, lakeside bush, earthquake-rent valleys, fiords, swollen rivers, windswept passes, remote bays, thermal areas and farmland abounding with sheep.

Marlborough Sounds, the final segment of his journey (which he had divided into sixteen sections, each separated by a populated area where he could resupply), was a joy, he adds.

"I'd never seen that maze of inlets and peninsulas," Žižka gushes. "The track just sticks to the crest of the peninsula. You can see such a long way."

Looking northwest from there toward Africa, Žižka says he felt pleased with his accomplishment, which included raising almost $1,600 for the Stephen Lewis Foundation.

"I'm happy. The main purpose is to raise awareness," Žižka says. "If we're going to solve those big problems, it's going to take more than donations. We need to have a big shift in how people think.

"It was a great experience for me personally. But I also feel it was a team effort. Meghan [Ward] did so much – the organization, logistics, looking after the website, getting in touch with sponsors. People were so helpful, including all the Kiwis. I never felt like I was alone, with so many people involved, working together and pushing in the same direction to make something happen. Hopefully it had some effects on people."

FINDING FARLEY: A FAMILY PILGRIMAGE (2007)

> ❯ Karsten **Heuer**, Leanne **Allison**, Zev **Heuer**
> and **Willow** the **border** collie

He did it on a whim.

Karsten Heuer sent a final draft of his book *Being Caribou* to Farley Mowat, prolific writer, activist and beloved Canadian icon.

To Heuer's delight, Mowat replied, on paper-bag-brown stationery, typed on his Underwood, his name in bold capitals at the top left corner, complete with typos and alive with spirit and vigour.

"I thought he might enjoy it," Heuer shrugs.

The story tells how Heuer and his wife, Leanne Allison, followed a caribou herd on foot for 1500 kilometres across the Yukon to Alaska and back for five and a half months in 2003, in an effort to raise awareness of the US government's plans to drill for oil in the caribou's calving grounds in the Arctic National Wildlife Refuge. Mowat didn't just love the book, he was downright sorry when he finished reading it.

A few days after Heuer and Allison received Mowat's letter, the phone rang in the couple's Canmore, Alberta, home. It was Mowat himself, inviting Heuer and Allison to visit him at his Cape Breton farm.

"He just called out of the blue," Heuer laughs.

Thrilled, the couple accepted, then immediately pondered how, as keen environmental stewards, they should travel.

"We get to visit with Farley Mowat, but we can't fly and we can't drive across the country," Allison says. "Then I tossed out – how about canoe?"

Within moments they were tracing potential routes on maps with their fingertips.

In early May 2007, Heuer and Allison walked the three blocks from their house to the Bow River, loaded their two-and-a-half-year-old son, Zev, and Willow the border collie into their canoe and started paddling. Nearly six months later, the family sailed into Mowat's bay on Cape Breton Island, after spending the previous month touring Newfoundland by sailboat and visiting the settings of Mowat's books *A Whale for the Killing* and *The Boat Who Wouldn't Float*.

Having corresponded with the young family throughout their journey via letters sent General Delivery to destinations such as Leader, Saskatchewan, and Arviat, Nunavut, an enthusiastic Mowat, his wife, Claire, and a National Film Board crew welcomed the travellers. Extending his greetings, the outspoken eighty-six-year-old turned to Allison and declared, "You canoed all this way? I want to see your pectorals!"

Laughing, Allison says she was only slightly embarrassed before coming up with an appropriate response.

"I said, 'How about my biceps?'"

The hardest part of any trip, Heuer says, is actually leaving. Once the organizing and the trappings of home have all been left behind and the journey is launched, everything falls into place.

So it was, as an entourage of friends and neighbours and reporters and cameramen paraded down to the banks of the Bow River that May morning. Then, with just a little more fanfare, Heuer slid the canoe packed with food, camping gear, still and video cameras (Heuer plans to write a book, Allison to make a film), into the aqua green glacier meltwater. A few strokes later, with Zev sitting up front "looking for rocks," they were following the Bow River east. A few days later they reached Calgary, and then they continued on to where the Bow joins the South Saskatchewan, which they followed north to Saskatoon – a route that included portaging around no fewer than seven dams, in anticipation of which they carried a set of canoe wheels.

"We just loaded Zev into the canoe with all our gear, and a couple of times even hooked up Willow to help pull," Heuer says. "It worked really well."

Before leaving Canmore, Heuer and Allison had plotted their route as best they could, all the while cognizant there were uncertainties about how time and logistics might fit with their plans, particularly for the second half of their journey.

Aiming to reach Hudson Bay by mid-August, before freeze-up and fall weather made travel difficult, they decided they would have to fast track from Saskatoon to Reindeer Lake in northeastern Saskatchewan.

FROM LEFT, GREG HORNE, DAVE PORS, LYNN MARTEL AND SEAN ELLIOTT UNFURL THE FLAGS OF THE ALPINE CLUB OF CANADA AND THE INTERNATIONAL YEAR OF MOUNTAINS ON THE SUMMIT OF MOUNT BROWN, CANADIAN ROCKIES.

LEANNE ALLISON STRADDLES THE CONTINENTAL DIVIDE NEAR HOLMES PEAK, BC

PAUL ŽIŽKA AT THE WEST EDGE OF ARTHUR'S PASS NATIONAL PARK, CRONIN GLACIER IN THE BACKGROUND, SOUTH ISLAND, NEW ZEALAND.

DANIELLE DROITSCH, FRONT, A JIM KIEVIT PADDLE DOWN T BOW RIVER, ALBER

KARSTEN HEUER, LEANNE ALLISON,
ZEV AND WILLOW TAKE A BREAK
ON THE THLEWIAZA RIVER IN
NUNAVUT TERRITORY.

FROM LEFT, MIKE DOBBIN, LORI DOWLING AND ANGUS TAYLOR SAVOUR THE MOMENT ON THE SUMMIT OF MOUNT ATHABASCA, CANADIAN ROCKIES.

MEMBERS OF
THE PORCUPINE
CARIBOU HERD
HIKE ALONGSIDE
LEANNE ALLISON
IN NORTHERN YUKON.

GREG MORTENSON WITH KHANDAY VILLAGE
SCHOOLCHILDREN, HUSHE VALLEY,
KARAKORAM, PAKISTAN.

**PAULA DUNCAN HIKES ALONG THE CARTHEW–
ALDERSON TRAIL IN WATERTON LAKES
NATIONAL PARK, CANADIAN ROCKIES.**

Picking up a local newspaper, they perused the classifieds and purchased an old Chrysler Magic Wagon minivan for $400. After topping it up with a couple of litres of oil, they drove to Reindeer Lake, where they traded the vehicle for a boat ride across the 240-kilometre body of water.

"Reindeer Lake is an end of the gravel road kind of place," Heuer says. "It was really great interacting with all these local characters, from the Hell's Angels who ran the car dealership to the Cree guy in his driveway with a Magic Wagon the exact same year and model."

While travelling through the prairies, the connection between the landscape and the writings of Mowat's youth was less pronounced, Heuer says, but not so north of Reindeer Lake.

They paddled up the Cochrane River for thirteen days, then down the Thlewiaza River (which involved another seven portages), following a route taken by Mowat sixty years earlier with trapper Charles Schweder, a journey that built the foundation for his writings about the north, including *No Man's River*, *The Desperate People*, *Lost in the Barrens* and his first book, *People of the Deer*.

"The scent of Farley really got strong," Heuer says. "We could discern rapids and portage trails, his descriptions were so vivid from sixty years ago. We found the exact same wolf den from *Never Cry Wolf*. Zev and I were able to crawl down and poke our heads into it."

They also found the exact trading post featured in *People of the Deer*.

"You knew you were in those places as soon as you got to them," Allison says. "It made our experience and our respect for these places so much richer. I knew how Newfoundland smelled before we got there because of his books."

Veterans of long, challenging self-propelled expeditions – which include hiking, skiing and paddling 3400 kilometres from Yellowstone to Yukon in 1988–99, and following the Porcupine caribou herd across hummocky tundra for five months in 2003 – Allison and Heuer admit that at first they thought Zev, who turned three right after they returned home, would be the "big unknown factor."

"We'd already done a couple of eight-day canoe trips before this, and there's actually a calmness that comes over him on these trips,"

Heuer says. "Then when we come home there are all these distractions with his toys and friends that almost overwhelm him."

"These trips are always incredible bonding times," Allison adds. "Zev was a big part of our motivation, I think. It's such a great time to expose him to travelling and sleeping on the ground, while his little mind is still forming. With these kinds of trips, too, it's a great way to slow life down. They're great time expanders. It's as if we live a lifetime in a few months."

At the same time, as parents, the couple did wonder, prior to starting out, how their adventure would take shape with the addition of a very young teammate.

"On a trip like this, things creep up on you, and you only notice change the moment after it happens," Heuer says. "There was definitely a bit of an adjustment period for Zev, just getting used to the fact that we were confined to a canoe. We're lucky; he's already got a healthy respect for danger. But the idea that we weren't going home tonight took a few weeks to sink in. And on the fourth day we stopped in Calgary and we were at Grandma's house."

The turning point, albeit subtle, happened farther downstream as they paddled through the Siksika reserve, when they were overtaken by a fierce windstorm with rain and hail.

"Zev was totally comfortable in it; we didn't go for shelter on the shore," Heuer says. "Leanne and I were astounded at his level of comfort and ease and how he adjusted to the elements. Zev has always loved camping and being in the tent. But a lot of our hopes came to fruition with how nature occupied him – the campsites, the animals and our daily experiences worked out really well."

Portaging in northern Saskatchewan on seldom used trails littered with debris presented an extra challenge, however.

"It was definitely a struggle," Heuer admits. "One of us would be at the campsite with Zev, cooking dinner, while the other carried gear for two kilometres. But we never had to carry Zev; he's a really good hiker."

Shortly before reaching Arviat, a village on the western shore of Hudson Bay, the family experienced one of the most magical wild-animal encounters of their entire journey, as they stopped to scout a route through some technical Class III rapids.

"The wind was blowing hard and I was looking at the system of ledges and waves and circulating holes," Heuer recalls. "Then I looked out at this big slab of rock and there was this polar bear climbing onto it. I turned to Leanne stunned – people had told us we'd never see a polar bear in that area."

Standing on the shore with 30 metres of rapids separating them, they watched the bear casually fish from his perch, blocking the only channel they could navigate through the rapids.

Fortunately, a strong wind kept him from being aware of their presence.

"We said, 'Zev, there's a polar bear,'" Heuer says. "Two minutes later Zev's saying, 'I'm hungry, can I have a granola bar?' For him this was no different from any of the other things that had happened. Fortunately, the bear quit fishing and crawled out to take a nap on a rock."

Seizing the moment, they hurried right by the bear to start their run, worried about Zev and hoping Willow wouldn't bark and blow their cover.

"It was the wildest moment in terms of feeling small and insignificant in a way that was thrilling to feel that insignificant," Heuer says.

By the time they reached Arviat, Heuer and Allison realized they'd have to modify their plans again, since their original idea of hitching a ride on a supply ship to travel down the eastern coast of Labrador would mean a month of waiting in Iqaluit.

"One thing we learned about travelling with a toddler – keep moving," Heuer laughs.

But at the same time, through his letters Mowat urged the family to consider another option, saying he hadn't spent much time on the Labrador Coast.

"There were three letters and a book waiting for us in Arviat," Allison says. "You could tell he was getting pretty excited."

Embracing their new plan, the family hopped a plane to Churchill, Manitoba, then settled in for a two-day, two-night train ride to Winnipeg aboard what Mowat dubbed the "Muskeg Special," which cruised along tracks laid in earth so soft it moved under their weight at a top speed of about thirty kilometres per hour.

"Some of the other passengers were complaining, but we thought it was plenty fast after being in a canoe for three months," Heuer jokes.

"The train excited us," Allison adds. "Farley took the train as a teenager and en route a herd of caribou came across the tracks and stopped the train for several hours. It was a very significant early wildlife encounter for him."

Before boarding the train they experienced another highlight of their pilgrimage as they paddled their canoe in the mouth of the Churchill River surrounded by 1000 beluga whales.

"Their backs looked like whitecaps on the water," Heuer recalls.

Continuing by train to Montreal, they hunted for a sailboat reminiscent of Mowat's persistently leaky thirty-foot craft featured in *The Boat Who Wouldn't Float*, about his adventures with stormy seas, whales and women and an eternally leaky boat. Disappointed, they could find only fibreglass and motor yachts, until serendipity intervened and through a friend of a friend they connected with Nova Scotia sailor Tam Flemming, who skippered a ten-metre boat he'd built himself of teak, fir and ash. Better still, he'd just finished watching *Being Caribou*, Allison's Gemini Award-winning film about their adventure living among the caribou. He promptly cleared his schedule to sail with the four-member family for the next month. Riding the train to Gaspé, they hopped aboard an archaic cruise vessel to rendezvous at Îles de la Madeleine, then promptly sailed for twenty-four hours across a stormy Cabot Strait to Burgeo, Newfoundland.

"We couldn't have asked for a better match, his great sailing skills and his mellow demeanour. He became Zev's uncle," Heuer says.

Their first-ever sailing adventure exacted something of a toll, and as Zev made himself at home in a hammock slung across the galley below deck, oblivious to the reeling boat, his dad suffered through some extreme sea sickness, and Willow couldn't get comfortable enough to relieve herself, not even on the bed of spruce boughs laid out for her. She threw up, too.

"Until then, our sailing experience was limited to sticking two canoe paddles through a tarp," Heuer says. "It was a huge adjustment for Leanne and I; we didn't know what to think. We had nothing to relate it to. Tam was so mellow, and it turned out, despite his trips to the Caribbean, on this trip he was exposed to the toughest-sailing seas of his life."

After Flemming clipped her into a harness on deck, Allison soaked in her situation.

"It was the wildest thing, looking up at the masts and the stars," she recalls. "But the best thing about sailing was arriving in the communities. There was no marina; you just pulled up beside a fishing wharf with all the guys getting up at 5 a.m. to go fishing. It really immersed us in the culture."

While sailing away from Burgeo, the setting for Mowat's *A Whale for the Killing*, the family was accompanied by four fin whales – creatures Mowat would consider the progeny of those he encountered long ago.

"It's kind of like these spirits in body forms today that would appear to us on our journey," Heuer says.

"The whale was quite a thrill; it was bigger than our boat," Allison recalls.

To finish their journey, they sailed right into Mowat's bay and were promptly invited up for a drink.

"We were struck by how incredibly modest and low key his home was, his farmhouse with his writing space in the guest cottage," Allison says. "His desk is an old door; his chair is covered in duct tape; he's got a plastic milk crate for a foot stool. There are posters of past books and films, and black and white pictures of people from the Arctic."

Staying for three days, Heuer and Allison exchanged stories with their still alert but aging hero.

"It was emotional for all of us, but for him to be mining all his memories as we were exchanging stories, it was exhausting for him," Heuer says. "A lot of the places that were powerful for us, whether because of the landscape or the people or the animals, turned out they were the exact settings in his life, relived through his autobiography, the same places of resonance in his life. Lots has changed, but there were also lots of core elements in people and landscapes that are the same."

"I think, in his heart, he wanted to stay up and talk with us all night," Allison adds. "One of the big reasons we wanted to do this trip was so his stories were not forgotten. He was a childhood hero of mine. *Owls in the Family* was my first real book that I read. And *A Whale for the Killing* was what got me to have my first World Wildlife Fund membership when I was ten. His stories are still relevant, and human beings are not the most important creature on the planet. But I think his stories have the potential to be forgotten. It's a chance to pay tribute to him. Through our trip we can bring them to light in a different way."

ALBERTA'S ALPINE BIRTHDAY BASH (2005)

> Angus **Taylor**, Jim **Comfort**, Nathan **Taylor**,
Mike **Sanders and** Joe **Belanger**

First there's the idea. Small, fleeting, a mere glimpse of the greater objective. Then the maps, spread across the living room carpet, and a pencil to trace potential routes. Friends are e-mailed, prospective partners are lined up and soon the idea mushrooms into a full-blown expedition. Endless lists are compiled – equipment, food, possible sponsors, transportation, logistics. There's a website to design and a volunteer to post regular updates. Digital cameras, batteries, recharging options to consider, media connections to make, press releases to send out ...

Not to mention the beer.

When Angus Taylor first dreamed the first twinkling sparks of his big expedition, the only can he was cracking open was a frosty root beer.

The year was 1980, Alberta was celebrating its seventy-fifth birthday and Taylor's uncle Jim Comfort threw a party that lasted all summer. A wide-eyed eight-year-old at the time, Taylor was perpetually fascinated by the steady flow of tired, dirty, bearded and beaming mountain climbers kicking back in his uncle's backyard, sharing a few celebratory cold ones and pouring out spellbinding stories of their alpine adventures.

"Listening to those climbers, to their passion, their excitement, the joy they found in climbing – it was infectious," Taylor recalls.

To commemorate his province's seventy-fifth, Comfort had organized a unique mountain climbing expedition by coordinating 300 familiar friends and complete strangers to climb seventy-five Alberta Rockies peaks over the course of the summer. Comfort's celebration created lasting memories not just for the climbers but also for young Taylor, who began planning his own birthday party a quarter of a century into the future – for Alberta's hundredth in 2005.

"It was in the back of my mind ever since I was a kid," admits Taylor, whose uncle also inspired him to make the small Rocky Mountain town of Canmore, Alberta, his home. "As we got closer to the centennial I figured I'd be the logical one for the job."

❯ One **Special** Ice **Axe**

Far beyond the Rocky Mountain barrier, the eastern horizon glimmered a rosy shade of peach as Lori Dowling's crampons crunched into the gradually inclining slope of the lower Athabasca Glacier, a snowfield corrugated with crevasses. In her hand she clutched her ice axe with an extra firm grip.

This was Lori Dowling's first time climbing the Rockies landmark, with its summit touching the fading August night stars high above the Banff–Jasper National Park boundary on the Icefields Parkway. But her ice axe was a veteran. The old-style wooden axe had belonged to her father, Bob Dowling, who first climbed 3491-metre Athabasca in 1962 with her mother, who'd been daintily dressed in pink pedal-pushers, one of her husband's shirts, a green chiffon scarf and borrowed hiking boots. The climb afforded the couple active membership into the Alpine Club of Canada, which at that time required a prerequisite significant climb.

Then, in 1980, Lori Dowling had volunteered to celebrate Alberta's seventy-fifth birthday by climbing Jasper's Roche à Perdrix with Jim Comfort. Serving as the provincial commissioner for the celebrations, her dad, Bob Dowling, had also climbed with Comfort, choosing Mount Athabasca and taking his trusty ice axe with him.

Now seventy-eight and eighty years old, neither of Lori Dowling's parents were interested in peak-bagging to mark the province's centennial. Instead they were content to relax at the Columbia Icefields Chalet while Lori carried on the family tradition, reaching Athabasca's summit with her partner Mike Dobbin, ACMG (Association of Canadian Mountain Guides) certified guide Marc Piché and Angus Taylor, as part of his own celebration of Alberta's hundredth anniversary.

"Dad was really pleased that I wanted to climb Athabasca, so I took his ice axe with me. It's a long-handled wooden one, and it was its fifth time on the mountain. And having Angus along was just the icing on the cake," Lori Dowling says.

Starting at 2 a.m., their twelve-hour ascent was pretty much perfect, Taylor adds.

"We had absolutely perfect weather, a good solid freeze-up overnight. There was no post-holing, nothing slid, not even close. It was uneventful, which is the way I like my mountaineering. And the view was spectacular."

But not all of Taylor's summits were so smoothly reached.

› Sled **Hell**

Clipping into waist harnesses to tow gear-laden plastic/polymer sleds, each holding forty kilograms of food, camping gear, batteries and cameras, with another fifteen kilograms each in backpacks, Taylor and four companions skied away from a mostly deserted, snow-covered parking lot at Upper Kananaskis Lake one sunny morning in March 2005.

Cruising easily across the windswept frozen surface, they soon ground to a crawl as they attempted to manoeuvre through tightly spaced trees, following winding creekbeds into the forest. On only the second day of a twelve-day traverse from Kananaskis to Lake Louise – the first leg of a journey that was scheduled to conclude at the Willmore Wilderness area 250 kilometres north of Jasper – their sleds began to break apart.

"We had a massive gear failure," Taylor says. "The sleds we were dragging behind us literally began disintegrating. They became completely unruly; it was impossible to ski with them. From day two onward we just had a complete nightmare with those things."

The team, comprised of Taylor, his brother Nathan, Mike Sanders, John Blerot and Taylor's girlfriend, Colleen Delaney, struggled to control the sleds after the joints connecting them by long poles to their waist harnesses began to crumble. Navigating through trees became impossible, and on the downhills the sleds overtook the skiers, threatening serious injury.

"They would stop you dead and then clothesline you at the waist," Taylor recalls. "It was awful; and they injured us."

Jury-rigging the system to the best of their MacGyver abilities, they carried on, lurching over fallen logs and bushes only partially buried in the meagre Rockies snowpack. One day, exhausted, they stomped out what little space they could to pitch their tents on a steep slope. Pulling out their maps, compasses and GPS in the fading evening light, they accepted the discouraging realization they'd barely travelled a couple of kilometres.

"We had quite a journey on our first leg," Taylor recalls. "Colossal equipment failure, high drama and some scary skiing. It was really heinous. We slept that night on the only flat spot on the entire slope."

When asked about the team's decision to ski through tree-choked valley-bottom terrain towing sleds, Taylor insisted the manufacturer had assured him they supplied the same sleds to the US military, which routinely "drag them through everything, hauling heavy equipment."

"That was a bit of a disaster," Taylor admits. "None of us had tried it before. The reasoning behind it was that we could go longer periods of time without resupplying. Probably comes down to our own naïveté about it. We figured we were getting something that could do the job."

Among seasoned long-distance ski mountaineers, the preferred strategy involves carrying an average ten-day supply of dehydrated food in backpacks between pre-dropped food caches and using sleds for travelling long distances across massive and relatively flat and open glaciers – such as those found in Yukon.

But for Taylor's team, with two skiers suffering knee injuries, continuing was unanimously decided to be unsafe. Only five days and twenty-five kilometres into an 850-kilometre ski traverse, Taylor was forced to modify his plans – for what was then the second time.

› Taylor **Dreams** Big

Taylor's Alberta Centennial Mountain Expedition (ACME) involved nearly 1,000 volunteers who registered their choices from a list of 100 Rockies peaks posted on his climbalberta.com website. Objectives ranged from casual Sunday afternoon family-friendly hikes, to committing and technical multi-day mountaineering expeditions. In addition to replacing commemorative summit canisters – some dating back to his uncle's 1980s celebrations – climbers recorded their ascents on digital cameras Taylor supplied, to share their adventures on the website.

The second component of ACME was the ambitious ski traverse. Taylor's team – none of whose experiences exceeded five-day backcountry ski trips on frequently travelled routes – planned to start from the Canada–US border at Waterton Lakes International Peace Park. They were to finish fourteen weeks later at Intersection Mountain, the geographic point at which the Alberta–British Columbia border becomes a line of longitude. The never attempted route encompassed 1200 kilometres, in stages, of dense BC forest, high alpine passes and expansive glaciers. It incorporated the twenty-one-day Great Divide Traverse from Lake Louise to Jasper, which crosses the whiteout-prone and frequently un-navigable Wapta, Freshfields, Mons, Lyell, Columbia, Clemenceau and Hooker icefields. The Great Divide Traverse is a challenging wilderness expedition that has only been completed a handful of times, and never from south to north.

Long before they packed their sleds, however, January's warm, rainy weather rendered the route unskiable between Waterton and Kananaskis Country. It was then that Angus modified his plans for the first time and decided to start the ski journey from Kananaskis. Ultimately, Angus and Nathan Taylor, Mike Sanders and Joe Belanger skied less than 500 kilometres, from Kananaskis Lakes to the Columbia Icefield in five stages, skipping the Lyell region completely.

"In retrospect, it was bittersweet," Taylor says. "We went a long ways and we saw some neat stuff, and we really enjoyed it. But we weren't able to accomplish our goals – a lot of it went undone. But I believe we made decisions for the right reasons: ultimately nobody got hurt; we all walked away in one piece."

Accomplishing as much of the ski traverse as they did, however, allowed Taylor to capture coveted film footage of the high mountains to be used as content for ACME's third component – creating a new educational program that will become part of Alberta's Grade 4 geography curriculum. Working on his masters in distance learning, Taylor secured grant money from Alberta Learning to develop his Educational Outreach Project. While most distance learning is linear, Taylor explains, his program – to which Delaney is a key contributor – makes geography more interactive, in a "Lara Croft, puzzle-solving kind of way."

"That's what we want to do with the geography and geology of the Rocky Mountains, so the kids can learn about rocks and glaciers and the national parks," Taylor says. "It will be quest-like. Rather than being tested through working through the program, they will show they've been learning through their choices."

› An **Old** Mountaineer **Is a Wise** Mountaineer

As alumni of the 1980 celebrations, members of Calgary's Grizzly Group (so named after an encounter with an actual grizzly, not because of their personal appearances), decided they would participate again in 2005, citing the education component as a selling feature.

"We all thought it was a really good event to profile the mountains as part of Alberta's heritage," says Mike Simpson. "It had a spin-off with the educational purposes after the event. A lot of other centennial events were one-day affairs, then forgotten. This one had lasting value."

All seasoned alpine veterans, Simpson, Lyn Michaud, Leon Kubbernus and Whistler's Karl Ricker – who'd been a member of Hans Gmoser's epic 1959 Mount Logan East Ridge expedition, which put the first all-Canadian team on Canada's highest summit – settled on not one, but three objectives: an easy hike on Mount Crandell (2381 metres), a scramble up Mount Blakiston (2910 metres) and a "real" climb, Jasper's Mount Geraldine (2900 metres).

"We've benefited from the mountains for many years and felt that participating in the centennial affair was one small way of giving back," Simpson says.

An easy scramble via its back side, Geraldine's north ridge promised a full day of 5.5 rock climbing along a quartzite ridge. But first they had to get there.

"The trail was sketchy at best," Ricker says. "It was primarily a bushwhack to get to the bivy site. In the morning, the troops did not like the looks of the weather. The black clouds rolled in. We couldn't see the summit of [neighbouring] Edith Cavell. Looking up at the first pitches of a vertical multi-pitch climb, there were signs that something nasty could happen."

Exhibiting the good sense that grants a climber the opportunity to climb another day, the group retreated. Exhibiting unusual fashion sense, the Grizzly Group, including some of their wives, who joined in for the easier ascents, summitted Crandell and Blakiston in period clothing, explaining, "We took some photos to replicate the clothing and gear of 100 years ago. Some of our climbers looked as if they were almost as old as Alberta!"

> The **One** that **Got** Away

Geraldine wasn't the only mountain that had climbers weathered out. Like his uncle Jim Comfort twenty-five years before him, who sat at its base watching rain pour down for a week, Taylor's own dream of climbing the Rockies' loosest, scariest and most elusive peak, 3619-metre Mount Alberta, were dashed, as record-setting June rains left excessive piles of snow on its ledges.

"It was a big disappointment. For the sake of the project, I'd really hoped to get that one done," Taylor says. "It just was not possible this year. But that's what climbing is all about. [Mount] Alberta has always had a certain mystique – for me and many climbers. It grants such a small window of opportunity each year; it just doesn't give itself up easily."

Taylor is a self-described weekend mountaineer and keen rock climber who has explored sport-climbing crags in France, Australia and Thailand, climbed 6000-metre non-technical peaks in Nepal, and a host of mid-range routes in his home Rockies. He did reach a dozen summits on the ACME list, including easy half-day hikes up Banff's Sulphur and Tunnel Mountains with groups of Banff and Canmore Grade 4 students, and Lake Louise's Mount Fairview with representatives of Edmonton's Swiss Consul. Taylor also made his way up 2240-metre Mount Yamnuska's backside scrambling route with Alberta Community Development Minister Gary Mar, who was led by ACMG guide and Kananaskis public safety manager George Field, as part of a sixteen-person entourage.

By the end of his summer project, however, organizing everyone else's climbs had become Taylor's biggest expedition of all.

"It had been my hope to spend the entire summer climbing and getting out with the various teams, but the organizing of the peaks was a big logistical challenge."

Triumphantly, about 1,000 eager Albertans climbed 100 Alberta Rockies mountains, plus a couple more for good measure. Just in time for the province's official birthday on September 1.

Happy peak baggers included members of Canmore's seniors hiking group, the Meanderthals, the Alpine Club of Canada and Trail Minders of the Bow Valley. Two groups from the same team climbed Mount Sir Douglas via different routes to rendezvous at the summit.

Impressively, among all those hikers, scramblers and climbers, not a single injury was reported. Credit, Taylor says, goes to organizers who planned outings with care and consideration for the participants' abilities.

"I'm overjoyed that we got it done," Taylor says. "This is the end of a four-year journey for me. I'm still amazed that that many Albertans wanted to participate. I'm especially pleased there were so many novices and first-timers reaching their first summits. It was a scene that played over and over, all summer long. They'll remember those for the rest of their lives."

Some of them might even start planning Alberta's 150th birthday.

LONG-DISTANCE HIKER FOCUSES ON THE IMPORTANT (2006)

> Paula **Duncan**

When it comes to long distance mountain hikes, Paula Duncan can't get enough.

With several Himalayan treks and a ten-day solo hike of Jasper's 192-kilometre North Boundary Trail behind her, Duncan decided to spend fifty-three days of the 2006 summer hiking the 1200-kilometre Great Divide Trail, from Waterton Lakes National Park to BC's Kakwa Lake Provincial Park.

Not content to simply walk the wilderness route that crosses the Continental Divide thirty times, Duncan was also hiking to raise money to benefit Child Haven International, a charity that runs homes for orphans and destitute women, children and seniors in India, Nepal, Tibet and Bangladesh.

"The long-distance hikes I've done have never seemed long enough," says Duncan, forty-three. "I love being out there. I love walking, the simplicity of it and getting in the rhythm of doing it day after day. Living out of a backpack helps cut through the superficial and superfluous that one tends to get bogged down in, and you come back more focused on what is truly important in life."

When Duncan reached the end of the trail on August 27, she happily embraced three of life's most important elements – her partner, Simon Bryant, and the champagne and chocolates he bore.

Having started out from Waterton on June 21, the summer solstice, and followed the scenic Carthew–Alderson Trail for twenty-three kilometres to the Akamina Creek campsite, Duncan said goodbye the next morning to Bryant, who had rendezvoused with her at the campsite for their last night together. Then, detouring from the main trail, she bushwhacked for half an hour to access steep, open slopes to the 2446-metre summit of Mount Rowe, from where she followed largely snow-free ridgetops for another fifteen kilometres.

"I like to go places I haven't been before," Duncan explains. "If I've done a section of trail before, I'll look for alternatives. There are always all these side trails. Sometimes I think every hike is just a reconnaissance for future trips."

Duncan spent nearly eight weeks hiking through remote Canadian Rockies wilderness, nearly all of it solo, and sometimes not seeing another person for up to six days. Likely the first woman to hike the route solo, Duncan says she was relieved her trip unfolded smoothly and without unpleasant animal encounters.

"I was so lucky – lucky with the weather and the kindness of strangers helping me out of the blue," Duncan says. "Everybody was asking about bears. I think some people were almost disappointed I didn't have hand-to-hand combat."

Prepared for encountering bears on the trail, Duncan says she carries all whistles, no bells, plus an air horn and bear spray.

"When you encounter hikers wearing bells, you often don't hear them until they are twenty feet away," she explains. "When I need them, my noisemakers can be heard over a kilometre away. I knew there would be situations in which I would be fearful, such as river crossings, or bear encounters, but I felt I had enough experience and skills to handle those things. I'm very careful with my food, and I'm very aware of bear signs. My general philosophy is to deal with things as they occur."

Her most memorable animal encounter happened one morning when she awoke to find her carbon-fibre trekking poles missing. They turned up seven metres away from the tent, carted off by a ground squirrel who had chewed up the handles and straps.

By journey's end, Duncan says her biggest challenge had been a whiteout brought on by a snowstorm while crossing a 2460-metre pass in the White Goat Wilderness Area, which forced her to navigate with compass and GPS.

"It was raining the night before with hail and thunder and lightning," Duncan says. "By morning it looked like it could go either way, but on my way up the pass rain turned to snow and the visibility dropped to about ten feet. I was counting the time between the lightning and thunder, first it was five seconds, then it was three. The snow came down so hard my map was sopping wet."

Before starting out, one of Duncan's biggest concerns had been unbridged river crossings – a concern she shared with another Great Divide solo hiker she met who was travelling from Jasper to Waterton. Comparing maps, GPS coordinates and creek crossings, neither had encountered anything higher than knee deep.

"You're at the headwaters of so many rivers where glaciers used to be and they're all receding," Duncan says. "You think about that a lot when you're out there – about our impact on the planet and my part in it. Watching glaciers disappear raises lots of questions. Then it hits you how so much of our society is petroleum dependent – our clothes, agriculture, everyday things – it's not just our cars."

Inspired by Dustin Lynx's *Hiking Canada's Great Divide Trail*, Duncan turned her attention to hiking the route after running Calgary's Burnco Marathon in 2005.

"After the marathon, I thought, this is just a different kind of marathon," she says.

She studied the route, bought a GPS unit and mapping software, researched lightweight backcountry equipment and prepared nutritionally dense meals in her dehydrator all winter long. At its heaviest, her pack weighed just fourteen kilograms, including rain gear, sleeping bag, tent, stove, fuel, food, toiletries and requisite mountain clothing. She and Bryant arranged for her to resupply along the way in Coleman, Alberta; Canmore, Alberta; Field, BC; and Jasper, Alberta.

While striving to keep her pack light, however, Duncan tried to replace lost weight when she stopped in towns. Before starting out, she purposefully gained five kilograms, but by summer's end she'd lost 6.5 kilograms.

"I put whipped cream in my coffee and butter on everything," she says with a laugh, all the while conscious of such North American luxuries, while she pointed out that in countries such as India and Tibet, destitute is measured at less than one good meal per day.

A licensed practical nurse at the Strathmore and Canmore, Alberta, hospitals, for nine years, Duncan has helped organize events with Calgary's Child Haven support group.

"After trekking in Nepal, I've found being involved with Child Haven is a great way to give back to a place that affected me profoundly," Duncan says. "I think what Child Haven does is very effective – raising children through vocational schools so they can grow up to be self-sufficient."

At last tally, she'd raised about $8,000, while many hikers she encountered along her route pledged to donate when they got home.

Although she feels fatigued now that she's home in Calgary, Duncan says she felt strong out on the trail.

"I can't believe how fast it went by," she says. "I don't want to say it was easy, though, because some parts were really hard."

Like the day Duncan arrived at her intended campsite to discover numerous bear tracks and scat piles.

"I had a really strong feeling, I just knew I didn't want to be camping there," she says. "It looked like a sow and a couple of adolescents. I don't usually get feelings that strong, but when I do, I listen to them."

Continuing over the next pass, the tracks disappeared, as did the feeling – but not her love for solo hiking.

"When you're hiking solo, you see more, hear more; it allows for a mindful meditation," Duncan says. "When you're with someone, you talk a lot and you miss stuff. I have a more profound wilderness experience when I'm by myself. It's wonderful to wander, to see what each day brings – new landscapes, challenges in terrain, and a further appreciation and gratefulness for being in a life and situation where I have the privilege to be out doing this."

JOURNEY A GATEWAY TO SOMETHING MUCH BIGGER (2005)

> Karsten **Heuer** and Leanne **Allison**

As they watched a grader smooth out one of five gravel roads in the Yukon village of Old Crow, Leanne Allison and Karsten Heuer, fresh off the land after living among the Porcupine caribou herd for five solid months, felt completely overwhelmed by the modern technology of the 300-resident community.

Watching the grader, however, was not nearly as overwhelming as the experience they shared – seven airports and barely a week later – in Washington, DC, where they met with aides for senators and congressmen in an attempt to lobby on behalf of the caribou.

"It was very surreal," Heuer recalls. "We were still searching for caribou tracks in vacant lots near Capitol Hill."

The couple embarked on their über trek in April 2003, and for nearly half a year followed the migrating herd from its wintering grounds at Old Crow to its calving grounds on the coastal plain of Alaska's Arctic National Wildlife Refuge (ANWR) – and back again.

For 27,000 years, the 123,000-strong herd has navigated different routes across the hummocky tundra, over steep mountain slopes and through raging rivers. Never knowing where the caribou would go. next, Heuer and Allison walked, skied and paddled 1500 kilometres, enduring fierce snowstorms, body-numbing river crossings, relentless insect swarms and the terror of being stalked by starving grizzly bears.

But they weren't just pursuing adventure.

Beneath the 1.5-million-acre coastal plain, and the precise strip of land where the caribou give birth every spring, is believed to be 3.5 billion barrels' worth of recoverable crude oil. The couple was following the trail of the caribou in order to experience, document and hopefully understand the daily hardships faced by the caribou as they journeyed along their annual migration path, all the while facing a potentially devastating threat as the US government proposed oil and gas development in the very heart of the calving grounds.

Over the course of their journey, Heuer and Allison pursued a quest that didn't only immerse them in the rugged landscape of the Arctic tundra but ultimately transported them to something resembling a shamanic journey into another dimension.

Heuer, a wildlife biologist, national park warden and author, was inspired to embark on the "Being Caribou" journey in 2001. While working as a park warden in Yukon's Ivvavik National Park, he spent two days hunkered down in the caribou's calving grounds, completely mesmerized as 20,000 caribou flowed incessantly around him. Watching the animals as they were swept down a turbulent river and mauled by hungry grizzlies, Heuer became curious about the reality of the animals' perpetual journey.

He also became concerned about how the herd might be affected by the intrusion of oil drilling machinery right in the heart of its calving grounds. Other caribou herds have survived despite drilling in their habitat, he explains, only because they found alternative calving grounds. No alternative grounds exist for the Porcupine herd, because its strip of land is so small. Adult females are in their poorest condition of the year when they arrive at the calving grounds, usually in the first week of June after weeks of arduous travel. After giving birth, they are dependent on the area's unique, high-protein cotton grass, which transforms half-starved mothers into milk factories for their rapidly growing calves. Due to the wet and flat nature of the coastal landscape, wolves don't dig dens there, while grizzlies, a nearly constant presence throughout most of the migration, find the area unattractive for unknown reasons and thus leave the newborns less vulnerable to predation.

Opening ANWR to drilling, Heuer explains, would threaten not only the caribou but also the golden eagles, wolves, bears and countless other animals that rely on the migrating herd for their own survival, as well as the traditional culture of the region's Gwich'in people, for whom the caribou are an intrinsic element of life.

All for an estimated six-month supply of oil.

"Too often we reduce things to numbers and economic forecasts," Heuer says. "Decisions are being made without people having any awareness of what's actually at stake."

"Being Caribou" was not the couple's first long-distance trek to understand the practical realities of wildlife survival. Over eighteen months in 1998–99, Heuer travelled by foot, horseback, skis and canoe, covering 3400 kilometres from Yellowstone National Park to Watson Lake, Yukon – the trek known as Yellowstone to Yukon, or Y2Y – with Allison accompanying him for the latter, and more challenging, half of the journey.

Long-time friends, they had attended the same kindergarten in Calgary, Alberta, in the early 1970s. They didn't encounter each other again until university, when Karsten's boss, who was also Leanne's good friend, insisted they meet because they were so much alike. Both loved skiing, whitewater kayaking, canoeing, backpacking and climbing. Through the following years they shared numerous outdoor adventures, but it wasn't until their Y2Y expedition that their friendship blossomed into romance. "Being Caribou" was actually their honeymoon.

From the very beginning, however, Heuer said "Being Caribou" was a very different journey. First off, maps were useless because the caribou didn't plan their route.

"The caribou are very unpredictable. They take different routes to the calving grounds every year," Heuer says. "We had to get used to travelling in circles, to not having a goal, to not having a destination."

Following the herd, on skis and then on foot, the couple laboured under sixty-five-pound packs laden with supplies that included a satellite phone to arrange for food drops, still and video cameras, and a solar battery charger – necessary tools for his book project and her documentary – as they struggled to keep pace with large numbers of caribou that literally flowed across the barren mountains, unaffected by deep snow or rugged terrain.

"It's just like gravity doesn't affect them," Heuer says. "We were just getting hammered over the head with exhaustion. We were overwhelmed with unknowns, the scale of the mountains and the difference in the experience from all our previous ones."

Eventually they stopped fighting their circumstances, surrendered, and accepted their fate. After two months, they reached the calving grounds. The cows, until then extremely tolerant of the humans' presence, became skittish at the slightest movement. Heuer and Allison were held hostage in their tent for ten days, crawling on their bellies to fetch water as calves were born all around them.

"When Leanne and I left the calving grounds, we pretty much stopped talking to each other. We were whispering," Heuer says.

"There was less of a need for words. A hushed quality permeated the rest of our days out there."

Then suddenly, the pace quickened as the caribou rushed toward the mountains to escape swarming mosquitoes and flies, some delirious in pain with flies so deep inside their heads that brown mucus gushed out their nostrils.

"The animals started to move at incredible speed, almost as if they were possessed," Heuer says. "Leanne and I had to move as if we were possessed."

They ate on the run and slept only a couple of hours at a time in an effort to keep moving through the twenty-four-hour daylight of the Arctic in summer.

"All these things together brought the next frame of mind," Heuer explains. "That line between dreaming and waking fused, blurred together. We were sleep deprived, hungry and dizzy. We started to get visions."

After not seeing any bulls for many days, Heuer dreamt vivid dreams. Upon waking he announced, "We're going to see bulls today."

Opening their tent flap, his dream played out before their eyes. From that point on they didn't need to follow tracks to find the herd. Instead they listened and moved in the direction of what Heuer called "the thrumming." As he attempts to describe the experience, Heuer's speaking tone changes from a neutral reporting of scientific fact to one of peaceful wonder.

"It was a different dimension, I guess," he shrugs. "It was probably always there. It just started to be accessed. The good thing is, we're disconnected but we haven't lost it. It's still this nugget that's inside all of us."

That kind of transformation, he adds, can only be discovered in big, intact wilderness.

"You won't get that from an hour-long run in the wildlife corridor – it's not long enough, but probably not wild enough either."

Native legends describe the local Gwich'in, Inuvialuit and Inupiat people on both sides of the Yukon–Alaska border, whose traditional way of life is centred on the caribou hunt, communicating with the caribou. Scientists and land-use managers are so easily caught up in correct terms and structured boundaries, Heuer says, that they forget about the thrumming.

"We should all make efforts to hear it," Heuer advises. "The vibration is still out there – the thrumming."

It's an effort he and Allison have struggled to sustain since they left the herd.

"All the barriers and layers we'd shed over those five months began to grow back," he says. "'Being Caribou' taught us about being human on a deeper level. We caught a glimpse into our own ignorance during the five months on the tundra, and so far as I can tell, there's nothing in the technological world that will help cure that ignorance. It's hard living in conventional society knowing that most of what occupies people detracts from the marrow of life. We are living in a world of distractions, and sifting through them to what's important is exhausting."

Rejoining everyday society presents an ongoing challenge, he adds.

"It's something we continue to struggle with, and may very well struggle with for the rest of our lives," he says. "Even now, months later, the transition is still happening. Leanne and I are changed people. It's a world we grew up in, but we're still struggling to belong. But this whole project has been a leap of faith without knowing how it's going to turn out, just knowing what's right."

While not everyone can experience the thrumming firsthand, he says, it's more important to embrace the surety of its existence.

"Everyone, I think, has had some sort of a connection with nature, and that's what I'm trying to build on in my presentations – to show how it's a gateway to something much bigger," Heuer explains.

"The thrumming is a symbol for everything magical and mysterious in nature, everything that we don't know about that gets destroyed when we push over a stand of trees for yet another building, or cut off another wildlife corridor so we can play a few more holes of golf. What's important isn't that people connect with the thrumming but that they connect with the idea of loss – losing something big, mysterious and mind-blowing without even knowing it exists."

A GIANT LEAP FOR THE COMMUNITY (2006)

> Greg **Mortenson**

In 1993 Greg Mortenson was an experienced American mountaineer who set off to climb 8611-metre K2, the world's second highest mountain, located in Pakistan's remote Karakoram Range. His goal was simple – to climb what many consider the world's toughest mountain to honour his sister, Christa, who had died of epilepsy.

After seventy-eight days on the mountain, Mortenson missed his own chance to summit after helping rescue a stricken fellow climber. Exhausted, emaciated and emotionally drained, he became separated from his teammates on the 100-kilometre trek back to the nearest town, and he stumbled into the uncharted village of Korphe. As the ethnic Balti villagers nursed him – the first foreigner they'd ever met – back to health, Mortenson witnessed a scene that would redefine his life.

"I saw eighty-four children sitting in the dirt, trying to learn their lessons and scratching in the sand with sticks," Mortenson recalls. "There were seventy-nine boys and five girls, and they were so keen to learn. I just had this Eureka moment – I hadn't reached the summit, but I could help here in this village."

He would build them a school.

Mortenson returned to California and his nursing profession. In between emergency room shifts, he pecked away at an electronic typewriter (he was computer illiterate), diligently composing no fewer than 580 letters to wealthy celebrities in an attempt to raise the requisite $12,000. His only response came from US TV news anchor Tom Brokaw, who wished him luck along with a $100 cheque.

Mortenson applied for sixteen grants, none successfully. Discouraged but undaunted, he sold his climbing gear and the Buick his grandfather had passed down to him, which he'd christened La Bamba and had used as his crashpad for a year and a half.

Then, on a visit to the elementary school in Wisconsin where his mother, Jerene, was principal, Mortenson gave a slide show. Unlike many adults, the kids embraced his message right away. Students filled two 150-litre trashcans with 62,345 pennies and sent Mortenson a cheque for $623.45.

"It wasn't adults who helped, but children who reached out across the world with no bias or prejudice," he says.

Finally, his luck turned when a short item in the American Himalayan Foundation newsletter intrigued Dr. Jean Hoerni, an ornery Swiss-born physicist, inventor, former climber and multi-millionaire, who donated the entire $12,000 on the promise that Mortenson wouldn't "piss it away smoking dope on some Mexican beach with his girlfriend."

Enthused, Mortenson returned to Pakistan with $12,800 in $100 bills stashed in a green nylon stuff sack – enough to build the school and cover his living expenses for several months. Aided by the watchman at his $2 per night hotel, he spent the next few weeks bargaining with local tradesmen for bags of cement, nails, sledgehammers and wooden roof struts, and drinking countless cups of tea throughout the negotiation.

Finally, he hired a 1940s Bedford truck and its driver, loaded it with building supplies and climbed aboard, heading toward northern Pakistan via the notoriously treacherous Karakoram Highway. After several days of swaying above 350-metre drops and avoiding oncoming traffic hurtling toward them on the narrow, bouncy dirt track, he and the driver finally arrived in Skardu, still an eight-hour jeep ride from Korphe. Here, he would have to store the building supplies until he could arrange for them to be transported any farther. Days – and numerous cups of tea and conversations later – Mortenson finally arrived by jeep at the Braldu River. Jamming his six-foot-four frame into a fruit crate held together by a few nails and suspended over the turbulent river from a 110-metre-long cable, he reached the opposite shore, where a familiar man greeted him.

"They were shocked; they couldn't believe I'd come back," Mortenson recalls. "Then they told me I'd made a couple of mistakes – you don't start building in late fall, and second, they would first need a bridge over the Braldu."

Mortenson's lessons were just beginning – and he had much to learn about helping people in remote regions.

"I went there to make sure I fulfilled my promise," Mortenson says. "I had no clue how I was going to do this. When I got there, I was feeling very fulfilled, very proud, that I'd brought the supplies to build them a school. I didn't realize I had a lot of lessons to learn."

Mortenson settled in, stayed the winter and learned the Balti language.

Having gown up on the slopes of Mount Kilimanjaro in Tanzania, East Africa, from infancy to the age of fifteen, where his father founded the Kilimanjaro Medical Centre and his mother started the Moshi International School, Mortenson felt at home among the Balti villagers, and they welcomed him as family.

By winter's end, Mortenson returned to the US, Hoerni wrote another cheque, and Mortenson made his way back to Korphe with enough money for materials to build a ninety-metre bridge over the Braldu, with all the labour carried out by local villagers.

He describes the building of the bridge in his book, *Three Cups of Tea*, written with journalist David Oliver Relin. The Herculean effort astounded him, as ten men carried each of the five 800-pound cable coils. For the men, many of whom had worked as porters, labouring that hard to improve life for their village, rather than carrying loads for foreign climbers chasing inscrutable goals, was a pleasure.

For Mortenson, however, the biggest lesson from building the bridge came as he attempted to micromanage the project. Locking away his receipts and his plumb line, a village elder told him to "sit down, shut up and let us do the work."

"I had to let go, let them be empowered," Mortenson says. "They have more to teach us than we can ever learn from them, and than we can ever teach them."

After thirty trips, totalling sixty months spent in Pakistan and Afghanistan over thirteen years, Mortenson, through his non-profit Central Asia Institute, has built fifty-five schools, helping educate 22,000 children, some of whom walk up to three hours a day to attend classes. A committee of elders guides each project, the community matches funds with equal amounts of labour and natural resources, and the teachers are locals.

Mortenson's priority is educating girls, which, he says, accomplishes three things: reduces population explosion, reduces infant mortality, and significantly improves basic health and quality of life in a region where one in three babies born alive doesn't reach its first birthday, and where the literacy rate is about 3 per cent.

"By educating girls, I don't mean not educating boys," Mortenson explains.

An educated girl, however, is more likely to return to her village and pass her knowledge on. An educated mother is less likely to support her son in terror activities, since a man must gain his mother's permission before embarking on jihad – holy war. And a literate boy , Mortenson continued, is less likely to be recruited into a Taliban-run madrassa, or school, that encourages terrorist activities.

As a climber, Mortenson says, despite growing up accustomed to abject poverty, on expedition to places such as Nepal he found the disparity bothersome.

"While I was considered poor in the us, it bothered me that I had all this free time to lollygag and climb," he says. "A lot of climbers and trekking expeditions feel they're bringing money into the economy. But a lot of the older women in the villages tell me now their workload is double. Men leave to work as porters or to build roads, leaving the women to work the fields, move heavy rocks."

Of the men who leave the villages, only half manage to find gainful employment, he says, which is measured at $1 day or about $400 year. Many of them sell their resources, such as a goat, to get that work.

"And what do they do with the money?" Mortenson continues. "Mainly, they buy white flour. Their socio-economics and their diet have changed. It's very prestigious for them to come back home with fifty bags of white flour. But if they'd stayed home, they could have been growing a lot more buckwheat and whole grains – which are more nutritious."

Mortenson's own story has become filled with adventure far beyond the realm of mountaineering. He speaks Balti, Farsi and Urdu, in addition to Swahili, which he learned as a child. He spends seven months a year raising two children with his wife, Tara, in Bozeman, Montana. The hardest part, he says, is being away from his family the other five months.

He's hunted ibex with villagers, crossing glaciers in his running shoes while the locals wore sandals, and slept in caves. He survived a firefight between Afghan opium smugglers. He's had two separate fatwas issued against him to banish him from Pakistan for educating girls – both rescinded by high-level mullahs. While venturing into Afghanistan unaccompanied by any locals, he was kidnapped and held captive in a small, dark room for eight days. Undeterred, and since then formally invited, Mortenson returned to that region to build several schools.

In the US, he's received death threats, and been "debriefed" by the CIA twice.

"I think it's interesting; what we're doing is more to promote peace than anything," Mortenson says. "I loathe the Taliban as much as I do some rednecks. They're hijacking society in the name of Islam."

For that reason, he admits the book's subtitle – *One Man's Mission to Fight Terrorism and Build Nations ... One School at a Time* – chosen by the publisher, is somewhat misrepresentative.

"I don't really care about fighting terror," Mortenson says. "The biggest issues in the world we need to address today are poverty, illiteracy, ignorance. Ignorance breeds hatred."

Calculated by UNICEF, the estimated cost of eradicating global illiteracy is $6 billion to $8 billion annually for fifteen years. In 2005, Mortenson says, the US spent $94.2 billion in Iraq, and another $14 billion in Afghanistan, fighting the "War on Terror."

"What the US military spends in eighteen months could wipe out illiteracy, globally," Mortenson says. "The US is trying to plug in democracy like it's electricity. Building democracy starts with education of boys and girls, and women's suffrage – including land ownership, the ability of women to own and inherit land. Without land ownership, people don't become invested in the communities."

While the political climate in the US and across Asia can be disheartening, Mortenson says he continues to believe in the inherent good in mankind.

"I look into the eyes of my children, and I see the eyes of children in Pakistan and Afghanistan," he says.

"When I see those little girls – their tiny bare feet, or in plastic Chinese boots, walking to school – those little footprints in the dust may be tiny, but I think of Neil Armstrong on the moon. She'll become a role model, a giant leap for her community."

ACKNOWLEDGEMENTS

They say it takes a village to raise a child; I believe it takes an entire community to nurture a writer.

To my Bow Valley community of Banff and Canmore, I must express enormous gratitude, particularly to everyone who has ever phoned or e-mailed me to offer praise or thanks for a story I wrote, for unceremoniously pointing out any errors I may have committed and for greeting me in the produce aisle with the phrase "You know what you should write about?..."

I could not imagine doing it without you.

Thank you to Suzan Chamney for her sound ear and for her willingness to share her valuable talents no matter how often I ask for help.

Thanks to Vi Sandford for her critical eye and her eagerness to share her time and insights.

I owe many, many thanks to Pat Morrow for generously sharing the rewards of his own hard-earned experience and for always adding a lively dollop of superbly sharp commentary to the conversation.

I also owe immeasurable thanks to Chic Scott for being a selfless routefinder on the challenging path of the mountain writer and for encouraging the generation behind him to record its own history.

Many, many, many thanks to Bob Sandford for being a real friend, for sharing his wisdom and experience, for believing in me and for always encouraging me to accomplish everything he knows I can.

Thank you to my writer friends who've taken the time over the years to answer my questions or to share a drink and a generous helping of high quality, stimulating, entertaining and inspiring conversation, especially Geoff Powter, Dave Dornian, Greig Bethel, Rob Alexander, Pam Doyle, Dahlma Llanos Figueroa, Christie Pashby, Jen Lutz and Michael Finkel.

Thanks to all the veteran climbers and mountain guides who have taught me so much about the unique mountain world in which I live, especially Lloyd "Kiwi" Gallagher and Hans Gmoser.

Many thanks also to Bernie Schiesser, Eric and Dorle Lomas, Sepp, Andre and Barb Renner, Brad Harrison, Dan Verral, Chris Espinel, Tannis Daikin, Larry Dolecki, Cori Brewster, Ruedi and Nicoline Beglinger and the Alpine Club of Canada for their generous hospitality.

. Thanks to Shawna and Brian Wyvill for letting me have the right home at the right time.

Thank you to Vermont artist Robin Mix and to journalist and author Laura Robinson for some valuable words of advice early in my career.

An extra big thanks to my awesome partners in mountain adventures and for the terrific conversations born of those adventures: Jennifer Erickson, Christina Brodribb, Andrea Pintaric, Michelle Gagnon, Crista-Lee Mitchell, Kim Csizmazia, Becky Bristow, Amanda Follett, Gail Crowe-Swords, Maegan Carney, Niki Lepage, Maria Hawkins, Gloria Folden, Marg Rees, Lin Heidt, Jordy Burkes, John Derick, Renee Meggs, Dale Bartrom, Judy Musselman, Catherine Kemp, Jackie Clark, Steve Fedyna, Doug MacLean and, especially, my very first adventure partner, Daisy Matheson. I've learned wonderful things from all of you.

Thank you to Karen McNeill for reminding me that being a girl in the mountains is a gift worth celebrating and to never stop aiming for the stars.

Thanks so very, very much to all the adventurers – and photographers, writers, filmmakers and mountain guides – featured in these stories for answering my phone calls and e-mails and for taking the time to send me photos and share their entertaining exploits with me in the first place.

Thank you to the editors and their assistants who've given me the pages on which to share my stories, especially James Little, David Leach, Jackie Davis, Kate Barker, Eric Rumble, Tom Gierasimczuk, Bob Barnett, Valerie Berenyi, Tom Maloney, David Chaundy-Smart, Mitchell Scott, Sherri Zickefoose and Kate Tooke.

Thanks especially to editor Dave Rooney for encouraging me to discover what I had to say.

Thank you to editor Dave Burke for giving me the best on-the-job education a writer could ask for and for making learning a lively, stimulating and rewarding pursuit.

Thanks to Tony and Gillean Daffern for recognizing the gems of the Canadian Rockies' unique culture.

Thanks to Don Gorman for sharing such keen interest in publishing this collection of stories.

And finally, I owe a huge, ongoing thanks to *Rocky Mountain Outlook* founder and editor Carol Picard for trusting her writers and photographers to tell the story of their world as they interpret it. This book could not have happened without her unflagging belief in the value of community.

RECOMMENDED READING AND VIEWING

> Books

Angus, Colin. *Beyond the Horizon: The Great Race to Finish the First Human-Powered Circumnavigation of the Planet.* Toronto, ON: Doubleday Canada (Random House), 2007.

———. *Lost in Mongolia: Rafting the World's Last Unchallenged River.* Toronto, ON: Anchor Books (Random House), 2003.

Angus, Colin, and Ian Mulgrew. *Amazon Extreme: Three Ordinary Guys, One Rubber Raft and the Most Dangerous River on Earth.* Toronto, ON: Stoddart Publishing Co., 2001.

Blum, Arlene. *Annapurna: A Woman's Place.* San Francisco, CA: Sierra Club Books, 1980.

Blum, Arlene. *Breaking Trail: A Climbing Life.* Orlando, FL: Scribner/ Lisa Drew, 2005.

Boles, Glen. *My Mountain Album: Art & Photography of the Canadian Rockies & Columbia Mountains.* Surrey, BC: Rocky Mountain Books, 2006.

Corbett, Bill. *The 11,000ers of the Canadian Rockies.* Surrey, BC: Rocky Mountain Books, 2004.

Davis, Steph. *High Infatuation: A Climber's Guide to Love and Gravity.* Seattle, WA: Mountaineers Books, 2007.

Finkel, Michael. *Alpine Circus: A Skier's Exotic Adventures at the Snowy Edge of the World.* New York, NY: Lyons Press, 1999.

Heuer, Karsten. *Being Caribou: Five Months on Foot with an Arctic Herd.* Seattle, WA: Mountaineers Books, 2005.

Heuer, Karsten. *Walking the Big Wild: From Yellowstone to the Yukon on the Grizzly Bear's Trail*. Toronto, ON: McClelland & Stewart, 2002.

Kobalenko, Jerry. *The Horizontal Everest: Extreme Journeys on Ellesmere Island*. New York, NY: Soho Press, 2002.

Macdonald, Warren. *A Test of Will: One Man's Extraordinary Story of Survival*. Vancouver, BC: Greystone Books, 2004.

Morrow, Pat. *Beyond Everest: Quest for the Seven Summits*. Camden East, ON: Camden House Publishing, 1986.

Mortenson, Greg, and David Oliver Relin. *Three Cups of Tea: One Man's Mission to Promote Peace ... One School at a Time*. New York, NY: Penguin Books, 2006.

Patterson, Bruce. *Canadians on Everest*. Canmore, AB: Altitude Publishing, 2006.

Powter, Geoff. *Strange and Dangerous Dreams: The Fine Line between Adventure and Madness*. Seattle, WA: The Mountaineers Books, 2006.

Ralston, Aron. *Between a Rock and a Hard Place*. New York, NY: Atria Books, 2004.

Sandford, Robert William. *Called by this Mountain: The Legend of the Silver Ice Axe and the Early Climbing History of Mount Alberta*. Canmore, AB: The Alpine Club of Canada/The Japanese Alpine Club, 2000.

Scott, Chic. *Powder Pioneers: Ski Stories from the Canadian Rockies and Columbia Mountains*. Surrey, BC: Rocky Mountain Books, 2005.

Scott, Chic. *Pushing the Limits: The Story of Canadian Mountaineering*. Calgary, AB: Rocky Mountain Books, 2000.

A Dog Gone Addiction. Dir. Becky Bristow. Prod. Becky Bristow/Wild Soul Creations, 2007.

A Russian Wave. Dir. Becky Bristow. Prod. Becky Bristow/Wild Soul Creations, 2004.

Amazon from Source to Sea. Dir. Ken Malestine. Co-prod. Angus Adventures/CTV, 2001.

Aweberg. Dir. Will Gadd. Prod. Will Gadd, 2005.

Beyond the Horizon. Dir. Colin and Julie Angus. Prod. Angus Adventures, 2006.

Cobra Crack. Dir. Sonnie Trotter and Paul Bride. Prod. Ivan Hughes, 2006.

Deep Seeded Instability. Dir. Dave Mossop and Eric Crosland. Prod. Rocky Mountain Sherpas, 2003.

Ice Mines. Dir. Will Gadd. Prod. Will Gadd/Gravsports, 2007.

Part Animal, Part Machine. Dir. Will Gadd. Prod. Will Gadd/Gravsports, 2003.

Shining Mountains Series. Dir. Guy Clarkson. Prod. Guy Clarkson, 2005.

The Fine Line. Dir. Dave Mossop. Prod. Malcolm Sangster and Eric Crosland/Rocky Mountain Sherpas, 2008.

The Liquid Truth. Dir. Alan Bibby. Co-prod. White Gold Productions and Bibby Productions, 2008.

The Second Step – Warren Macdonald's Epic Journey to Federation Peak. Dir. Gary Caganoff/Lysis Films. Prod. Suzanne Davies for Kaganovich Productions/Part Animal Part Machine (Australia), 2002.

The Yenisey River Expedition. Dir. Colin Angus, Remy Quinter, Ben Kozel, Tim Cope. Prod. Colin Angus, Remy Quinter, Ben Kozel, Tim Cope, 2003.

University Wall. Dir. Ivan Hughes. Prod. Fringe Filmworks Inc., 2006.

PHOTOGRAPHERS

P. 49 Andy Evans is all smiles on the summit of K2, Karakoram, Pakistan. Photo Andy Evans collection.

P. 49 Peter Arbic takes in the view on Howse Peak in the Canadian Rockies. Photo by Tim Auger.

P. 50 Nancy Hansen on the summit of Mount Clemenceau, Mount Shackleton in the background, Canadian Rockies. Photo by Doug Fulford.

P. 51 Aron Ralston. Photo by Donald Lee.

P. 52 Abby Watkins climbs Rocky Mountain Horror Show, at the Cineplex, Canadian Rockies.

P. 52 Kim Csizmazia swings onto Ain't Nobody Here but Us Chickens, Canadian Rockies. Photo by Will Gadd.

P. 53 Catherine Mulvihill leads up the pillar on Ice Nine on the Icefields Parkway, Canadian Rockies. Photo Catherine Mulvihill collection.

P. 54 Zak McGurk training hard at Grassi Lakes, Canadian Rockies. Photo by Sarah Fuller.

P. 55 Mark Heard. Photo by Craig Douce.

P. 56 Rick Collier in the Vowells, Bugaboos, BC. Photo Rick Collier collection.

P. 56 Karl Griffiths climbs above Camp 2 on Ama Dablam, Nepali Himalayas. Photo by Grant Meekins.

P. 105 Colin Angus and Ben Kozel explore the Amazon River delta. Photo by Scott Borthwick.

P. 105 Kari Medig pulls his sled toward Mount Logan on the Hubbard Glacier, Yukon Territory. Photo by Kari Medig.

P. 106 Arlene Blum treks in the Himalayas. Photo by Richard Isherwood.

P. 107 John Martin and Chris Perry at the base of Casino Wall, Cougar Creek, Canadian Rockies. Photo by Kristen Wood/*Rocky Mountain Outlook*.

P. 107 Carlos Buhler. Photo by Crista-Lee Mitchell.

P. 107 Glen Boles on Mount Karnak, Purcell Mountains, BC. Photo Glen Boles collection.

P. 108 Marko Prezelj works out the moves on the North Face of the North Twin, Canadian Rockies. Photo by Steve House.

P. 109 Sean Isaac works his way up Slovenian Death Water, Cairngorm Mountains, Scotland. Photo by Simon Richardson.

P. 109 Jen Olson and Lilla Molnar on the summit of Brakk Zang, Karakoram, Pakistan. Photo by Lilla Molnar.

P. 109 Eamonn Walsh negotiates Mount Alberta's precipitous summit ridge, Canadian Rockies. Photo by Raphael Slawinski.

P. 110 Marko Prezelj susses out the route up the North Face of the North Twin, Canadian Rockies. Photo by Steve House.

P. 110 Katherine Fraser, Katy Holm, Aidan Oloman in the Four Girls Mountains, China. Photo Katy Holm collection.

P. 111 Jeff Boyd, Tod Gourley and Mark Heard paddle the Lohit River, Arunachal Pradesh, Indian Himalayas. Photo by Kim Hartlin/Thunderbow Expeditions.

P. 111 Logan Grayling in Vietnam's central highlands. Photo by Ben Marr/Young Guns Productions.

P. 111 Ben Firth explores the cliffs of Wadi Rum, Jordan. Photo by Chris Kalous.

P. 112 Karen McNeill and Sue Nott, Mount McKinley, Alaska. Photo Sue Nott collection.

P. 112 Pat Morrow savours his moment on the summit of Mount Everest. Photo Pat Morrow collection.

P. 161 Barry Blanchard considers his next move at Nuptse, Nepali Himalayas. Photo by Marko Prezelj.

P. 162 Ken Wylie in his favourite classroom. Photo by John Irvine.

P. 163 Denise Martin is all smiles at the South Pole, Antarctica. Photo Denise Martin collection.

P. 164/65 Alex Taylor loving the cold and the scene in Antarctica. Photo Alex Taylor collection.

P. 167 Ola Dunin-Bell takes a break from clinic duties, Mount Everest in the background, Nepali Himalayas. Photo Ola Dunin-Bell collection.

P. 168 Wally Berg hiking to work in the Nepali Himalayas. Photo Wally Berg collection.

P. 185 Richard Else. Photo Richard Else collection.

P. 186 Ivan Hughes carries the tools of his trade. Photo by Angela Heck.

P. 187 Dave Mossop. Photo by Dave Mossop.

P. 188/89 Guy Clarkson. Photo Guy Clarkson collection.

P. 190 Chic Scott and Franz Dopf at the base of Spitzmauer in Austria, which Dopf and Hans Gmoser climbed as young men. Photo by Roberta Dopf.

P. 191 Becky Bristow. Photo Becky Bristow collection.

P. 192 David Lavallée does research on the Columbia Icefield, Mount Andromeda in the background, Canadian Rockies. Photo by Johnathon Charron.

P. 241 Jerry Kobalenko stops for a self-portrait in Labrador, then and now. Photos by Jerry Kobalenko.

P. 241 Will Gadd soars into the sunset over the Andes, Chile/Argentina border. Photo by Christian Pondella/Red Bull Photofiles.

P. 242 Sonnie Trotter makes it look easy on Cobra Crack, Squamish, BC. Photo by Paul Bride.

P. 243 Steph Davis aims high on the Salathe Wall, Yosemite, California. Photo by Jimmy Chin.

P. 244 Ben Firth sticks his tools into an iceberg off the Labrador Coast. Photo by Andrew Querner.

P. 244 Baiba and Pat Morrow. Photo by Pat Morrow.

P. 245 Logan Grayling takes a big plunge on the second descent of Johnston Falls, Canadian Rockies. Photo by Ryan Creary.

P. 245 Sonnie Trotter works out the moves on The Path, Back of the Lake, Canadian Rockies. Photo by Cory Richards.

P. 246 Will Gadd climbs some funky ice in an abandoned mine shaft, Dannemora, Sweden. Photo by Christian Pondella/Red Bull Photofiles.

P. 247 Will Gadd handles his flying rig. Photo by Christian Pondella/Red Bull Photofiles.

P. 248 Warren Macdonald climbs Mount Kilimanjaro, Tanzania. Photo by Jeremy Smith.

P. 248 Colin Angus and Julie Wafaei (Angus) work the oars on their journey across the Atlantic Ocean. Photo Colin and Julie Angus collection.

P. 297 Greg Horne, Dave Pors, Lynn Martel and Sean Elliott unfurl the flags of the Alpine Club of Canada and the International Year of Mountains on the summit of Mount Brown, Canadian Rockies. Photo Lynn Martel collection.

P. 298 Leanne Allison straddles the Continental Divide near Holmes Peak, BC. Photo by Karsten Heuer.

P. 299 Danielle Droitsch and Jim Kievit paddle down the Bow River, Alberta. Photo by Dave Kalbfleisch.

P. 299 Paul Žižka at the west edge of Arthur's Pass National Park, Cronin Glacier in the background, South Island, New Zealand. Photo by Paul Žižka.

P. 300 Karsten Heuer, Leanne Allison, Zev and Willow take a break on the Thlewiaza River in Nunavut Territory. Photo by Karsten Heuer.

P. 301 Mike Dobbin, Lori Dowling and Angus Taylor savour the moment on the summit of Mount Athabasca, Canadian Rockies. Photo Angus Taylor collection.

P. 302 Members of the Porcupine caribou herd hike alongside Leanne Allison in northern Yukon. Photo by Karsten Heuer.

P. 303 Greg Mortenson with Khanday Village schoolchildren, Hushe Valley, Karakoram, Pakistan. Photo courtesy of Central Asia Institute.

P. 304 Paula Duncan hikes along the Carthew–Alderson Trail in Waterton Lakes National Park, Canadian Rockies. Photo by Lynn Martel.

P. 347 Lynn Martel. Photo by Amanda Follett.

A NOTE ON THE STORIES

Some of the stories in this collection appear in their barely altered original form, while others were extended and significantly modified specifically for this book. The original versions appeared in the following publications:

Adventurous
Avenue West
Banff Mountain Film Festival Magazine
Calgary Herald
Canadian Alpine Journal
Canmore Leader
explore
Gripped
Medical Post
Rocky Mountain Outlook
Ski Press
The Fitzhugh
up!
Vancouver Province
Whistler Pique Newsmagazine

> Lynn **Martel**

Lynn Martel grew up in Montreal, where she studied creative writing at Concordia University while wholly embracing the lifestyle of dance clubs and popular fashion. Upon visiting Banff in the early 1980s, before she could graduate she fell madly in love with the mountain environment and has made her home in the Canadian Rockies ever since. An avid backcountry skier, mountaineer and backpacker, Martel writes about mountain culture and history, mountain adventure and personalities for various newspapers and magazines, including the *Rocky Mountain Outlook*, *Whistler Pique Newsmagazine*, *Calgary Herald*, *explore* and *up!* (WestJet).

Adventurous Dreams, Adventurous Lives
Collected & Edited by Jason Schoonover
Foreword by Meave Leakey
ISBN 978-1-894765-91-6
$29.95

My Mountain Album
Art & Photography of the Canadian Rockies & Columbia Mountains
Glen Boles
ISBN 978-1-894765-78-7
$64.95

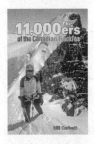

The 11,000ers of the Canadian Rockies
Bill Corbett
ISBN 978-1894765-43-5
$29.95

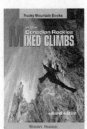

Mixed Climbs in the Canadian Rockies
Second Edition
Sean Isaac
ISBN 98-0921102-96-0
$24.95

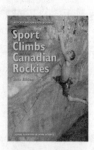

Sport Climbs in the Canadian Rockies
Sixth Edition
Jon Jones & John Martin
ISBN 978-1-894765-67-1
$34.95

The Weekender Effect
Hyperdevelopment in Mountain Towns
Robert William Sandford
ISBN 978-1-897522-10-3
$16.95

Water, Weather and the Mountain West
Robert William Sandford
ISBN 978-1-894765-93-0
$19.95

Powder Pioneers
Ski Stories from the Canadian Rockies and Columbia Mountains
Chic Scott
ISBN 978-1894765-64-0
$29.95

Pushing the Limits
The Story of Canadian Mountaineering
Chic Scott
ISBN 978-0921102-59-5
$59.95